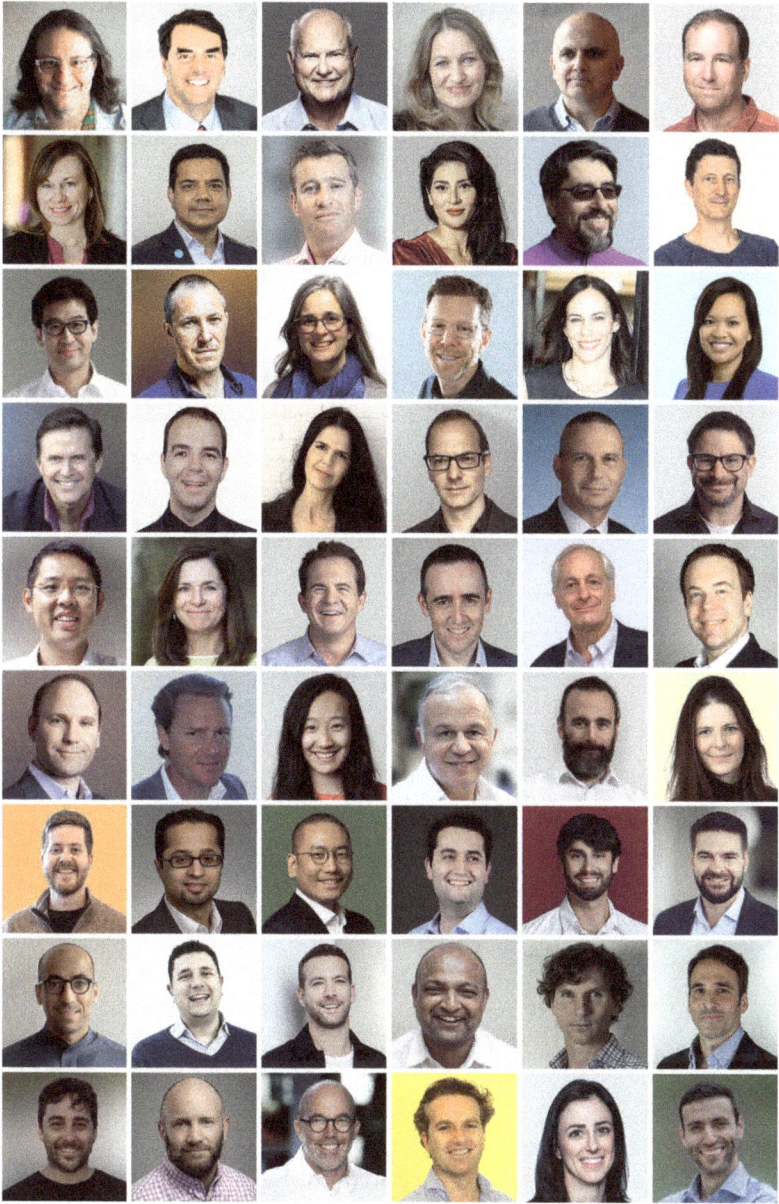

VENTURE ADVENTURE

STARTUP FUNDRAISING ADVICE FROM TOP GLOBAL INVESTORS

AMIR HEGAZI

TRANSFORMENA
PUBLISHING

ʟ ʝ
TRANSFORMENA
PUBLISHING

Disclaimer: The expressed opinions of each contributor and interviewee in this publication do not represent whatsoever the opinions or views of the author. They also do not in any way purport to reflect the opinions or views of other contributors and interviewees. The following material is for informational purposes only. It does not represent investing, legal, or personal advice. The author does not claim or take responsibility for the accuracy of any expressed opinions or views put forth in this publication. The enclosed information is meant for consideration only. It does not constitute advice or recommendations.

Ordering information: Special discounts are available on quantity purchases by governments, NGOs, schools, companies, associations, and others. For details, contact the publisher at www.CapitalDemocracy.com.

Hegazi, Amir. Venture Adventure. TRANSFORMENA PUBLISHING, 2022

Hardcover print ISBN: 978-1-7325421-7-4

Paperback print ISBN: 978-1-7325421-8-1

Ebook ISBN: 979-8-9858401-0-0

1. Venture Capital, 2. New Business Enterprises, 3. Entrepreneurship

First Edition

Cover and interior design by www.meadencreative.com

www.CapitalDemocracy.com

"Follow your bliss and the universe will open doors for you where there were only walls."

—JOSEPH CAMPBELL

CONTENTS

FOREWORD

By Brad Feld

In 2011, I co-authored the first edition of *Venture Deals: Be Smarter Than Your Lawyer and Venture Capitalist* based on my experience as a venture capitalist working with other venture capitalists, lead partners, angels, and founders. The goal of the book was to help founders develop an effective fundraising strategy, understand all the aspects of a venture capital financing, and learn how venture capital firms work. At the time, venture capital and entrepreneurship were highly localized phenomena in a few major cities, with much of the focus on Silicon Valley.

The last decade has seen global democratization of entrepreneurship. Companies are now being created across the United States and throughout the world. In addition, major technology and entrepreneur ecosystems have emerged in cities including London, Berlin, Stockholm, Tel Aviv, Tokyo, Shanghai, Shenzhen, Bengaluru, Singapore, São Paulo, and Dubai. As the concept of a "unicorn" went from a new and mythical idea in 2013 to a pervasive global phenomenon, companies all over the world have received funding at valuations like their US counterparts and are generating corresponding returns. I'm constantly reminded of this trend as I interact with founders through Techstars, a global accelerator I co-founded in Colorado back in 2006, which has grown to support and fund over 2,500 startups all over the world.

Today, there is an extraordinary amount of capital available to fund new companies. If you are an entrepreneur with a vision to build something new, now is a great time to take advantage of the fundraising opportunities available to you. As you start a fundraising journey, this book will help you get inside venture capitalist's heads so you can chart your path more strategically.

Venture Adventure provides a wide array of bite-sized and practical advice, tips, and lessons from dozens of investors from around the world and is a resource for every entrepreneur raising capital. Even if you are a seasoned founder with sizable funds raised and multiple funding rounds under your belt, there are plenty of nuggets and pointers in this book to help you be even more successful during your fundraise.

I'm increasingly optimistic about the globalization of entrepreneurship and the resulting access to investors for entrepreneurs all over the world. This results in new opportunities for founders to succeed and have impact, regardless of where they live. I believe entrepreneurship is foundational to the economic health and development of cities, states, and nations, and venture capital is an important component in the creation of companies. This book is an exciting addition that will advance the field of knowledge around venture capital and financing.

—**BRAD FELD,** Co-Founder of Foundry Group, Co-Founder of Techstars, and Author of *Venture Deals: Be Smarter Than Your Lawyer and Venture Capitalist*

PREFACE

What you have in your hand or on your screen is a different kind of book. This book will help you understand the mindset of venture capitalists (VCs). You will once and for all grasp how they think and what they look for in the investments they back, and figure out how you can essentially "speak their language." This book does not speculate on what might work for fundraising based on a top-down, academic, or one-dimensional perspective. On the contrary, it takes a bottom-up, practical, and multi-perspective approach from the same global VCs you might want to approach someday.

With dozens of investors featured from every corner of the globe, each providing their latest and greatest fundraising advice and tips on a wide array of fundraising-related topics, you're getting the most current, comprehensive, and actionable takeaways. It's information that can put into practice immediately to raise capital. Combined, these VCs oversee hundreds of billions of dollars in assets under management. All of their advice is presented in bite-sized sections, so it is easy for you to follow, wrap your head around, and apply intelligently and successfully to achieve your fundraising goals.

My moonshot aim for *Venture Adventure* is to help educate and inspire startup founders and founding teams on all aspects of VC fundraising and, in effect, help flow massive amounts of venture capital—in the order of billions of dollars—to promising and game-changing startups everywhere. In doing so, I hope to not just help ensure their survival, but also accelerate their growth. Our global economy and forward progress depend on their success.

PREFACE

I genuinely hope you find value in the following pages and decide to apply whatever lessons you may learn. I would very much enjoy hearing from you.

Happy venture adventure!

—AMIR HEGAZI, February 2022
amir@capitaldemocracy.com

CONTRIBUTORS

AHMED EL ALFI—Co-Founder and Chairman at Egypt-based Sawari Ventures

AHMAD ALNAIMI—General Partner at Saudi Arabia-based STV

FEDERICO ANTONI—Founder and Managing Partner at Mexico-based ALLVP

CAIO BOLOGNESI—Partner at Brazil-based Monashees

SIMON CANT—Co-Founder and Managing Partner at Australia-based Reinventure Group

JASON CHAPMAN—Managing Partner at Colorado-based Konvoy Ventures

SHUO CHEN—General Partner at San Francisco-based IOVC

SHANE CHESSON—Founding Partner at Singapore-based Openspace Ventures

UZMA CHOUDRY—Investor at London-based Octopus Ventures

DAVID COHEN—Founder and Chairman at Colorado-based Techstars

JAMES CURRIER—General Partner at San Francisco-based NFX

FILIP DAMES—Founding Partner at Berlin-based Cherry Ventures

BYRON DEETER—Partner at San Francisco-based Bessemer Venture Partners

FRED DESTIN—Co-Founder and General Partner at London-based Stride. VC

CAMILLA DOLAN—Partner at London-based Eka Ventures

TIM DRAPER—Founder at San Francisco-based Draper Associates and DFJ

BRAD FELD—Co-Founder of Colorado-based Foundry Group and Techstars

CONTRIBUTORS

JENNY FIELDING—General Partner at New York-based The Fund

ZACH FINKELSTEIN–Co-Founder and Managing Partner at Class 5 Global

ISABEL FOX—General Partner at London-based Outsized Ventures

FABRICE GRINDA—Founding Partner at New York-based FJ Labs

MARY GROVE—Managing Partner at Minneapolis-based Bread and Butter Ventures

OLIVER HOLLE—Co-Founder and Managing Partner at Austria-based Speedinvest

DAVID HORNIK—Founding Partner at San Francisco-based Lobby Capital

ALI KARABEY—Managing Director at Turkey-based 212 Ventures

ROB KNIAZ—Co-Founder and Partner at London-based Hoxton Ventures

VINNIE LAURIA—Founding Partner at Singapore-based Golden Gate Ventures

JENNY LEFCOURT—General Partner at San Francisco-based Freestyle Capital

TIM LEVENE—CEO at London-based Augmentum Fintech

SETH LEVINE—Co-Founder and Managing Director at Colorado-based Foundry Group

BILL LIAO—General Partner at Ireland-based SOSV

NATHAN LUSTIG—Managing Partner at Chile-based Magma Partners

MANUEL SILVA MARTINEZ—General Partner at London-based Mouro Capital

ELISA MILLER-OUT—Co-Founder and Managing Partner at New York-based Chloe Capital

GREG MOON—Managing Partner at Japan-based SoftBank Vision Fund

PATRICIA NAKACHE—General Partner at San Francisco-based Trinity Ventures

JIMMY FUSSING NIELSEN—Co-Founder of Denmark-based Heartcore Capital

SAJITH PAI—Director at India-based Blume Ventures

CONTRIBUTORS

KELLY PERDEW—Co-Founder and Managing General Partner at Los Angeles-based Moonshots Capital

BILL REICHERT—Venture Partner at San Francisco-based Pegasus Tech Ventures

GARY RIESCHEL—Founding Managing Partner at Shanghai-based Qiming Venture Partners

ANDREW ROMANS—Co-Founder, CEO, and General Partner at San Francisco-based 7BC Capital

JENNY ROOKE—Managing Director at San Francisco-based Genoa Ventures

DANIEL ROSEN—Founder and General Partner at San Francisco-based Commerce Ventures

CHRISTOPHER M. SCHROEDER—Co-Founder of Next Billion Venture

IZHAR SHAY—Venture Partner at Israel-based DisruptAI

WAYNE SHIONG—Partner at Beijing-based China Growth Capital

JON SOBERG—Managing Partner at San Francisco-based MS&AD Ventures

THOMAS SPERRY—Co-Founder Managing Director at Oregon-based Rogue Venture Partners

NOOR SWEID—Founder of Dubai-based Global Ventures

YINGLAN TAN—CEO and Founding Managing Partner at Singapore-based Insignia Ventures Partners

ANIS UZZAMAN—Founder and CEO at San Francisco-based Pegasus Tech Ventures

BILAL ZUBERI—Partner at New York-based Lux Capital

KEET VAN ZYL—Co-Founder and Partner at South Africa-based Knife Capital

LIST OF ABBREVIATIONS

AI – artificial intelligence

ARR – annual recurring revenue

B2B – business-to-business

B2C – business-to-consumer

CAC – customer acquisition costs

CEO – chief executive officer

CFO – chief financial officer

CM – compound metric

CMO – chief marketing officer

CRM – customer relationship management

CTO – chief technical officer

CVC – corporate venture capital

FOMO – fear of missing out

GMV – gross merchandise value

ICO – initial coin offering

IPO – initial public offering

KPI – key performance indicator

LOI – letter of intent

LP – limited partner

LTV – lifetime value

M&A – mergers and acquisitions

MENA – Middle East and North Africa

MRR – monthly recurring revenue

MVP – minimum viable product

NDA – non-disclosure agreement

NFT – non-fungible token

NPS – net promoter score

NVCA – National Venture Capital Association

O2O – online-to-offline

P&L – profit and loss statement

PR – public relations

ROI – return on investment

SaaS – software as a service

SAFE – simple agreement for future equity

SAM – serviceable available market

SOM – serviceable obtainable market

SPAC – special purpose acquisition company

TAM – total addressable market

UI – user interface

USP – unique selling proposition

UX – user experience

VC – venture capital/venture capitalist

PART I

SETTING THE STAGE: PLAN & PREPARE FOR FUNDRAISING

1. PLANTING THE SEED

Locate to a Tech Hub City if at All Possible

By James Currier, General Partner at NFX

One way to maximize your chances of securing fundraising and ultimately scaling your startup is to physically move to a tech hub city and start building a close-knit network of people who are knowledgeable about fundraising, startups, and VCs. This will help you get on the inside track and learn the language of this game. There is a local language that people speak to communicate in any creative industry. Whether it's the language of Hollywood for the movie industry, or Washington, DC, for politics, or New York and London for finance—there's a language that is used to communicate very precise and nuanced things. You need to learn that language. That's going to help you with your fundraising process two or three years after you learn the language and build your network. You also have to learn what's hot, what's stale, and what's out of vogue at that moment. For example, VCs are tired of hearing that your company is "the next Uber" for whatever. This may have worked six years ago; it does not work today. That's an example of the kind nuances you need to be on top of if you want to be most effective.

Being in the right environment, surrounded by like-minded people, isn't just inspiring—it influences how you think and approach your business. It puts you at the forefront of the latest trends and on the cutting edge. It opens doors for you because you meet people you wouldn't have run into otherwise. By attending conferences and events, you get to mingle with other entrepreneurs and VCs and warm up to them. Ninety-five percent of all investments made by good investors result from warm relationships. That alone gives you an edge over anyone who's outside the loop. All things being equal, a founder who is based in a tech hub city has far greater chance of success than one who isn't. Their speed of leaning, making connections, recruiting, and, yes, raising capital will be much higher. Locating to a tech hub city maybe the best move you can make, if you're not already in one.

We live in a virtual world, which is great. It allows people to learn and interact remotely. However, face-to-face interaction and physical presence is always going to be more effective than Zoom. There's no substitute for going to a conference, meeting up with people face to face, and actually sharing personal stories over a drink, hearing the real scoop, and building relationships in the real world. After all, 60 percent of what is true and important to people will not be written down or available on the internet. A lot of communication gets lost when you are stuck in a virtual world.

You don't have to relocate to Silicon Valley. There are a couple dozen or so tech hubs around the world and they're growing: New York, Boston, Boulder, Toronto, London, Berlin, Tel Aviv, Shanghai, Singapore, Dubai, and many others are viable options. Obviously, some might be better for you than others, depending on your sector and the markets you're focused on. The point is to make the physical move to be in the action if you want to set yourself and your business up for the greatest chance of success, including raising capital.

Leverage Thought Leadership to Attract Investors

By Yinglan Tan, CEO at Insignia Ventures Partners

It's always better to catch the attention of investors and have them reach out to you than the other way around. There are many ways for you to create this "pull" effect for investors in a cost-effective manner. This is where thought leadership can come in handy. This may include doing podcasts or writing LinkedIn or Medium posts, and essentially creating a brand around one's expertise in a space. The concept is for you to create a "halo effect" that builds outside interest in the work you're doing—in this case, building a venture-backable tech startup—because you have shown that you know what you are talking about when it comes to a specific subject or topics that are related to your company.

Thought leadership does not mean having to talk about your company all the time. It is actually better to be stingy with the details and strategically choose which aspects to be public about, so that investors then have to reach out to you to learn more. For example, you might talk about industry pain points and your own personal stories experiencing those pain points, and how you are currently solving them. Or tell stories about your experience building companies and products in your sector. You may also choose to be completely transparent by openly sharing your indicators of growth and customer feedback.

You can distribute this thought leadership to your prospective investor audience in various ways: generating highly personal content from your own personal and social media channels, gearing the company's content marketing strategy toward an investor audience, and becoming a contributor or regularly quoted personality in media outlets. You can even leverage the marketing channels of existing investors. Investors tend to be connected with other investors, so contributing to or getting featured on investors' channels can give you exposure and establish your thought leadership and credibility in the VC community.

Creating a "pull" effect is meant to amplify your company's story of growth independently from the funding it is looking to raise. It is easy to latch growth on to funding, but startups are not built for the sole purpose of being venture-backed. It's a subtle shift in messaging from "we need the funding to grow"—which is more of a "push" approach—to "we are growing well, and we can potentially be your fund returner"—which is more of a "pull" approach.

From a more practical standpoint, focusing on "pull" approach enables you to potentially reap more connections for the amount of effort you put in than doing one-on-one outreach, ultimately saving you time. An ideal combination would be for you to leverage "pull" strategies to generate top-of-funnel interest and engage one-on-one with the right contacts for you from there.

It is important to not just put out signs for investors to find, but also build many pathways for investors to reach out to you. You want to make it easy for investors to get in touch and engage with you, especially those who are relevant to your market or industry and who can provide value beyond capital. Ultimately, the goal is to build a top-of-funnel network of investors to tap into at all times. After all, the best venture-backed founders never really stop fundraising, even when they are not formally doing so.

———————

Nurture Key Relationships Well Before You Fundraise

By Isabel Fox, General Partner at Outsized Ventures

As an entrepreneur, you should be fundraising in one sense or another all the time. You don't necessarily need to always be in full-fledged fundraising mode, but you should at least always be thinking about and planning your next round. Whether you just started or just closed a round, you need to identify your most likely funding options and your most likely funding parties, whether you're eyeing a Series A, B, C, or D round. Once you've identified the right target investors based on your geography and sector, and the size of the round that you're doing, the next step is to start building those relationships.

For instance, don't wait six months from your Series A round before you start to think about fundraising. You want to start thinking about it as soon as you raise your seed. List your target dozen investors or so, and figure out what milestones you need to hit to formally approach them. Then, start planting seeds with those investors and get a dialogue going with them as soon as possible. The sooner you can start building those relationships, well before you go to market to raise capital, the further ahead you will be when the time comes. The concept is that you want to get on your prospective investors' radar as early as possible and slowly and consistently warm them to your business over time.

Some savvy entrepreneurs actually engage with investors a full 18 months before they plan to do their round. Start building those relationships, telling your story, feeling out investors' appetite, and gathering their feedback. Really get to know them and understand what is likely to move the needle regarding their funding decision. The beauty of that approach is that it removes the pressure from the relationship and creates an authentic and long-term connection between you and the investors as ecosystem colleagues. It's far more casual and friendly, without having an ask or either side having a formal agenda. You are literally just meeting up, exchanging thoughts, sharing insights about the industry and observations on certain trends, and building your rapport and credibility. You can follow up these interactions with personalized update emails or more formal company newsletters. The idea is to try to keep your target VCs within arm's reach as much as possible and abreast of your progress. The more you can show them that you have a plan and you're following through—"We said we were going to deliver such and such and here's what we did"—the more confidence they will have in your and your team's ability to execute.

The point of the updates is not simply to highlight the big wins; you need to also acknowledge what's not going well. Every investor knows that no business is perfect and every startup, by definition, is in an ongoing struggle. That transparency with potential investors demonstrates humility and openness. It shows that you're willing to acknowledge challenges and learn from mistakes. Ultimately, it cultivates greater trust with investors, who will appreciate your sharing a candid picture of where your business stands, as opposed to merely sending out promo material. If you play this well, it will be much easier to transition into "I'm going to be putting my next round together, and thought we could chat about it." In addition, by then your potential investors will already be familiar with your story and your evolution, which essentially puts you further ahead of the game than someone starting from scratch. Going through this process will also help you eliminate any investors who you think are less likely to invest or are not the right fit for your business, so you can focus on the ones who are more responsive to you, generous with their time and advice, and more engaged and excited about your business.

———

Be Wary of Getting Dragged into the Fundraising Process When You're Unprepared

By Patricia Nakache, General Partner at Trinity Ventures

Oftentimes, particularly in the heated investment environment that we're currently in, investors will proactively reach out to entrepreneurs to try to pre-empt a fundraising process. They will approach an entrepreneur who is not yet even in the market raising money. The entrepreneur may have not yet prepared a deck, let alone set up a data room. They may have little prepared in terms of materials for fundraising. What a savvy investor might do in this situation, if they're interested in learning more about your venture, is to encourage you to have a conversation with them about raising money with the promise that it will be a very quick and easy process. They might tell you not to worry about making a deck and getting a data room ready. They might imply that you could raise money from them without having to go through the more involved, typical fundraising process in terms of pitching, due diligence, and so forth.

This is what's referred to as "single threading," meaning you have just a single conversation with one venture firm about raising money. It's a practice that you should be wary of, because generally you're likely not prepared for the conversation. You don't have all your fundraising material ready, including an investor-tailored pitch deck, financial model, and other supportive material. You're also likely to have not thought properly about your fundraising strategy or process. As a result, more often than not, you're not in a position to put your best foot forward or leverage a compelling and complete story to generate your optimal valuation and deal terms. The venture firm that has approached you to try to pre-empt the fundraising process and has promised a quick and easy process would have no competition, and thus have all the leverage they need. As such, the balance is tipped in favor of the venture firm.

Also, even though they might have promised a seamless process with little due diligence, there is often diligence creep. They start asking for more and more information and data points, which you have not prepared. They also have no time urgency to reach a conclusion to their process. Certainly, if they do ultimately decide to give you a term sheet, there's no pressure from a valuation perspective. What's more likely to happen is that the undertaking ends up consuming more time than you thought and can often end in rejection. Worse still, the word can sometimes get out that that XYZ investor has taken a look at your company and passed, which doesn't put you and your company in the best light when you try to do a proper fundraising round. It's always better for you to control the fundraising process and not let a venture firm try to pre-empt your process and control it.

If you find yourself in such a situation, you can simply say, "We don't have our deck, financials, or investor materials ready at the moment, but we would love to circle back when we are prepared to launch our process. When we're ready to fundraise, you will be in my first cohort that I talk to. In the meantime, I'd be delighted to have a conversation with you, share with you my vision for the company, and highlight some of our accomplishments and the milestones that we've already hit." Meanwhile, make sure you don't engage in fundraising discussions in any meaningful capacity. It's obviously great to always be developing relationships with investors, so go ahead and have an initial conversation. Get to know the investor and establish a strong rapport, but don't get sucked into single-threaded process.

The one potential exception is where you're approached by a global brand or a potentially valuable strategic investor that can add tremendous value to you in addition to the capital, and you gather that they have a mandate to invest in your space. In such instance, where there's a timeline on their offer and delaying your engagement with will close the door on any future prospect of working with them, you'd have to exercise your own judgment and perhaps take your chance. Suppose, for example, you were approached by Tiger Global, SoftBank, or Google to engage in fundraising and you realize that if you don't engage, they will hit up your competition. You certainly want to explore further while the window is open. Perhaps consider trying to find some middle ground where you can quickly get yourself in a position to launch a proper fundraise process. Finally, just because an investor has invested in your competitor doesn't mean that you won't be able to attract capital from an equally worthy investor.

Write a Business Plan for You, Not for Investors
By Izhar Shay, Venture Partner with DisruptAI

Write a thoughtful, detailed, and meticulous business plan for your and your company's sake, not for investors. It is safe to assume that investors are never going to take the time to read a lengthy business plan. Granted, they will want to know the basic tenets of the plan and even dig deep on particular areas during their due diligence, but rarely will investors ask to see a detailed business plan. In almost every case, they will ask for a presentation or pitch deck and financials. They might also ask for supplemental documents on specific areas of operation, such as the technology, the product, the market, customers, financials, and so forth.

That said, you should take the time to document a comprehensive blueprint of your business. You can write it in whatever format you like. You can also even skip designing, branding, or making it aesthetically attractive as you would a pitch deck, for example. Just make sure you cover all aspects of your business in a very detailed and thoughtful fashion. You should look into market trends and conditions, the market opportunity, the growth of the various factors within your market, the competitive landscape, your competitive advantage, and risk analysis. You should look closely at your financials, metrics, economics, and growth margins, as well as the product roadmap.

Creating this plan has nothing to do with optics or convincing someone to invest in your business, or even recruiting a senior hire. On the contrary, it's an internal, live, dynamic document that you should refer to and update to guide your entrepreneurial journey. It will help you stay focused on what matters in your business and detect flaws in your thinking or gaps that you need to fill. Given what's at stake and the fact that, by definition, a startup is an all-consuming effort that demands your time and literally every ounce of your mental and physical energy, and it's something you will likely spend a lot of time building for many years, you cannot afford to skip this invaluable business planning. Remember, fundraising and building a business are entirely different undertakings that require different kinds of planning and documentation. Don't fall into the trap of thinking your wonderful pitch deck is sufficient as a guiding document for your business, irrespective of how much it helped you raise in VC capital.

Be Honest About the Gaps Between the Present Day and Your Ultimate Vision

By Jenny Rooke, Managing Director at Genoa Ventures

It's important to take a step back and take a long, hard look at the gaps between where your business is today and where you want it to go. This often can be a challenging exercise for extraordinary entrepreneurs because part of your strength is viewing your ultimate vision as inevitable. That can make it difficult for you to think about risks, milestones, and all of the elements that you need to think about when planning a financing journey.

VCs view potential investments in terms of risk, which can be a difficult framework for a passionate entrepreneur to relate to. Entrepreneurs are often more wired to see and be sold on the upside, and neglect to equally assess the risks involved. Identifying gaps between where you are today and where you want to be 5 or 10 years from now can help you prioritize which gaps you need to address, and in what order, over time. This can be particularly helpful in clarifying your key hires and specific milestones for each round.

This is an essential exercise to wrap your head around well before you approach investors. Subsequently, you should be able to address those risks—and your plans to mitigate them—with investors, should the topic come up. You could even prepare a slide on those gaps outside your deck, which you keep in your back pocket and pull out when you get related questions from investors. You will need to be able to speak to it and demonstrate to investors that you are cognizant of and realistic about the challenges you anticipate your company will face down the road, and that you're well prepared for them.

Identify Your Business Needs Before You Go Fundraising

By Jenny Lefcourt, General Partner at Freestyle Capital

Identify your business needs well before you go fundraising, because if you understand what needs you have, you will know which VCs are most likely to help you where you need help the most. Think about whether you are trying to create something, trying to figure something out, or looking to scale. Some VCs are quite good at the early stage and enjoy rolling up their sleeves and being part of the team and helping you execute. Some don't have the operational appetite and would rather provide their strategic input periodically. Meanwhile, others are better at the scaling stage, especially knowing how to scale certain metrics, how to recruit top-tier talent, and so forth.

You need to also look at seemingly minor but important aspects when you're making your needs assessment. For example, do you need lots of introductions? Or is it more about needing a thought partner? Do you need technical help or go-to-market help? Different investors bring different kinds of help to the table. Once you identify your business needs, you will then be able to decide who you want as your lead investor based on what essential needs they can fill for you. Then, ideally, for any leftover needs you can build a syndicate on your cap table that fills in the holes your lead may not cover.

Remember, you are solving issues beyond just capital when you are looking for a VC. It's a worthwhile exercise to identify, for instance, three areas you would want your VC to help with. Knowing those will provide you with the clarity to know whose door you want to knock on and which door you ultimately want to choose. You can take a top-tier VC brand that has all kinds of great success stories under their belt, but if they haven't worked in early stages, they are probably not going to be particularly helpful to you if you're in that stage. On the other hand, if you are looking for a VC who has a great brand name that you can leverage to attract other investors, partners, and clients, then that's a different approach. Obviously, your needs differ from one stage of the business to the next and from one fundraising to the next, so different kinds of investors will be more suitable than others at different times.

Laser In on the Right Milestones for Your Next Round

By Isabel Fox, General Partner at Outsized Ventures

As an early-stage startup founder, there will always be a lot to do, key performance indicators (KPIs) to hit, and targets to reach. That said, in the context of fundraising, it's critical that you focus on a few key inflection points and milestones and make great strides on those. The further along you can get on those milestones, the more traction you will be able to demonstrate, and the more credible and convincing you will come across to investors. Obviously, you need to make sure you identify the right milestones to begin with—not all milestones are created equal. The right kinds of milestones are ones that combine where the business needs to go with what needs to happen to prove your concept beyond a doubt, convincingly demonstrate product–market fit, and ultimately help de-risk the investment. You need to ask, "What do I need to achieve to close the next round of funding and secure that big valuation?" Typically, there are just three or four key metrics that will make a big difference as to whether you will succeed or fail with your fundraising.

Go speak to investors, including your existing investors, well before your next round to understand what they expect from a company at your stage in order to fund. What revenue and other metrics, such as customer base and gross margin, for instance, are they expecting? What does the team need to look like? Where does the product need to be? It's super important to define and focus on those areas to pave the way for your fundraising. It's never too early to start this process. If you just closed your Series A and expect that those funds give you an 18-month runway before you go out to market for your Series B, you need to figure out what your next 18 months should look like. What are the milestones that you need to reach to move the needle and set you up for your next round? How is that reflected in your business plan? Is it mainly a product, revenue, or customer growth plan? Finally, how is that reflected in what you are doing on a daily basis? From there, you can identify the key milestones you need to focus on over the months to come, so when you finally show up in front of investors on your next round you'll have the ammunition you need to set yourself up for a successful, efficient, and smooth fundraise.

———

Beware of Your Dilution Level's Impact on Future Rounds

By Sajith Pai, Director at Blume Ventures

Beware of ownership dilution levels and how they impact your future rounds. You shouldn't come into a seed round, for example, with more than 40 percent dilution. As a founder, you should not control less than 60 percent at the seed round, and ideally much more. If you're planning to raise your Series A, you should not control less than 50 percent going into it. It is seen as a very negative signal to VCs that you aren't protective of your shareholding if you have less. At the pre-seed stage, make sure not to dilute by more than 15 to 20 percent. Ideally, 15 percent should be the maximum allocated to angels and any pre-seed micro VCs. At the seed and Series A stage, 20 to 25 percent is fine, but ideally stay closer to 15 or 20 percent, and don't go above 25 percent.

Later on, as you move into Series B and Series C, your dilution should come down a bit to 10 to 15 percent. In general, be careful not to dilute a lot to angels, because you will be left with very little for the founders. This becomes a big problem. VCs often pass on many cap tables where there is some angel investor sitting with 20-25 percent. Typically, you want angel investors to have no more than 10 to 15 percent. You may think you can live with the dilution on the premise that your business will be a unicorn. You might be thinking that 3 percent of a billion-dollar businesses is still a lot of money. In reality, that's not how VCs will typically see it. They want to see founders who have more skin in the game and they are concerned that if you dilute too much and give too much to angel investors, you may not be incentivized enough.

---

2. EXPLORING FUNDRAISING OPTIONS

Always Be in Fundraising Mode

By Ali Karabey, Managing Director at 212 Ventures

Fundraising should be an everyday activity for any company, from a grocery store to a billion-dollar e-commerce marketplace. You need to think of your funding and your working capital every day, just like you do about your product, technology, and customer service. You need to know where your next dollar will come from if something good or bad happens.

Should a great opportunity arise or something terrible happen tomorrow, you need to know exactly how much money you can get and from whose pocket. This could be a bank, a VC investor, an angel, or other parties you can go to—that's why you should always be in fundraising mode. As such, it's never too early to understand and build relationships in fundraising-related areas you might need when the time comes. You should go to a bank at least once a year to take out a loan. Not because you need the money, but to get familiar with the process. You need to know exactly how much money you can get at what interest rate if you were to apply for a bank loan tomorrow. You need to know which bank to approach. Who will give you the best upside and is the easiest to deal with? Along the same lines, you need to know which investors or funding channels you could tap into if you needed money fast, whether for an emergency situation, a contingency plan, or even a great opportunity with a limited window. For instance, there might be an opportunity to bring key senior talent on board, acquire or invest in a new technology, or set up a new fulfillment center. In these scenarios, you won't have time to go fundraise first; you need to be ready to move fast.

Money is becoming more of a commodity right now, which wasn't always the case. There's a ton of money and liquidity in the market today. If you're not able to raise it tomorrow, you didn't plan properly and it's essentially your own fault. The only reason to go to a VC is to get better terms and better support; a good VC can bring tremendous value in terms of strategic and network support. That's obviously your ideal scenario. Still, it's important to line up your default options for fast money. You don't necessarily have to go and get a bank loan if you don't need money. You just need to know how much you qualify for, who to talk with, and which employee needs to sign what, for you to get, for example, a $100,000 loan from a bank tomorrow. At minimum, knowing that such options for fast money are available to you will orient your mindset to be more creative and opportunistic.

Another channel you could also feel out is your corporate customers. You can approach them to see if they would be willing to provide upfront funding in exchange for a discount. Enterprise customers have deep pockets, so they might jump on the opportunity to save money they would otherwise pay you. In that case, you don't have to worry about interest or complicated bank procedures. Especially if you're in a business-to-business (B2B) sector, it helps to know whether your corporate clients can front you some cash, if and when you need it.

Be on the Lookout for Alternative Sources of Financing to Venture Capital

By Elisa Miller-Out, Managing Partner at Chloe Capital

There are all types of funding out there for all different types of founders and businesses. Some investors want a big financial return. However, believe it or not, there are other investors who actually don't care about financial return at all and may invest for pure impact return. There are also some investors in the middle who want some of each. Some investors might be OK with even a negative return on an investment if they are looking to achieve a particular outcome or societal contribution.

There are other types of financing channels, including crowdfunding. Equity crowdfunding is a very popular way to raise money. That's an alternative to typical venture capital in some cases, and synergistic with venture capital in others. Crowdfunding is sometimes used to generate market interest and a community of excited and engaged customers.

In some cases, you can also fund your business through your customers. One of the best ways to prove product–market fit is to have customers who are willing to invest in your company, either as formal investors or, in some cases, just by paying up front for your product or service. If you can get advance payments from customers, that shows that there's a real demand, and you can use that to help fund the operations of your business, depending on your business model.

There are obviously many creative ways to fund businesses with tokens and initial coin offerings (ICOs). That craze has come and gone to some degree, but there are still lots of models out there for ICOs and similar things in the crypto world.

You can also fund businesses the old-fashioned way: with loans. There are lots of types of business loans you can get. You can even fund businesses on your credit cards—this is not ideal, but a lot of startups have to do whatever it takes, especially in the early days when you're just proving out the model.

Much of this depends on what kind of business you run. There are founders who are focused on running lifestyle businesses that throw off a lot of cash, rather than a VC-based business that needs an exit or a liquidity event in order to pay its investors back. If you are running a lifestyle business, some of those loans or certain other models might work a lot better than venture capital.

Explore Non-Dilutive Sources of Funding
By Shuo Chen, General Partner at IOVC

You should explore non-diluted sources of funding whenever possible, particularly before you fundraise. Non-dilutive funding is any capital you can secure that doesn't require you to give up equity or ownership. However, just because you don't give up equity or shares doesn't necessarily mean the funding comes with no strings attached; there may be conditions to qualify for the funding or to fulfill afterward. If you explore this approach, it's important that you make sure that whatever obligation you commit to (if any) is something you can live up to, and ultimately that whatever downside involved is less than the value attained from the funding.

There are plenty of non-dilutive sources of funding available in the US, predominantly for research-oriented startups. If you are building something that is based on, for example, biotech research or some type of hardware research, plenty of universities will offer unique networks that help you plug into funding sources. The National Science Foundation is a great platform for you to plug into—it is an independent agency of the US government that supports fundamental research and education for everything that's non-medical. It spans across all sciences and engineering. There are also plenty of equivalent foundations that fund medical research, as well as many other foundations that support science-enabled research. Other forms of non-dilutive funding include crowdfunding, contributions from donors, tax credit programs, vouchers, grants, competitions, government relief programs, licensing, product royalties, and awards such as public grants.

Traditional bank loans are more difficult to secure, given their regulatory restrictions. Thus, banks loans are more attainable for established enterprises with greater cash flow, credit, and collateral (typically in the form of hard assets), as well as a favorable debt-to-income ratio. As a startup founder, most of the time when you are raising early money, you are raising a convertible note anyway. A convertible note is equivalent of a loan, except you haven't yet decided on what specifically its value is until the next round, though typically there is a valuation cap. Raising on a convertible note or a simple agreement for future equity (SAFE) by Y Combinator is actually a great way to move forward, because it's so much faster than if you were to go through a bank to get a loan.

Venture debt is another form of non-dilutive finance that's available only to VC-backed companies. It is issued from a specialized venture debt lender, such as a hedge fund or private equity. There are plenty of examples of well-established companies that have used venture debt to finance their operations and secured mid-term loans. Airbnb and Uber are two such companies.

On the other hand, the time trade-off that is required for you to raise non-dilutive sources of funding may not be worth the effort. But it's always important to think about whether a non-dilutive source of capital is an option for you as the first step, before you start looking at venture capital.

———

Fully Use Social Media to
Tap Funding Channels

By Anis Uzzaman, CEO at Pegasus Tech Ventures

Fundraising is difficult, especially if you're in a country where there are not many VCs and angel investors. How do you solve that problem? How do you fundraise when you do not know anyone, or you have not done a startup before? The internet has brought the world into closer proximity, but trying to use social media and internet resources effectively to raise your early money is extremely difficult—more difficult than you think.

LinkedIn, the professional social network, has brought the business world together. Using LinkedIn—and even Facebook and Instagram—is an effective way to reach out to investors in remote locations. These platforms have made our lives easier in this regard. Still, you have to reach out to a larger number of investors, especially if you have no fundraising background and don't know many investors. If you're reaching out to, say, 10 or 20 investors, your chance of success is going to be extremely slim. You should reach out to 100, 200, or even 300 investors. Then, your possibility of raising capital will be higher.

Also, look at crowdfunding platforms. A lot of companies sitting in remote locations are raising money successfully through these platforms, because you're able to raise money from around the world if you have a good idea and a promising product in place. There are many crowdfunding platforms out there that you can use to take your business to the next level. One that has become very popular recently is Indiegogo. Indiegogo has one of the best-performing fundraising traction levels among crowdfunding platforms, and lot of startups have raised seed capital there. Other ones that have done well include GoFundMe, StartEngine, and Mightycause. Many entrepreneurs have also used these platforms, and other types of angel platforms, to raise funds. Patreon is another platform that many entrepreneurs have used successfully. A traditional one that has been around for some time is Kickstarter. There are also platforms like LendingClub and CircleUp. Kickstarter and Indiegogo are the two most famous ones, and a lot of entrepreneurs have raised money through them. Crowdfunding platforms allow you to raise capital from anywhere in the world. Some entrepreneurs have raised $300,000 or more, and a few have even raised more than $1 million on these platforms.

Crowdfunding platforms work best for companies that have a physical product—say you're developing a next-generation toothbrush or household appliance. Crowdfunding platforms have also worked well for hardware products and other consumer products that can be pre-ordered, where you can attract buyers who essentially fund your launch.

Manage Friends and Family's Expectations if You Choose to Get Money from Them

By Izhar Shay, Venture Partner at DisruptAI

Before you seek VC money, you want to look at other options out there, explore whether they're right for you, and make sure you exhaust those options first. For example, debt financing in the form of loans, as well as investment from friends and family, are a couple of common starting points. Raising money from your friends and family doesn't mean that you disregard their interests; it doesn't mean that you can take them less seriously than you would a professional investor. On the contrary, this is an even more significant decision, because you are taking money from people you have a personal relationship with. You have to deeply respect their investment and manage their expectations. In this regard, the rule of thumb is to take money only from people you're confident you will be able to stay on good terms with if things go south—that is, if your business fails or their money gets blown away, it will not impact your personal relationship with them going forward.

To navigate this delicately, you also need to be up front with them about the potential upside and downside involved in your business. Definitely share your excitement with them—talk to them about your big dream and how you are going to disrupt an industry and change the world—but also warn them in great detail about the various associated risks. Tell them about the very problematic statistic that the vast majority of early-stage high-tech ventures fold within five years. Explain to them what it means to fund a startup, including the odds of success and a healthy return on investment (ROI). Make sure they're fully aware of the big picture and what they're getting into.

———————

3. DECIDING TO RAISE VC CAPITAL

Grasp How Venture Capital Works

By Izhar Shay, Venture Partner at DisruptAI

Understand the venture capital model so that you're in a good position to align your interests with your investor partners'. As an entrepreneur, you're excited (and rightfully so) about your business, your technology or product, or your service—whatever you're offering that you feel will make a significant positive change in the world. That said, you have to remember the interests of the investors that put money into your business. Yes, they are also excited about your business, but investors also have fiduciary obligations. Especially if they are venture capital investors, they have to provide returns to their limited partners (LPs) or limited liability investors who financed them in the first place.

A venture capital investment firm is a financial platform somewhere along the food chain of the flow of funds between investors and high-tech startups. As such, venture capital investors have to carefully choose their investments. Their number one obligation is to provide returns to their investors—this is very important for you to realize and understand. You also have to understand that VCs have a limited timeframe to realize returns; that's just is the nature of the industry. VC firms typically have an expiration date, which could be in 7, 10, or 12 years. Whatever it is set at, it's a finite time limit that can be extended only under special provisions. Thus, investors have a limited time to choose the right investments and help their portfolio companies scale, and also to realize returns. That's why investors need to think about an exit strategy for any company they invest in, or some other way to provide financial returns to their LP investors.

This could take the form of a secondary investment event, where somewhere down the road someone comes in and buys those investors' shares. This is the case with many early-stage investors today, who sell their shares to later-stage investors. This provides positive returns to the investors and the company continues to run its business.

As an entrepreneur, you have to be aware of that significant interest of your investors. You also need to align your interests with theirs in terms of growing the company and identifying opportunities for their stakeholders. Often, misunderstandings, clashes, arguments, dysfunctional boards, and severed relationships result simply from a lack of understanding of the dynamics at play in terms of investors' drivers, and a mismatch between what investors need and what entrepreneurs want.

Granted, no one can force entrepreneurs to do something against their will. If an entrepreneur wants to sell their company, eventually the investors will have to agree. If the entrepreneur wants to continue to run their company, it will be very hard for investors to convince them to sell it. Still, within those very general guidelines there is a lot of room for agreement and alignment of interests or, in many cases, serious clashes that could have a significant negative impact on company performance or, sadly, ultimately result in company devaluation or even demise.

Understand the Mindset of a Venture Capitalist

By Jenny Lefcourt, General Partner at Freestyle Capital

Before you go fundraising, try to understand how a VC thinks and operates, what their day looks like, and what they are looking for in a startup. Because when you do, it will change your perspective, your mental game, and how you go into a pitch—you won't just go in there and try to sell. This will help you to not be intimated by the undertaking, to be more relaxed, and to enjoy the fundraising process.

A typical VC has their days full of meetings. They're excited about novel ideas and innovative approaches to tackling big problems and capturing big opportunities. They are excited to meet brilliant, action-oriented founders and founding teams. Typical VCs want to be generous; they want to add value. They are also constantly looking to learn and grow. If you know this, you won't go in a meeting with VCs and just try to sell whatever you built. You will go in and be curious throughout the whole meeting, including when challenges are brought up.

You should also understand that VCs usually have a short attention span. They are typically making a judgment about you and your business much earlier in the meeting than you imagine. The best founders are the ones that walk that tightrope between having conviction and self-belief and being open to learning. That's the kind of balance you want to strike. VCs want to work with founders who are very curious, want to learn, and are good listeners, but who also have strong convictions and are thoughtful about what they are building and doing.

If you approach a low-probability investor meeting with the attitude, "Well, I am not sure if I am going to get any money here, but I am going to learn something from this meeting," that attitude will show up in how you pitch, converse, and take feedback. You will likely learn from literally every pitch meeting because VCs see so much.

You're ultimately more likely to raise capital this way than if you don't capitalize on the opportunity to meet VCs as a learning journey.

Remember that VCs are not your adversaries—they are your potential partners. VCs want to be partners with the founders that they back, so they want to know that they can have honest conversations with people who are confident and determined about executing their vision, but who also have the humility to learn from others and from their mistakes. VCs absolutely think long term; they are trying to add long-term value. You do not have to be fearful that VCs are going to rip you off or be combative. They are typically trying to do the exact opposite. You should understand that they can be trusted and they probably have some great insights and value to add. If you understand the typical VC's mindset, then you can go in there and enjoy meeting them to talk about your business as if it's a free business consulting meeting that is likely to help you.

Today, VCs are increasingly rooting for founders everywhere—both the founders they work with and the founders they don't work with. VCs are usually optimists and founder-friendly. In the past, when there was less capital in the market, the power was more titled in favor of the VCs, but the best VCs didn't want to take advantage of that power dynamic. They genuinely wanted a partner, and they wanted to do their part (and let the founders do their part) to help make the company super successful. Nowadays, there is so much capital in the market that there's a better balance of power between the founder and the VC. In addition, because of social media, founders are more connected and VCs' conduct and reputation can spread like wildfire, for better or for worse. More than ever, VCs are conscious of this, and they're keen to do the right things, all of which obviously works in favor of founders.

Be an Avid Student of the VC Game

By Brad Feld, Co-Founder of Foundry Group and Techstars

As an entrepreneur, it pays to study and stay abreast of what's happening in the VC world. The best way to be a student of the VC game is to read. One of the challenges with learning is that people tend not to go deep enough into a topic to really master it; instead, they skim the surface of things. When you are trying to get a handle on how venture capital works, you have access to a lot of different sources of content from lots of different places. Twenty years ago, there was very little writing about venture capital, with most of the literature being theoretical and academic. Today, every VC has a blog. There are numerous books about venture capital. There are many articles about investing and how to invest, along with tons of podcasts. VCs are talking all the time about what they do and how they do it.

That said, when I say read, I really mean read. Watching videos and listening to podcasts is additive, but if you don't read the original source material, you won't master the basics. If you don't read what people write, whether in published books or articles, what you get is a lot of sloppy thinking. When people write, they tend to be more crisp, concise, and structured with what they say than when they are interviewed or talking on podcasts. While you will get a lot of anecdotes and stories in videos and podcasts, which can be entertaining, you'll often be learning at surface level.

Another key to learning is to engage and participate. It's one thing to be an intellectual student of venture capital; it's entirely different, and much more powerful, to participate by being an entrepreneur and by talking with VCs instead of being a passive observer.

If you're a first-time entrepreneur or new to venture capital, it doesn't matter which aspect of the field you start learning about. You want to start broadly and cover a wide range of different topics. Absorb as much as you can early on across the full spectrum. Reading about the fundamentals, such as learning about how term sheets work, and getting exposed to material that investors have written about how they started their venture capital fund is a great place to start.

Once you have grasped the fundamentals, you can go deeper into the specific areas you are most interested in. Are you an early-stage or growth-stage founder? Are you operating in climate tech, blockchain, or crypto? Are you interested in B2B software as a service (SaaS)? Go deeper into specialized areas to try to understand those markets and environments. Then, read some stories about successful companies in those spaces and how they navigated their fundraising, grew, and developed their businesses.

Focus on the evolution of super successful companies to understand how these companies evolved over time. There have been a number of great books written about the evolution from the early stages of Facebook, Amazon, Google, and many other remarkable companies. Go back even further and look at the early stages of Apple, Microsoft, HP, Intel, and IBM. Learning the startup history of these companies will give you a much broader perspective than just studying what is going on today.

Explore what has happened in multiple geographies. Instead of just reading about US venture capital, read things like Christopher Schroeder's great book about the Middle East, *Startup Rising*, as well as *Startup Nation*, which is about Israel's remarkable entrepreneurial ecosystem—those are classic. You could also learn about Alibaba and how it grew into a global powerhouse out of a humble apartment in China. Understanding how these startups and startup communities developed and evolved in different geographies, beyond just Silicon Valley, is important. Then, cut across that and instead of focusing just on venture capital, learn more broadly about entrepreneurship and startup communities. Understanding how entrepreneurial ecosystems grow and develop will give you the big-picture perspective you need to understand the interplay between the different components of this world.

While some things with respect to early-stage investing have remained the same in the last 30 years, many things are quite different today. The arc of an entrepreneur and the development of an investing profile have changed a lot, along with how VCs invest in today's market environment. If we go back to the mid-1990s, there were very few geographies where there was a lot of VC investing, and most of it was concentrated in the San Francisco Bay Area, Boston, and a few other places. Today, venture capital is increasingly being globally democratized. You now see angel investors and VCs investing in every major city, all over the world, and lots of non-major cities. This change occurred alongside the idea—amplified by the Covid-19 crisis—that investors no longer have to be physically close to the companies they are investing in. Countless other aspects of venture capital investing have changed in the last decade, including how to engage, pitch, negotiate, and secure fundraising, along with navigating your entire relationship with your investors after fundraising.

Make Sure You Absolutely Need to Raise VC Capital

By Izhar Shay, Venture Partner at DisruptAI

When it comes to fundraising, the two fundamental questions you should ask yourself first are, "Am I absolutely sure that I must raise money from professional investors or venture capital firms?" and "Am I absolutely confident that I have explored all other options and determined that VC financing is the right approach to building my business?" This might be your only option. For example, if you are building a capital-intensive, very fast-growing business, where you are going to need a lot of money at high risk, then venture capital is the right option for you. On the other hand, if you're building a business that will be generating positive cash flow quite quickly, that doesn't necessarily need millions and millions of dollars as a starting point just in order to get a product out of the door, then venture capital is not necessarily for you.

Take a deep, hard look into your business plan and your financial needs before you commit to the VC fundraising route, because it comes with a lot of ramifications, including giving up equity as well as the toll it takes in on you and your business in time and focus.

Fundraising can indeed be a very time-consuming undertaking. Granted, in today's market conditions, it may be a bit faster than it used to be. Still, when you decide to play the VC game, you need to learn and adopt its rules. If mismanaged, this undertaking could drag your attention and resources away from the business, and ultimately hurt business performance, before you raise a single dollar.

Additionally, partnering with VC investors means a whole set of rules of engagement: educating investors on the specifics of your business, raising those funds, managing those funds, partnering with investors along the way, growing your company, and making decisions jointly with people who did not start your business with you. It also means formal reporting, board meetings, board decisions, longer processes, and so on. You have to know that this is the world that you are entering; these are the rules of the game that you will have to abide by and learn to play with.

You have to take all that into consideration. There are no major decisions that you are going to be able to make without the appropriate approval, consent, and agreements (amicable or not) of your investors. That's something you have to thoughtfully and seriously consider before you decide to raise money from a professional investor.

Go for It, Your Timing is Perfect

By Christopher M. Schroeder, Co-Founder of Next Billion Venture

You've decided to raise venture capital and you're debating whether this is the right time. My advice is to go for it, since your timing couldn't be more perfect, as of the writing of this book—assuming, of course, that you've created an investable business and you're investor-ready. This moment is, far and away, the most entrepreneur-friendly environment for investing. The good news for you is that there's a tremendous amount of new capital that's available in the world. You have a lot of investors, whether they're single investors or funds, looking at opportunities globally, not just in the US, in ways that they've not looked before. There have never been more funds rising than now. From a range of very early-stage investors who are writing big checks, to later stages with bigger funds and wider investment themes and scopes, to corporate VCs that feel the pressure to diversify and embrace new digital trends and emerging technologies, and finally to family offices that are now in the hands of the younger generation, who want to provide venture capital, there's a significant amount of capital and liquidity in the market.

As a result, you can dictate your terms when negotiating with investors a little bit more than has been the case historically. You can get very good valuations, which means you don't have to get diluted as much. That's all great. What entrepreneurs may be missing in this narrative, however, is that the story isn't just about money: it's about choice. If you can get money anywhere, you may be tempted to take the best valuation. The opportunity you're missing is that in addition to all this capital out there, there's also expertise. This is not just an era of inflated valuations and money, it's an era of entrepreneurs' opportunity to surround themselves with the women and men who can help them win in the future.

Also, in terms of timing, what's been unleashed in technology over the last five to seven years (and accelerated by Covid-19) is widespread access to technology. It's almost as if a billion new customers have appeared almost overnight, because they not only have access to the technology, they also have the mental capacity, desire, and experience to want to use it in new ways. Once you've been forced to buy items for the first time and have them delivered to your house, e-commerce doesn't look scary anymore. If you've never had access to a bank account, and thus you've never been able to borrow money except from your family or from some loan shark, and suddenly you have access to mobile money and you can get credit, that's a game changer. All of these things become multiplier revolutions in consumer behavior. It's like those billion customers just got released into the global economy. The implication for you, when it comes to fundraising, is that a significantly greater number of VCs are recognizing these opportunities and looking to take advantage of them. This works in your favor, of course. As long as you can position yourself to ride this new technological wave and have built a sustainable business that addresses a real problem or opportunity in the market, you have greater access to capital than ever before.

When you combine this with the availability of talent everywhere, a greater ability to tap into that talent virtually, and greater access to data—all of which is leveling the playing field—you no longer to have to be in Silicon Valley to build a world-class company. While being in a certain geographical location—such as a tech hub—still has advantages, those on the outside are no longer excluded from the global arena. There are actually some advantages to being in an emerging market, including lower cost of operating and cheaper talent. Granted, the network effect of talent in a single geographic location remains a powerful dynamic, which will not go away entirely. Certainly, if you're in Silicon Valley, New York, Boston, London, Singapore, Dubai, or São Paulo, you have a greater opportunity to meet and network with investors. But the world is becoming more connected and the trend of remote investing, which was already happening, has only accelerated (as did remote working in general) as a result of Covid-19. The former requirement that you must be in a certain physical geographic hub to scale a startup and tap into international markets to raise capital is no longer the case.

As a result, exceptional entrepreneurs and startups are springing up everywhere, even in unlikely places. Consequently, VCs are becoming more geography agnostic and globally minded than ever. They're realizing that innovation can come from anywhere, and they've set their eyes on what's happening beyond their backyard. They're looking at what's happening in Latin America, Southeast Asia, Africa, and the Middle East. As a founder, no matter where you are, your access to global capital has never been greater. There's no guarantee that it will stay that way, so take advantage of this window while it's open and don't delay this step any longer if you decide it's the right path. Simply, go for it!

Raise Money When You Need It

By Shuo Chen, General Partner at IOVC

The best time to raise capital is when every single dollar that you put into your startup can spit out a multiple of itself. The right multiple obviously varies from company to company and from sector to sector, but at a minimum it is anything more than one. Of course, the bigger that number, the better. If you have yet to develop a scalable business model where your startup is ROI positive, then you're not in the right position to ask for money. If you do, you're probably going to unnecessarily dilute yourself. Many founders tend to equate how much funding they have managed to raise with success of the startup, whereas the real metric of how successful your startup has become is how scalable your business model is.

You might be in a capital-intensive sector like hardware, where you do need that upfront capital investment, but even then you should try to explore non-diluted sources of funding as early as possible to work out a minimum viable product (MVP) and proof of concept before you go to fundraise. On the other hand, the vast majority of tech sectors—for instance, software and enterprise SaaS—are not as capital intensive. In those cases, you should focus on building your product before you go to raise money.

One question that you should ask before you go to fundraise is "If I were able to raise 10 times the funding that I have now, what would I actually do with that money?" Not because you are anticipating that funding down the line, but because you are being creative as to how you can scale your current business even faster. Let's say you are going to the market trying to raise $10 million; what would you do if you brought in $100 million instead? It's actually a lot of pressure to have that much money, because you wouldn't know what to do with it and where to spend it. Challenge yourself to be creative from a business-building perspective. What would you do with this capital that would actually be conducive to building your business faster and better?

Raise Money When You Can

By Jimmy Fussing Nielsen, Co-Founder of Heartcore Capital

A common mistake entrepreneurs make is to say we just need to build this feature on the product, we need to launch in this new country, or we need to hire these senior executives before we go fundraising. Their rationale is that if they fix these things, they will get a higher valuation. At face value, this may be true, but this will be true at any point in time in a company's life. However, the risk of delaying is that you may encounter an unanticipated variable or an event outside of your control that can derail your fundraising altogether. For instance, you might be in a buying market and friendly environment now, and just three weeks from now things could dramatically change for some reason. Nobody really knows how the market will behave and when, and consequently how it will influence investors' behavior. If you're in a position to raise funds at meaningful valuations that are not too punitive and raise an amount that sustains you for 18 to 24 months, then I say: take it; don't delay.

The most successful companies out there typically raise often. They don't just raise when they need funds, they also raise when they can. This means that in good times, they will usually raise every eight or nine months, whereas in bad times, they will usually raise every two years.

You shouldn't wait for a commercial or operational milestone to secure capital that may later become substantially more difficult to raise. As a startup, the risk of running dry is often much greater than the upside of maximizing valuation. If you have a good opportunity to get a quality investor in at a fair value round, and maybe get diluted say just 15-20 percent in the current market, you should take the money rather than defer to a later time.

Tragically, there have been too many good companies that couldn't raise funds because their timing was wrong—for example, after the 2008 financial crisis. Fortunately, that hasn't been the case during Covid-19; the market and investors' appetite is holding strong. Still, the market can be volatile at times and could flip in a blink, so it's better to raise when you can.

———

Pursue Growth Capital Only When Your Playbook Is Working

By Jimmy Fussing Nielsen, Co-Founder of Heartcore Capital

In an effort to demonstrate traction, momentum, and scale to investors, many founders focus too much on revenue and growth velocity and not enough on whether their unit economics work at scale, and they cut corners around fixing their product. Because of this, they never establish a clear product–market fit. They try to jump ahead to generating revenues, and focus on such areas as performance marketing and public relations (PR) to drive growth. Their rationale is that if they can go big fast, they will attract investor dollars—but then they hit a ceiling when they blow through a lot of cash and the product–market fit isn't there. When there's no product–market fit, there will be no stickiness. You then run the risk of depleting your marketing channels while watching your customer acquisition costs balloon. You never achieve organic or viral consumer uptake: a recipe for stalling.

You can cut corners by moving too fast and skipping critical foundational steps and even try to raise international expansion capital. I have seen this happen quite a bit, and it almost always ends in a lack of focus and wasted time and resources, and ultimately hinders growth and future fundraising. As an entrepreneur, especially an early-stage one, never try to expand without a sufficient proof of concept and a strong foundation. Skipping this step will likely come back to bite you over time.

Weigh the Pros and Cons of VCs, CVCs, Strategics, and Family Offices

By Simon Cant, Managing Partner at Reinventure Group

One question on many early-stage founders' minds at the beginning of any fundraising is what type of investors should they pursue. Should you pursue a traditional VC or go after corporate venture capital (CVC), strategics, or family offices? There are certainly pros and cons to each type.

One of the strengths of VCs is their alignment around the startup's success. VCs are set up as independent firms with the standard carry management fee model, where the partners only get paid when they exit. They get around 20 percent of the upside after the capital has been returned. This makes VCs a natural fit for high-growth startups and scaleups, since their interests are clearly aligned with those of the entrepreneur. Both are striving to generate a solid return from the startup that they have poured their time, effort, and resources into. That's the beauty of the venture capital model.

On the other hand, occasionally VCs' incentives can create a problematic alignment. One of the traps that you need to watch for with a VC is being forced into a "grow or die" mentality. A lot of larger VCs will have a minimum amount that they need to deploy every year. That means that if they are investing in your Series A, for example, they will be doing that with the intention that they need to be able to put to work at least two, three, or even four or five times the capital that they have initially invested over the life of the startup's expansion. Thus, they will push you very hard toward an aggressive growth trajectory. If that is not something that your business is ready for or well suited to, it can create an environment where they pressure you to spend too much money too fast, sometimes doing what's been described as premature scaling. In fact, according to surveys on startup failure, premature scaling is one of the key causes. Being driven toward premature scaling by VCs that need to deploy a minimum amount of funding can significantly hurt your business and even cause it to fail. That's certainly a situation you want to avoid.

Another type of investor is strategics, typically in the form of an alliance or a joint venture with a larger corporate investor. The opportunity with strategics lies in the fact that strategics typically have some assets that, if unleashed, can be powerful tools in the hands of the startup. That in itself can be a massive upside, in addition to the capital infusion. The downside with strategics is that if the corporate fund is not set up well, it might have misaligned incentives compared with the startup's objectives. After all, the fund will be primarily focused on meeting the aims of its parent corporation. Consequently, the aims of the startup are often a secondary priority to those of corporation; and where a potential conflict of interest might emerge—as in the case of the startup working with a corporation's competitor—the corporate relations could prevent or limit such a collaboration.

If you are dealing with a strategic, it's therefore important to understand what their alignment and incentives are. You need to ask that question and understand their underlying agenda and objectives. You also need to know the particular executives' incentives. Often, the incentive may just be salary, or salary with some kind of bonus structure. It's important to understand that bonus structure, because it's likely to indicate how they will operate as an investor over the long term: where that bonus demonstrates a short-term incentive, they will not be aligned with the startup's long-term ambitions. They may in fact operate in a way that's misaligned with the startup's long-term interests. That's something you want to watch out for. Be careful, because they may end up pushing you to accept a particular short-term outcome that isn't necessarily going to drive the long-term success of your company.

When you are dealing with strategics, it's also important to understand how long the partner associate you're dealing with has been in the role. One of the challenges with strategics is the high turnover among staff. You need to ask what the typical tenure of people in the corporate venture investing role is. That will give you some indication of how long you can expect that person to be on your board. When you are dealing with an investor who isn't the same person who made the investment, it's more difficult to get them to fall in love with your company, let alone get them up to speed. One way to mitigate this risk a bit is to make sure that you build relationships with a range of people within that corporation. That way, if your point person moves on and you lose your champion, you've got other people who you can deal with. You want to make sure you're not vulnerable to any potential key personnel turnover that could derail your plans and your business at large.

It's also worth understanding other types of investors, such as family offices, which will also have slightly different incentives from VCs. Family offices can be quite good investors, because they often are prepared to take lower returns than a VC fund. A typical VC fund is looking for a minimum of 10 times their invested money on any individual investment. That's because the economics of venture capital only work at such ROI levels. On the other hand, family offices are much more prepared to invest in something where they might get three to four times their money, perhaps with a high level of confidence. They're not necessarily looking for stellar growth or unicorn-type exits; family offices will give you much more leeway in terms of potential exits. Whereas a VC may shoot down, for instance, a $100-million-dollar acquisition, a family office investor may jump on it.

The other thing to bear in mind when you're dealing with family offices, and particularly angels, is how savvy these people are as venture investors. Sometimes they're inexperienced as investors and thus have dramatically unrealistic expectations about when they're going to get their money back and how startups work. They may also lack the domain expertise to support your business or the deep investor network to help you secure your next fundraise. Occasionally, they may want to exercise too much control, particularly negative control with respect to authorizing certain business decisions. There are situations, for instance, where an angel with a 1 percent share of a company refuses to sign the shareholder agreement for the round to close unless they get their money back out of the business as part of the transaction. These kinds of dynamics can also turn VCs away from future rounds, because they typically want to see a capable founder who is in control and well incentivized to build the business.

It's important to understand the various types of investors out there and the upside and downside of each, and to know which one is best suited to your business. You also need to look at the impact of bringing a particular type of investor on board in terms of your business needs and future rounds. What additional business support beyond cash, if any, can they offer you? Do they have enough capital and will they be willing to deploy it to finance your next round? Are they committed to the relationship, and can you count on them in the long haul, especially if you don't hit your targets? Or will they lose interest? What kind of controls and approvals will they exercise? Will they be micromanaging business decisions and spending, for example? How flexible are they about accepting certain exits or outcomes for the business?

Know Exactly What You Want if You're Taking Money from a Corporate VC

By Manuel Silva Martinez, General Partner at Mouro Capital

When you take money from regular VC, you know exactly what they're looking for. They're looking for financial return—that's the main thing they care about. It's very easy as an entrepreneur to align with what VCs want: to maximize upside and financial return. On the other hand, if you take money from a corporate VC, it's very important that you understand their agenda behind the investment, to the extent that they invest strategically. They will normally also want financial returns, but they may have an additional interest in partnering with you. Instead of waiting for them to tell you what you need to know, it's better for you to ask them. You also need to define what synergies and collaborations with the corporate you will be able to tap into. Those can come in a variety of forms: revenue, accessing their customer base, de-risking an international expansion, profiting from brand affiliation, etc. Make sure you align with them on the objectives of the relationship very clearly and very early on. That way you can assess the value of the partnership and the feasibility of the aspirations on both sides.

Be very specific about what you want but also what you can offer. If the expectations are unrealistic or misaligned at the outset—or there is not a clear roadmap for building the relationship that makes you comfortable that there is a win-win at the end of the tunnel—those are sure signs that the entity shouldn't be part of your cap table. Including them could complicate things down the road and potentially slow you down and hinder your growth, especially to the extent that they have some governance controls or decision-making authority. You should make every effort to avoid that.

Prepare to Adjust Quickly if You're Unable to Secure Financing

By Jon Soberg, Managing Partner at MS&AD Ventures

If you ran a fundraising process and you were not able to get enough investor commitments (or any), depending on how much time you have in terms of runway, you will likely need to make some drastic changes. You will absolutely have to cut your burn rate (i.e., your spending) due to lack of financing. You might also need to piece smaller checks into a bridge round or an extension to the last round. If you were planning to raise, say, $10 million and only managed to raise $1 million or $2 million, you will likely have to take a bit more dilution than you wanted to. Perhaps the market is telling you that you are not ready for a $10 million round, because all the investors said no.

Acknowledge what the market is saying and adjust your plans to deal with the lack of financing. Most importantly, try to keep everything alive and keep moving forward. Also, take whatever feedback you received from investors and address it in your preparation for your next fundraising. If you get a bunch of investors saying no—and "a bunch" can be subjective, in terms of how many that is—it's not worth beating your head against the wall for months. The markets have already basically told you that you are not ready. Furthermore, the VCs know each other, so they already know that you are in the market and that your metrics were not quite there.

You really have to think about your new reality operationally. Try to cut down your costs, find ways to piece together maybe a third round, or extend the last round to give yourself some more runway, and essentially buy yourself more time to regroup and then hit those milestones for the next round. It's a painful process. Make the necessary changes, get some additional metrics, and maybe get back out to fundraise in a few months when you're in a better position.

———

4. PLANNING TO FUNDRAISE

Plan and Budget Resources Before You Undertake Fundraising

By Caio Bolognesi, Partner at Monashees

Fundraising can be an overwhelming and very time-consuming task. As such, you want to plan ahead and budget time for it. Don't expect that you will be able to run your business as usual and juggle a full fundraising process in the background; there's just too much to be done, especially if you're looking to maximize the probability of successful fundraising. Many entrepreneurs make that mistake only to see their business's performance drop as they get dragged into more demanding and longer-than-expected fundraising. You should start thinking about your backups well before you start fundraising. Think about who on your team is going to fill in for you, and in which areas, while you're preoccupied with fundraising. Make sure they're capable and empowered to make as many decisions as possible, so you can remain attentive to fundraising. You will need to give them more autonomy than usual, and prep them beforehand accordingly.

You will also need to set up efficient check-ins to stay abreast of things and provide counsel on any critical issues. Your role should transition to be strategic rather than operational in scope during your fundraising. Granted, that's easier said than done in the face of emergencies and your typical startup's fire drills. Hence, the better you plan ahead, the less likely you are to drop the ball on the business or have to compromise fundraising to attend to business needs.

What you don't want is to go to market and start talking to investors while your business metrics are deteriorating in your absence, then have this become a concern or even a red flag to investors in terms of the sustainability of the business or the strength of your second in command and your management team. Investors like to see consistency when it comes to performance metrics. They also want to see that the management team in place is capable of executing in the absence of the founder. If you, as founder, take your eyes off the ball for a couple of months and then suddenly your business growth halts—or worse, drops—it certainly won't reflect well on you and your team, and on the business as a whole, to investors. It might not necessarily be a deal breaker with VCs, especially if you're further along in the fundraising process and, for example, you're already beyond term sheets. Still, you are likely to have some explaining to do to the investors. All this, of course, can be avoided by picking a good time to fundraise, budgeting the time it will need, and placing and preparing the right team members in key areas.

Most notably, if you're anticipating a major event you need to attend to, then it will be better to defer fundraising until after it. For example, if you're an e-commerce business and you expect Black Friday and the holidays to be your busiest time, then that's probably not the time to start raising capital unless you absolutely have to. The rule of thumb is to start fundraising at a moment where the company can operate without you.

You can also slightly increase in your marketing spend while you're attending to investors, to make sure business growth continues. Granted, VCs will ask you for a breakdown of marketing investments and acquisition channels; still, it's always positive to see the line go up.

Sometimes founders also time a press event or cover story in a business or industry publication to correspond with fundraising in the hope that investors will be impressed by the additional buzz. This rarely works. VCs are desensitized to any media and PR-related coverage for companies. If it's overdone, it can actually backfire. That is, if investors perceive a founder to be very involved in speaking at media events, they may question his or her focus on the business. That's not to say that all press is bad, just make sure you're not simply trying to hype the business for the sake of fundraising. Of course, if the press coverage is organic and more related to business performance and drivers—for example, an industry award for best product or best marketing campaign or customer service—then that's great to showcase to investors.

Fundraising is a burden for founders and startups; however, if it's well planned in terms of time and resource allocation, it can be manageable. In most cases, the time and attention you put into the process will be strongly correlated with the outcome.

Go for a Bridge Round if You Haven't Hit Your Milestones

By Jon Soberg, Managing Partner at MS&AD Ventures

One topic that comes up often within companies and boards is whether and when to raise bridge capital. This discussion should come up earlier rather than later. As a founder, you don't want to put yourself in a corner where you have a short time horizon before you run out of cash, or before you hit your milestones. As always, if possible, you want to have as much buffer time on your side as you can. You should be planning and working on your financing round six to nine months ahead of time. Take a hard look at whether or not you're likely to hit the milestones and metrics that make your traction compelling for your next round, especially in relation to the funding you received on your last round. For example, say you raised $15 million on your last round a year ago, and you've only grown by 20 percent since then and your annual recurring revenue (ARR) is $1 million, that might not be an impressive enough record to leverage for your planned next raise of $30 million. If you think you're not going to hit your numbers within the timeframe, or you're not sure about it, then that's when you should be looking at creating a wedge in the form of a bridge round. Ideally, it could be an internal round with existing investors, but it may involve new outside capital as well. The idea is to provide you with a quick capital infusion that's just enough to give you additional runway to hit your target milestones. This is not the ideal scenario, but it's a practical one under those circumstances.

The worst-case scenario is that you go to market without those milestones and metrics, you get a bunch of nos from VCs, and then everybody knows a few months later that you failed to raise and assumes that it's probably due to lack of traction. Then, the general perception among VCs will not play in your favor. Investors are probably not going to take another look at your business for another six months or more because trajectories usually don't change that fast. You might find you have to try harder to get their attention the next time around. In this situation, you're better off going for the smaller round and getting back to focusing on your business, rather than wasting time swinging for the big raise and coming up empty-handed.

Weigh the Pros and Cons of Convertible Notes
By Elisa Miller-Out, Managing Partner at Chloe Capital

A convertible note is used quite often by founders. It's basically a simple vehicle for making an investment. It is a debt instrument with a loan, but it's a special kind of loan that has some optionality around whether it stays as a loan and gets paid back with interest or, under certain circumstances, whether it converts to equity in a priced equity round and can be then converted to shares in the company instead of being paid back as a loan. It's a vehicle that's sort of a hybrid between debt and equity.

Convertible notes are quite popular, especially in seed rounds. The reason they are popular with both founders and investors is simple: they are cheaper and easier to do legally than doing a priced equity round. There's less paperwork, so it doesn't cost you as much in legal fees. There are also some well-established templates available that can be used to help speed up the process and make it even cheaper.

When you are at a seed stage and you are not raising quite as much capital, it makes sense to spend a little less on legal fees. Using convertible notes also doesn't force you to set the valuation in stone yet. Most convertible notes have what's called a "valuation cap," where you can set an upper limit on what the valuation will be for those note holders when they convert their notes to equity. However, that does not mean that the cap limits the valuation for all the other investors coming into that next round. It allows you to wait until you have bigger and more professional investors at the table before setting a fixed valuation for your company in a priced equity round.

Additionally, it provides flexibility for early investors and for founders. There may be situations where paying back the note actually makes sense for you—for example, if you realize that the business is moving in a different direction, and the venture track no longer is the best option. As a debt, there is more risk to the founder with a convertible note than with pure equity. You may have to pay it back; that's one of the risks. It can also be harder to tell how diluted your shares will be once the notes all convert to equity. That's because, again, the valuation is not fixed until the subsequent round, so there's a lot of fluidity in terms of how the numbers will shake out in the subsequent funding round in which the notes convert to equity.

It's important to solicit good financial advice here and weigh out your options. Take the time to do a variety of scenario planning and financial modeling. You can model out the different scenarios and see exactly what is going to happen to your shares and to your dilution based on different kinds of outcomes in the next round and where the valuation ends up landing. If you can do that financial modeling exercise, or get a financial advisor or part-time chief financial officer (CFO) to do it for you, that can be quite helpful in mitigating that risk of not knowing exactly how things are going to look once your notes convert to equity, and how your cap table is going to look at that point.

Think Twice About Choosing a Convertible Note or a SAFE over a Priced Round

By Jason Chapman, Managing Partner at Konvoy Ventures

One decision that founders have to weigh out when they undertake a fundraise is speed versus proper structure. In just about every scenario, an actual priced round makes more sense than a convertible note or a SAFE, which an agreement drawn between you and the investor. This is because priced rounds provide clarity, and clarity helps you to avoid sticky situations down the line. When you do full documentation and a priced round, even if it's a smaller round of $1 million or $2 million, its pays dividends in the long run. When you go through the negotiations and then properly frame the relationship, you leave no room for ambiguity or confusion. On the other hand, when you sign a convertible note or SAFE, sometimes there are terms that come up later with your investors, where they're frustrated because they had a different interpretation or assumption about how you're going to deal with them.

The main argument for a convertible note is simplicity and speed, but what you're sacrificing when you take that speed is confusion, misalignment, and potentially fracturing relationships with your investors. The other thing that gets overlooked is that when you take a convertible note, you're going to eventually go raise another round, and what most likely happens is that all those people get lumped into the new, current rounds. Let's say that you then have to establish a new option pool. You're essentially just going to be diluting yourself in that scenario; you're not actually going to dilute the previous investors on the convertible note. What ends up happening is that you create an option pool that's quite diluted just to the founders, not diluted to the investors, because they're converting that same share class.

Think twice before choosing a convertible note or SAFE over a priced round. Price rounds have become dramatically cheaper to do than they were historically. It's worth taking the time and being a little patient and not too antsy to just get the deal done. Proper priced round documentation should cost around $20,000 to $30,000 and should never exceed 2 percent of the total round size for the seed rounds. Once the round size gets above $2 million, it shouldn't get above 0.5 to 1.5 percent. Use that as a frame of reference to keep legal teams and legal fees in check.

Be Careful Not to Raise Too Many Convertible Notes

By Mary Grove, Managing Partner at Bread and Butter Ventures

You can raise capital across a variety of instruments, ranging from convertible debt notes to SAFEs to priced rounds. In terms of what vehicle to raise, whether it's equity or debt financing, one thing to keep in mind especially at the early stage is to try to avoid note-stacking or raising too many convertible notes and SAFEs on top of one another. You want to make sure that owners have a very clear view of ownership across the board.

Founders often perceive the valuation cap on a particular note as the future floor for an equity round; they assume that discounts on notes constitute the minimum premium on a future equity round. As a result, they fail to calculate their dilution properly and figure out the impact on their dilution from these notes converting to equity.

For example, let's say you raise a convertible debt note, and then nine months later you raise another convertible note, and then you raise another one. At that point, you have raised three times at, say, $5 million capital to date at various caps with various discounts. When you go to raise that first priced round, you still have to factor in the fact that you have $5 million that needs to be converted into equity, with certain discounts and valuation caps. Make sure that throughout the fundraising process, particularly when you are not raising priced equity rounds, you have an eye on dilution and ownership, and a clear understanding of what percentage of the company you have already sold.

Know the Good, the Bad, and the Ugly of Secondaries

By Andrew Romans, CEO at 7BC Capital

In the ancient times of the 1990s and early 2000s, secondaries were terrible. If Bill Gates is the CEO of Microsoft and he's selling his stock in Microsoft, he knows more of the insider trading information than we do. So as outside investors, we should then all dump our Microsoft shares before they go down in price. That was the old view. The new view of things for privately held companies is different. If Microsoft is private and Bill Gates wants to sell some shares, maybe it's because he wants to make a philanthropic donation or buy a house or invest in a startup. It doesn't necessarily mean that the stock is worthless. Also, after the dotcom crash in 2001, the Sarbanes-Oxley Act came in, and we entered a period where no one could have an initial public offering

(IPO) without having top-line revenue of hundreds of millions of dollars and six consecutive quarters of profitability.

As a result, companies stayed private much longer. Founders were sitting on a founder salary that was not so big and, in many cases, unable to provide sufficiently for their families. Meanwhile, investors—especially if they were investing other people's money from outside limited partners and their VC funds—didn't want to sit there illiquid, waiting 15 years to get their money back. That's when the secondaries market evolved, where founders and investors sell shares in a privately held company that's not publicly listed on a stock exchange. Investors sell some of their stock to another buyer who wants to increase their ownership or gain ownership in this asset in a company.

Secondaries are becoming extremely common. As VC funds have gotten larger, the number of VC funds out there has also increased, and many of them have minimum ownership target percentages. They want to own at least 20 percent of the company, but perhaps the company is only selling 10 percent in this financing round, existing investors are taking a third of it, and there are new investors coming in. In this scenario, there is not a lot of inventory of shares to buy in the company. Normally, when an investor invests, they are buying preferred shares that have terms such as blocking rights and other kinds of rights and privileges. The founder typically owns ordinary founder stock that has fewer rights and privileges. So it might be that the price for founder stock is lower than for the preferred shares.

For example, we have seen some of our portfolio companies raise something like $15 million that goes into the company, and another $32 million in the same financing round where secondaries and investors are buying shares from the founders or from early investors. As a founder, you should consider whether it makes sense to structure your next funding round with a secondary. Typically, as a general rule, you shouldn't sell more than 10 percent of the stock in your company. You want to send the signal to investors that you're highly motivated to sell your stock at a much higher valuation down the road, and thus give investors the confidence that you believe in the long-term prospects for the business and that your company is indeed a good investment.

Generally speaking, it's negatively perceived for a founder to seek to sell their founder stock as a secondary. It's better if the investor is the one asking, "Can we do a secondary as a way of creating more room for me on your cap table?" If you try to sell shares on the secondary market for a pre-revenue company, that often raises a red flag for investors that the entire thing might be a scam.

If the company is generating decent revenue and you are hitting your Series C, or possibly as early as Series B, you should see some appetite for secondary investment. The playbook probably says nothing about secondary; it says only that you are selling 20 percent of the company for this amount of funding at that valuation. When the round is heavily oversubscribed, you can decide among the founders whether you want to sell anywhere from zero to 10 percent of what each individual owns to accommodate those investors that want more. Or you may want to reach out to your early investors and say, "Would anyone like to sell some of their position in this company at this valuation?" In that case, you would actually be selling preferred shares.

By accommodating secondaries, you might make some of your founders, early employees, or early investors happy and you might be able to get a deal done. If Lightspeed wants to write a $47 million check and you are only selling $15 million of stock, Lightspeed may not do the deal. If they get $47 million worth of stock, they may take their two board seats and do the deal. The good, the bad, and the ugly of the secondary market is important to understand—including that some people feel negatively about it, and how those perceptions are changing over time.

———

Skip Fundraising Through NFTs for Now

By Jason Chapman, Managing Partner at Konvoy Ventures

In the era of blockchain and crypto, a lot of companies have looked at raising their seed round through non-fungible tokens (NFTs). What might come back to bite them down the line is that they're going to raise money through these assets that they sell to their community, but they're not delivering any kind of clear timeline. When you're looking at a fundraising target, typically you're working with professional investors. You go raise $2 million, $5 million, or $10 million for specific milestones you're trying to reach, and you're held somewhat accountable to that, which is healthy and good. You have a board; you have advisors; they're pushing you; they're questioning you if you miss a delivery date. On the other hand, with NFTs, there's not quite the same accountability to your community.

With NFTs and assets that you sell to your community, the community is your users, not just your investors. In fact, your users *are* your investors. The main downside to this approach is that you're exposing yourself to a level of volatility that isn't appropriate for early companies to experience. A lot of entrepreneurs overlook this aspect, driven by a quick cash grab in the moment. NFTs are not the ideal fundraising tool by any means. Not to be confused with blockchain and crypto, which are quite promising, NFTs are not a viable option from a fundraising mechanics standpoint, at least currently. There is no need for you to replace traditional financing rounds with NFT raises.

5. TAKING THE FIRST STEPS TO RAISING CAPITAL

Measure Your Customer Engagement Data

By Shane Chesson, Founding Partner at Openspace Ventures

An important aspect of your pre-fundraising planning is to measure your customer engagement early. Whether you're at seed or Series A, you need to understand how your initial customer ramp is proceeding, not based only on the basic numbers, the roll numbers, but also in terms of how those engaged customers are acting. Are they coming back? Are they using your content? Are they starting to consider transacting or moving down the transaction pipeline? Are they thinking about extending the types of services that they are using? Are they referring to friends or talking about your product or service with their friends? You need to capture this data early and build it into your story. Find impressive and suitable metrics to track those data points, and present them as some of the leading indicators when you pitch VCs.

Obviously, which set of metrics is right for you depends on the type of business you run. One common strategy, however, is to run a customer survey that measures your net promoter score (NPS). NPS will give you an indication of what percentage of your customers will recommend your product or service to others. The challenge with this kind of survey is that it's somewhat subjective and doesn't capture every customer. You will have to combine the results with your analytics. The basic metrics should tell you what percentage of your customers are coming back. How much time are customers spending interacting with your product or service? Are customers referring other users, and if so, what is the conversion rate of those referrals? In addition to such metrics around acquisition, activation, retention, referral, and revenues, other useful metrics to consider capturing are average transaction value (ATV), lifetime value (LTV), and annual revenue per user (ARPU). There are many analytics solutions in the market to help you in this regard, including Google Analytics, Mixpanel, Flurry, Loyaltics, QlikView, and others.

A lot of early-stage entrepreneurs haven't booked much revenue yet. They may be early in their overall development, but if they can demonstrate strong customer engagement, they will have a more solid case to prove product–market fit. This, in turn, will further build investor confidence in their business.

Audit Your and Your Team's Social Media Image Before Fundraising

By Zach Finkelstein, Managing Partner at Class 5 Global

While fundraising processes rarely live or die by a founder's social media presence, there are things entrepreneurs can do to optimize their chances of success and avoid unnecessary embarrassment. A thoughtless photo or post can kill a fundraising process, while the right content can even help land an investor. Depending on a founder's personality and proclivities, they may use social media as a key channel to reach potential employees, customers, and even investors. But even for the majority who do not, social media cannot be ignored outright. The good news is that simple common sense is the most important attribute for an effective social media presence.

Not all investors will conduct detailed due diligence on a founder's social media, but most of them will check a founder's LinkedIn profile. This is where they will try to develop a sense of the founder's professional background. A founder's profile should clearly, concisely, and truthfully lay out their professional history. Ironically, many VCs are very bad at this and tend to list every minor position the have ever held. Do not use us as examples! Descriptions should be brief and clear and are only necessary if a position is not self-explanatory. As with most things, an appearance of effortlessness is usually optimal. LinkedIn posts can be a powerful tool, but also a potential pitfall. LinkedIn is a powerful content platform with a huge reach. Founders can easily have their posts seen by tens or even hundreds of thousands of users. However, founders should use these posts to show genuine insights where possible. Otherwise, founders risk appearing like they have nothing better to do than share shallow and unsolicited business insights. In summary, LinkedIn is a platform for putting your career history on display. It can be a lot more powerful if content is used correctly, but it can easily hurt as much as help.

Twitter is another platform that can present advantages and risks. Many VCs spend a lot of time on Twitter (perhaps too much). Inserting yourself into interesting conversations in areas where you have insights to offer can be a great way to engage with them. Again, if you don't have anything insightful to say, you may risk looking like you have nothing better to do—so be careful here, too. And most of all, remember that some subjects carry downside risks: notably politics. While it may be your right to speak your mind, some VCs may find your posts indiscreet or disagreeable. To minimize risks, its often best to confine your Twitter posts to professional subjects.

Other media, such as Instagram and Facebook, tend to present risks without upside. Not all VCs will check these platforms, but in order to be safe you should assume they will. And setting your profile to private may not help. VCs may know your contacts and use them to view your posts. Assume the worst and be careful on these platforms.

In sum, LinkedIn and Twitter can be powerful tools. Most founders do not find them necessary to reach investors; however, a clear LinkedIn profile is usually a necessity. Most other platforms offer more drawbacks then benefits, but common sense is enough to keep most founders out of trouble. Also, remember that investors are investing in you and your company's potential, not your ability to come up with interesting content for social media. Focus on building a great company and investors will come.

Determine the Right Amount of Capital to Raise

By Camilla Dolan, Partner at Eka Ventures

When you're determining the right amount of capital to raise, a few questions that might be helpful include: First, what am I looking to use this capital for? For example, what team do I need in place to execute for the next 6, 12, and 24 months? Are there game-changing senior hires that I could bring in early to accelerate the business?

Second, what am I looking to prove out with this capital so that the valuation of the business increases exponentially before I need to fundraise again? For example, what product–market fit signals am I looking for, and how can I evidence those? In an app company this might be the cost of acquisition or the retention rate of customers, whereas in a deep tech business this might be proving certain types of effectiveness through an experiment

Third, how will this fundraise exponentially accelerate the growth in value of my business? This is one of the questions that investors are going to be focused on, so being able to articulate this well will be helpful and provide a valuable sense check to investors as to whether the capital is being effectively deployed.

Every business operates differently. The average cadence between venture capital rounds is less than 24 months, and in the current environment many companies are raising again in under 12 months. If raising venture capital regularly is the path you want to pursue, it helps to be crystal clear on what you are trying to prove out with each investment round and how that accelerates the long-term value of the business. Every time capital is raised, the bar of what the company needs to achieve to be successful is raised.

Once you have worked out what it is you are going to try to prove with the fundraise, take that as a starting point and work backward to figure out how much you think it is going to cost to achieve each of those milestones. Then add a significant buffer because it often takes longer and costs more than expected to reach milestones. This process should get you to a ballpark figure for how much to raise.

Once you've figured out the amount, it is worth sense-checking that amount by benchmarking it against other companies in your space that you respect. If the amount you estimate you need is very different to what you have seen competitors raise in the market, try to understand why and double-check your assumptions. It could be that there is a great reason that their funding requirement is different. If it is, then it is helpful to be able to articulate why.

In the early stages it is fine to have a range, as long as you have clarity on the impact to the business of raising less or more capital and how you will adjust the business plan and strategy accordingly.

Find Funder–Founder Fit Before You Begin Fundraising

By Elisa Miller-Out, Managing Partner at Chloe Capital

It's very important that you think carefully about your fundraising goals and figure out which venture capital funders are the best aligned with you, and what types of capital you want to raise once you're set on raising VC capital. To do that, you need to understand the investor's strategy or thesis very well and approach the investors whose strategy and thesis match what you are doing with your company. Some of the things to consider in looking at that fit are aligning your goals and timeline for how soon you want to exit from your company, and how soon your funder wants to see an ROI; timeline is therefore important. Timing is also important in other ways. For example, the VCs that you speak with have their own fundraising cycles and their own cycles with their funds, so it's important that you are approaching them at a time when they are actively deploying capital to new investments. They may be at a place where they are winding down a fund and deploying capital only to their existing investments as follow-on investments, but not actively making new investments. They might be waiting until they raise their next fund to deploy capital to new investments. Figuring out when the timing is right to approach them and understanding where they are in their own fundraising and fund lifecycle are important.

Investment themes are another important aspect. Look at what themes the investor is focused on, whether it's climate, education, health, or deep tech. There are all kinds of different industry frames that different investors look at, and you need to make sure they're aligned with your business. Be precise about who you approach and make sure there's an alignment with a given investor regarding investment themes and sector focus.

Geography is also important for funder–founder fit, and that can mean the investment geography. It's important to look at whether that fund or investor focuses on a regional approach or whether they invest nationally or globally.

You also need to be looking at size of check or ticket size range for their typical investment. Make sure their check size and the percentage of that round they want to take are aligned with the size of your round and the amount you are raising.

They might not make the investment, even if it's a great fit in some ways. For example, if that investor is used to writing $5 million checks and you are raising a $1 million round, it seems like they should be able to invest in you because clearly they have plenty of money available. The reality is that they will be unlikely to make that investment because it's just not the size of investment they typically make. Even if they have the capital to do it, it's not part of their strategy. Make sure you understand which investors are a good fit for the amount of capital you are raising for that round.

Investors are also looking at the stage of your company, whether it's seed stage, Series A, Series B, or beyond. Some investors are more stage agnostic and focus on a wider range, but most tend to have a few specific stages that they focus on. Make sure to align on this aspect as well. Early-stage investors will be focusing on pre-seed or seed deals. They are going to be looking at very different things than investors who focus on later, bigger rounds. Then there are growth-stage investors who focus on Series C, D, and beyond.

Finally, look at the special interests of the investor. If it's an individual investor, like an angel, they may have certain passions or interests that lead them to make certain investments, and there may be certain types of people who interest them. There also can be special lenses that an investor looks through; for example, they might have a gender and diversity lens. Others might have an impact lens and be looking for certain types of positive contribution in society, whether it's environmental or social impact in a certain area—social justice, for instance. Those are all aspects to look at in an investor, and how those aspects align with your company.

Build Your Investor Tracker from the Start

By Jenny Fielding, General Partner at The Fund

As you start thinking about raising capital, it's critical that you get organized right from the start. Begin by creating a master investor tracker spreadsheet that serves as your fundraising pipeline. It will take a few weeks to build an incredible investor pipeline document, which is a simple yet effective tool to help you manage your fundraising process. You can set it up as a Google sheet or in any other format, so long that it's shareable and editable by multiple people within your team. This will help ensure it is up to date at all times. It will list all your prospective funds according to your sector and ticket size, as well as whether you are running a seed, Series A, B, C, or D round. You can also narrow down your target investor list according to their investment range or "sweet spot" based on your research, and make sure it matches your ask. You'll also want to eliminate any investors whose geographical scope falls outside your markets.

Once you have your initial target investor list (which obviously will change quite a bit as you go), much like a sales pipeline, you want to designate where each target stands in terms of their stage in the fundraising lifecycle: contacted, interested, pitched, due diligence, term sheet, closed, and so on.

You should approach building this document like a great client relationship management system for sales. It should help you to keep organized so that you follow up and give those nudges to the clients. You will also want to input all the information about the customer, who in this case is the investor. What is their target check size? What are their preferred verticals? Who in the firm is experienced in your space? Make sure to keep it super organized. Then take that document and share it with five to ten existing co-founders, investors, mentors, and friends who are experienced in VC fundraising and ask for their feedback. They can weigh in on whether they think these are good investors for you, and whether they know any of them and could make introductions or suggest other relevant investors. Building out the pipeline from the beginning is critical. This is all well before you hit the pavement and start approaching investors—even before you send a single email or make a single call to a prospective investor, and well before you get any introductions. Without an organizing document like this, you're likely not going to be very well positioned to properly manage an effective and efficient fundraising process.

Work with Advisors with Open Eyes and Be Ready to Step In

By Tim Levene, CEO of Augmentum Fintech

One of the criticisms of venture capital in the past is that it's been the preserve of only a few. Some entrepreneurs, especially seasoned ones, have a fantastic investor network who they can go to directly when raising capital. This isn't a luxury that the majority of early-stage entrepreneurs have, particularly those from underrepresented backgrounds. If you are one of those entrepreneurs who doesn't yet have the who's who of VCs in their contact list, then deciding who to bring on board to help you on that journey is an incredibly important decision.

The first question you have to answer is: "Should I use an advisor, and if so, who?" Picking your advisor is as important as making the decision to use an advisor in the first place. There are some VCs who are critical of entrepreneurs using advisors, because they are "outsourcing" a critical skillset that an early stage company needs to demonstrate. However, that attitude is exactly why we have such an imbalance in European VC, where the vast majority of funding goes to white male entrepreneurs.

Ironically, the smaller the raise, the harder it typically is to find an advisor. Some advisors charge a retainer fee, but ultimately a percentage of the amount of capital that you raise will be their compensation in the form of a success fee. Typically, the total fee impacts the quality of the advisor. There is a fine balance to be struck when agreeing on fees, however. I have seen entrepreneurs choose well-regarded advisors and set the fees so low that that the advisors weren't motivated enough to do an exceptional job, or they simply allocated the raise to an inexperienced employee. Entrepreneurs would be better off paying more and using someone they trust, who is experienced and motivated to deliver. After all, a good advisor will earn their fee many times over and save the founder a huge amount of time and effort.

When it comes to selecting an advisor, don't just take them at their word. Do as much due diligence on them as they are doing on you. Ideally, test them out on some informal introductions and see how responsive and effective those are. Be specific in identifying the help you actually need. Do you need them to help raise capital? To help you frame the story? To help you create the pitch deck? To create or refine your financial model? To set up your data room? To interface and negotiate with investors on your behalf? To advise on term sheets? Any combination of these could form the advisory engagement framework. Different advisors have different strengths and perform different roles, so you need to choose the one who is best placed to help deliver on what you need. It is important to work closely with your advisor to define the scope of the project and set an aggressive yet realistic timeline on deliverables or milestones for specific stages.

To me, it is not a negative sign if a Series A company uses a reputable advisor, in particular if the entrepreneur can qualify why they needed this help. Insightful advisory support and warm introductions to VCs always help. One common mistake that a lot of entrepreneurs make is expecting the advisor to go and raise the money for you. Ultimately, the advisor can only help so much. If you fail to do your job as a founder of engaging and exciting prospective investors about your business, no advisor will be able to save the day. They can certainly help refine your pitch and coach you during the process, but the investor is still investing in you: your story and your vision for the company. No one should be able to sell the story better than you.

As with any hiring decision, you need to make this choice with your eyes open and choose someone who can help bridge any fundraising gaps you have. A good advisor typically comes with fundraising experience, whether as a seasoned entrepreneur, investor, investment banker, or corporate finance professional. They should bring with them an extensive network and relationships with VCs. Their job is to pique investor interest and put you in front of enough of the right investors that you are in the best possible position to complete a successful raise, ideally with a cohort of investors who can deliver value for your business beyond their capital.

Another common mistake entrepreneurs make—particularly those with less experience—is that they assume their story and pitch deck are in good shape simply because they feel they know their business inside out. An investor pitch deck is very different from other types of marketing presentations. Failing to see your business through a VC lens could ultimately be the difference between securing capital or not. This is another area where an external advisor can look at your material with fresh eyes and help you tailor your message for the right audience. Given how high the stakes are and the fact that you typically get only one shot to engage any given investor, it is worth the time and effort to leave no stone unturned when it comes to framing your story and reflecting this in your pitch deck and verbal articulation.

Take Selection of Your Attorney Seriously

By Gary Rieschel, Managing Partner at Qiming Venture Partners

You have to realize that, as an entrepreneur, there are a handful of advisors and confidants who can be incredibly valuable in your fundraising journey. One such advisor is the attorney or the law firm you choose to work with. As with your ultimate selection of investors, you want to select an attorney who can add value to your fundraising, beyond just reviewing term sheets.

First and foremost, you want to talk to the individuals at the law firm who are going to be involved in supporting you. You want to find references that tell you how responsive they are, from both startups and VCs they work with. You want to understand their workload. You have to be realistic—as a small company, you may not be getting the full attention of a senior partner at a firm. Once you start to provide significant business or you start to look like you are going to be a very successful startup, then you can perhaps expect more. You need to get a sense of the culture around the support, because the first call you are going to make when you have a problem is probably to your attorney. Treating them as anything other than a full partner in the business is a terrible mistake.

Any law firm that has any significant presence in venture capital should be able to provide you with insider info on the VCs they work with, in terms of their style and what it's like to work with them. If you are with a smaller law firm, or with a specific attorney because of a personal relationship, they still should have worked with another law firm that has more experience with venture firms and would be willing to share some information.

Adding a great attorney to your support team is paramount. Don't take this decision lightly. Most entrepreneurs take the choice of an attorney too casually.

———

Set Aggressive yet Realistic Timetables

By Tim Levene, CEO at Augmentum Fintech

It is important when fundraising to set an ambitious yet realistic timetable for closing the round, and there are key considerations at both ends of the spectrum. On one hand, when a founder is well versed in raising capital, they may like to work with a very aggressive timetable, suggesting something like holding investor meetings over a two-week period and then expecting a term sheet in four weeks. That can be seen as an artificially accelerated timeframe that doesn't allow investors time to run their processes and conduct effective due diligence. If you set too short a timeframe, you may be setting yourself up to fail, because inevitably it will need to be extended and that sends a negative signal back into the market.

The flipside of the story is that you don't set a definitive timetable to begin with and you let rounds extend indefinitely. Your CFO, investment manager, or financial advisor may say, "Let's start to have some soft conversations, test the market, and then have some more formal meetings later on." Some soft, friendly VC warm-up conversations can be useful prior to launching the round formally, but ultimately the lack of a defined timeline will create a longer process than you would like. Rounds that drag on tend to create a sense of uncertainty among investors, and give them the opportunity to continue to ask questions and watch how the business trades over a multi-month period rather than making a commitment. Building in a sense of urgency can be effective. You should set that tone with your CFO, investment manager, or financial advisor, while being careful not to cut corners or get sloppy in your execution. Urgency can help build momentum and competitive tension between the various investors you're speaking with, which can play in your favor to raise at the terms you want within a reasonable timeframe.

You also have to determine the point at which you, as the founder, bring the investment round to a head. Do you try to corral prospective investors to co-invest together? If you are fortunate enough to be oversubscribed, do you push them to increase their valuations? Your advisor should be speaking to investors behind the scenes, updating them, and maintaining a sense of urgency and competition. There is no one-size-fits-all in these situations, so it is important to stay close to what is happening and assess the ramifications of your actions and investors' perceptions every step of the way.

PART II

PACKAGING THE INVESTMENT OPPORTUNITY: NARRATIVE, PITCH DECK & DATA ROOM

6. CREATING YOUR STORY

Create Your Fundraising Narrative

By Andrew Romans, CEO at 7BC Capital

Storytelling is incredibly important at every stage of a startup, from early stage right up to post-IPO, and it's imperative to fundraising. As an entrepreneur, you need to identify the best story to get people and investors to buy into your business. Why should your business get better treatment on the multiples, more favorable valuation, and a larger appetite for support than other companies?

I suggest you get into a room with some of the existing supporters of your company. Gather your co-founders, angel investors, advisors, and supporters, and conduct a whiteboard session. Ask everyone, "What is the one thing that is special about this company?" Get each person to weigh in from their perspective. This is a useful exercise when you're trying to formulate your company thesis statement. You also need to identify the three or four data points to back up that thesis statement. Once you define your company's differentiators and what makes it special and great, you then need to frame them in a logical order (e.g., A, B, C). Then you might need to re-order them (e.g., B, C, A) if that makes more sense in terms of flow and building the argument of what makes your company special.

It's important to have that session to gather some outside views. This should be done before putting together the next deck when you are going out for fundraising. To the extent that you can undertake this exercise and define a differentiated story for your fundraising narrative, you'll be in better position to present a compelling and cohesive pitch to investors and ultimately engage investors and secure funding.

Craft and Practice an Investor-Friendly Story
By Isabel Fox, General Partner at Outsized Ventures

When it comes to pitching, great founders are typically very good at storytelling. They are able to condense quite difficult technologies or problems into a very simple and easy to understand dialogue. That's important for a number of reasons: it will attract investors, but it will also attract employees and talent, and it will help generate sales, partnerships, proofs of concept, and customers going forward.

However, in highly technical domains, like deep tech for example, founders often focus extremely heavily on the technology, whereas if you get your brand assets, your message, and your clear and compelling story right, it will be more impactful. Achieving the right balance between explaining the technology and the overall positioning and explaining the story is key. It's important that you strike that right balance with all of your investor communication, not just in your pitch deck. This can be particularly challenging for technical founders, especially when they're speaking to an investor who doesn't share a similar background. If you are a technical founder, make sure you define the essence of the technology or the technical aspect of what you're doing, and be careful not to oversell the technology. You'll definitely need to know your audience, and tailor your pitch differently to different investors. Most importantly, you need to make sure that you're pitching the forest not the trees, so to speak. This is especially important in the first meeting, unless the investor wants to deep dive on the technology or look closely at some features of your product or service. Never lose sight of communicating as clearly as possible the fundamentals of your company: Who are you selling to? What is the product? What does it do and for whom? And why is it important to them? Envision a pyramid, where the top level is your vision, the "why," then the middle level is about your "what," and finally the bottom level is your "how." That's a good frame to follow in telling your story.

Spend some time working on and refining your message until you have a strong story, well before you contact investors. Never assume that just because you've been eating, drinking, and sleeping this business for years and you're constantly talking about it, that your messaging is investor-ready and you can just wing it. Effective investor-specific communication is very different from everyday business communication. If this isn't your forte, get someone who can help you, such as an advisor or a mentor, especially in the early stages where you might lack experience interacting with investors. These people can help you position and craft your idea.

Define a Clear, Compelling, and Credible Value Proposition

By Bill Reichert, Venture Partner at Pegasus Tech Ventures

Believe it or not, most VCs do not invest only with their brains; they invest with their hearts as well. As an entrepreneur, if want to break through all the noise of other companies pitching these VCs, you have to figure out how to get the VC to say, "Wow, that's amazing. Tell me more." To get to wow, you've got to get beyond the brain, down to the heart. Not only do you have to get my attention as an investor, you also have to get my heart beating faster. Wow is not an intellectual response. Wow is not an analyst's data response. Wow is an emotional response.

The problem that many entrepreneurs have is that instead of focusing on making clear what is amazing about their company, they try to explain their company and describe their product and technology in detail and tout their team. Sure, something in there might be truly amazing, but it often gets lost among other non-essential details. Hence, it's critical that your messaging be concise and strictly focused on what's special about your business.

Most importantly, you should focus on figuring out the compelling value proposition that you can deliver to customers that no one else can deliver—the thing that is going to make customers scream for your product. What gets VCs excited is when you say that you can deliver something that is massively superior to its market counterpart, be it 10 times better, 1/10 the cost, 10 times longer lasting, or some other extraordinary benefit. That's what I call getting to wow. That's what gets VCs excited—not data charts, hockey sticks, pie-charts, or lots of text and graphics. Ultimately, it's about how sticky your product or service is, and how likely it is that your customers will love it and use it, and in some cases tell others about it.

You have to be clear what it is you are doing. A lot of entrepreneurs might say they're going to disrupt the multi-billion-dollar X industry. They think that's their wow, but it's not. An aspiration is not a wow, especially when it's not clear how you're planning to get there. All investors know is that the pitch is asserting some hyperbole that they're skeptical about. You must make it easy for investors to see how you're going to win the customer and, ultimately, market share. It's astonishing how many entrepreneurs don't realize that after delivering a lengthy and comprehensive pitch, investors are still not entirely clear on what they're doing and how the various pieces of their story fit together. As many as half of all pitches, perhaps more, fall into this category and fall by the wayside for this reason.

You also have to come across as credible to investors. Many entrepreneurs don't when they're pitching. Most go through their pitch asserting a whole bunch of claims and aspirations without backing them up with impressive traction, especially from credible third parties. As a VC, if I cannot see how you've got this stellar start where you've proven your concept beyond the shadow of a doubt, how can I trust that you will be able to scale the business in the long haul?

Defining a clear, compelling, and credible proposition is critical to winning investors' hearts and minds, and getting to wow. The more you can do so, the more likely you will be able to engage investors and raise capital.

Emotionalize Your Story

By Jimmy Fussing Nielsen, Co-Founder of Heartcore Capital

As an entrepreneur, you need to incorporate emotion into your narrative. It's not enough that your pitch is sound and makes economic sense. You need to find a way to make it appealing at a human level, not just an investor level. The reason is that investors are captivated and remember emotional stories, and so do your customers and your employees. Part of being a visionary is being able to engage people on an emotional and personal level and paint a picture that's relatable. The reason that Hollywood can crank out good movies is that they have a formula for how to tell stories. This is a skill that you can also learn. For instance, Disney has online material available that can teach you how to tell a story.

No matter who you meet with, they are going to represent your investment opportunity to fellow co-partners, to an investor board, an investment committee, etc., which is not a direct route to those who will take the decision. By emotionalizing your story, you are making it memorable, and the story will be easily communicated by others to the ultimate decision makers. It can be linked to the reason that a founder is launching this business, usually through a personal experience and often a painful one. People can relate to that and remember the story.

This is particularly important during the earlier meetings, when you need to articulate your story emotionally and demonstrate to prospective investors that you're indeed tied to this dream. Whatever problem you're trying to solve, you need to evangelize them and get their buy-in on the importance and timeliness of your vision. In do so, you will further underscore your commitment and your ability to recruit future employees, partners, and investors.

In short, you need to articulate and sell the dream, and do so in a captivating way. That doesn't mean, of course, that you shouldn't present a strong financial case with the right metrics. After all, investors are in the business of making money. Still, the more you can communicate your story in an emotional and aspirational way, the more you can stand out. Often, this can be the difference that gets you over the finish line with fundraising and elicits the kind of long-term personal attachment and support you need from your investor partners.

Perfect a Five-Minute Pitch

By Jenny Rooke, Managing Director at Genoa Ventures

When you're prepping for your investor pitch, create a mini-pitch—say, five minutes in length—and practice it rigorously until you perfect it. Five minutes is the right amount of time to force extreme prioritization in your messaging, while still giving you just enough time to touch on all of the high points that should be in your pitch. People talk about the elevator pitch, which is more of a teaser. But your five-minute pitch is a stand-alone pitch; it effectively strips your typical 15 or 20 slide pitch to its bare essentials. In doing this, you'll certainly have to leave out a lot of information and data points. This may feel a bit unnatural and counterintuitive, especially when you're always going to be tempted to say more to sell your business. But you must stay disciplined and stick to covering only the bare bones of the pitch.

Of course, 30, 45, or 60 minutes allows a lot more conversation and double-clicking on details. On the other hand, forcing yourself to tell the complete story end-to-end in just five minutes and a few slides is an excellent exercise to help you prioritize your communication. One of the benefits of doing this, in both your slides and your speaking around those slides, is that it creates a lot of mental space and conversational space for dialogue during a longer pitch. You typically have 30 or 60 minutes with investors, so once you've learned to communicate concisely and only touch on what matters, you'll discover you have so much more room to really listen to them and tailor your message to their needs, and to ask them questions.

This is an exercise you should do offline and you may never use it. Nevertheless, have a five-minute version of your pitch, with five minutes worth of slides and five minutes worth of speaking prepared. You may record yourself using your phone or a professional video camera giving the full five-minute pitch while going over the slides. You may also send this video by email to investors as your teaser, along with your short teaser deck. They will be more likely to open your email and watch it. Investors might not take a 30- or 60-minute meeting, but if you tell people, "Here's a five-minute, bite-sized video that tells the whole story," that's more doable for investors and easier to commit to and engage with. It's a great entrée, in effect, for connecting with investors. You would typically want to send out this video along with a short blurb with no more than a handful of bullet points of key highlights about the investment opportunity. That's one trick to try to engage investors. Another tool you want to have handy is crafting one sentence that encapsulates what you do as concisely and vividly as possible, which you should memorize verbatim and use whenever it is needed to help frame any new discussion or communication you undertake with potential investors, partners, or clients.

———

7. PREPARING A PITCH DECK

Develop Different Pitches for Different Sets of Investors

By David Cohen, Chairman at Techstars

If you are raising $2 million you shouldn't be pitching Tiger Global, for example; that is not the kind of ticket size they focus on. It is OK to have a plan A and a plan B, and to present either depending on who you're talking with. In other words, if you have a $2-million raise, you are talking to angels and seed funds using plan A. It is OK to then present plan B to a Bessemer or a Sequoia about a $10 million-dollar round, because that is what they do. Obviously, if you go to a Bessemer or Sequoia and you pitch a million-dollar round, that is not a fit for them, and their view is going to be that you haven't done your homework or that it is just not a good use of their time or yours. So make sure you know who you are pitching to, and it's fine to have multiple financing approaches in mind as you are exploring the market, and even to work with multiple financings. The smaller financing can be in your back pocket and you can use it as leverage for a larger one in some cases. The key point is to know your audience and not pitch a micro-fund on a $15-million investment check size. It's not going to be a fit.

Get Your Deck in the Right Logical Order
By Bilal Zuberi, Partner at Lux Capital

It's important that you get your deck in the right order, so your story flows logically and investors can follow along easily. At a basic level, the first slide should be your cover slide, which consists of your company name and logo and a description statement or tagline. You can leave date out; there is no need for it. Ideally, this slide specifically, if not your whole deck, should be designed in your company brand colors and look and feel. The second slide is "about"—this is what we do. The third slide should be "this is the problem that we're solving," which is essentially addressing why your business matters and why investors should care about this business. Put that up front and back it up with data, even if it's something obvious like "America suffers from high levels of obesity and my weight loss system will help solve this." Then the fourth slide will address your solution at a high level, so the investor can see a strong logical link between the problem you presented and the solution you propose.

Problem and opportunity can be used interchangeably here. You might discuss a sizable gap in the market you have identified and intend to fill. For example, you could talk about how you believe that a big portion of manufacturing is trending toward 3D printing for many reasons. Then move on to the next slide, which is the solution, and talk about how your company or technology is well positioned to take advantage of this massive opportunity. You can also present the problem and the solution (or the opportunity and the solution) on one slide. The next slide should be, "This is the team that that we've built so far. This is their experience that's relevant to the business."

The slide after should be a snapshot of the business in terms of current performance statistics, as well as some historical statistics to demonstrate the evolution of the business. This is where you describe something like: "We've existed since 2018. We have 40 employees.

We've raised $7 million so far. We're doing $2 million in ARR. We have 1.5 million users, or we have signed 75 corporate clients." Whatever performance metrics are relevant and help paint the picture as to the current state of your business. This is a good place to also show your margins or unit economics. You then segue by saying, "This is where we are today. Now I want to take the rest of time to tell you what we're building." And then you start talking about your future plans.

Up to this point, it's about getting the foundation right. The foundation is presenting all the facts straight up front even if, for example, your team isn't as complete or experienced as you would like. You still want to show investors where you are. It's somewhat awkward to talk about the business without touching on the people who are running it. Investors may pick on any attempt to hide certain facts or skip over them, and take that as an implicit acknowledgment of a weakness. Better to be up front and present a complete picture from the start.

By now, you're halfway or so through the deck, and that's when you can explain your product or service. First, you want to present a high-level overview, and save any technical detail for follow-up discussions. If your business is multifaceted or complex, you may consider adding a slide that diagrams your business model, essentially describing how your business works. You can add this in place of the product or service slide, or in addition to it.

You then move to the market slide, and initially talk about the size of the market. This matters because it's directly linked to how far the business can grow before it hits a ceiling, which also reflects on the potential exit value of the business. You can also touch on your customer profile, in terms of demographics if you're a business-to-consumer (B2C) business or verticals if you're a B2B business, and talk about how you intend to capture those customers.

The last slide in this section is where you present your competition and where you're positioned in the landscape, typically presented by an XY axis graph. Depending on your sector, this may or may not be the best way to present this slide. Alternatively, you can create a gird showcasing how you stack up against your top competition in various areas. You can also address your competitive advantages or any barriers to entry you might have. The main thing you want to address is, "This is how we're different and defensible."

Next is your financials slide, where you show historical accounts and your forecast for the business. Don't make the mistake of cramming a bunch of figures onto this slide, as many entrepreneurs do. As far as you can, try to present the information visually with graphs and charts.

Finally, the last slide should cover your funding history and how much you're looking to raise—your "ask." Your planned use of proceeds should be presented, typically as a pie chart with various percentages of the funds allocated to different areas, such as product development, team building, sales and marketing, and so forth.

This is, in a nutshell, the basic skeleton of a deck you would want to lead with to engage investors from the outset, whether through your initial email contact or during your initial pitch meeting. Obviously, you have the option to dress up these various core components or insert supplementary material in an appendix and use it for long investor discussions. Just remember, the best decks are simple and both easy and quick to read, so less is definitely more when it comes to decks, and order matters.

Make Your Pitch Deck Coherent and Interesting

By Bill Liao, General Partner at SOSV

With respect to pitch decks, your goal, first and foremost, is to try to make it coherent and interesting. A typical VC sees thousands of pitch decks in the course of a year. It doesn't give them comfort, improve their mood, or make them more likely to invest to see the same language in pitch decks from company after company, day in and day out.

Tell the investors about the opportunity you're tackling or the problem that you are solving. That should be the very first thing that you present. Then tell them the surprising thing that you have discovered to tap that opportunity or solve that problem, and how much effort you have put into figuring out that customer value proposition. Once you have done that, and only then, tell them how your solution works and how much it costs. After, tell them how much people will pay for it and how many people could pay for it. Finally, tell them how much money you'll make over a few years. Give investors some actual concrete evidence that you have built something that works. All these things should be in your pitch deck in roughly in that order.

You also need to include, somewhere in the deck, not just that there are competitors in the market, but a detailed comparative analysis. Tell investors specifically what your competitors' costs are and why they are not growing. Educate them on what's happening in the landscape and how your company is different. Whatever big undertakings you decide to do, demonstrate to investors that you have a great plan in place. If you must get regulatory approval, for example, break down the findings you've uncovered, outline the pathway that you're taking, and mention the pre-meetings that you have had so far and the outcome of those meetings. Whether you're planning to launch a new product, tap a new vertical, or enter a new market, demonstrate that you are a subject-matter expert, and that you know what you are talking about.

Present your expert knowledge as interesting stories and anecdotes; do not just throw data at investors. If you go to the pub, you do not want to end up at the bar with the person who just spouts on about every possible detail of Corvette maintenance, right down to the thickness of the valve covers. That's data; it's not even information. Investors don't want incomprehensible and fragmented data. You need to paint a picture with your words that investors can believe in, so they can then test and see through the data that it's concrete. Never just throw data and facts at investors without fitting in the big narrative, no matter how relevant the data may be. Be interesting from the get-go. You have 30 seconds to catch someone's attention. If you catch it for 30 seconds, you will be more likely to keep it for an hour. If you keep it for an hour, you will be more likely to catch a million bucks or more. The thing that will get you the investment is when you can make an investor go, "I get it. Aha! Yes, right."

Create a Concise, Cohesive, and Engaging Deck

By Jon Soberg, Managing Partner at MS&AD Ventures

Investors typically have very little time to read decks, and most don't actually read the detailed text, so it's more like scanning a resume than it is reading up close. One trick that has proven to be quite effective is to put PowerPoint into outline mode and write titles for each of your slides before you work on the presentation. If you can read that story, and it is completely intact and makes sense without actually reading anything on the slides, then generally you have a pretty good, cohesive story. After all, the deck is not about telling a historical story of what the company does as much as it is about giving a complete picture of what the investors want to see.

A mistake many entrepreneurs make is to waste the title space on their decks. It's good practice to write a full sentence as your title, as opposed to just a title that says "market size" or "financials." They basically have taken a big chunk of their real estate on the slide and wasted it by using a generic title, where they could be saying "Our financials are growing by 100 percent year-on-year," for example. If your metrics are remarkable in a specific area, you'll want to highlight them in the slide title. For instance, you could state "Remarkably fast user acquisition at low cost," or something to that effect. That's more likely to catch investors' eyes and help you in your storytelling.

You also want to try to make each slide as a stand-alone, single, focused message. For example, on your team slide, don't just state "Team." Frame it along the lines of "Diverse team of industry experts and world-class developers," or whatever is special about your team. You want to frame or contextualize each slide in a way that makes it easy for your audience to digest its key point, while ensuring that the various parts fit into a cohesive and compelling story.

Since VCs have limited attention to give to any presentation, especially early on, you're better off showing graphics and images than text in your deck. If you fill your presentation with a lot of text, you should assume that it's probably going to be skipped over, especially as your font size gets smaller. On the other hand, if you have effective graphics and maybe a little bit of text to give some context, that's more of an effective combination. Look at some of the best presenters ever: Steve Jobs had almost no text on most of his slides, and he was an extremely effective presenter. You don't necessarily have to go to that extreme, but remember that less is more when it comes to pitch decks.

Finally, rather than cramming your deck with extra information and slides beyond your core message, you're better off adding things to your appendix. You can also actually create a second, more comprehensive deck that you forward to investors at a later stage.

―――――――

Don't Start with the Problem, Start with Your Solution

By Bill Reichert, Venture Partner at Pegasus Tech Ventures

Contrary to common belief, you don't always have to start with the problem statement in your pitch deck. You can start with your solution. If you tell VCs what your solution is, they are going to know the problem you are solving. Most of the time entrepreneurs spend too much time describing a big, obvious problem. If you're a cleantech startup founder, don't waste investors' time by talking about the magnitude the climate change crisis and the problem with carbon. They already know about that. More importantly, what are you doing about it? Similarly, if you're a life science startup founder, don't walk into a VC's office and spend the first five minutes talking about how many people die from cancer every year. Investors know that cancer is a massive problem. They get it. Tell them how your solution is going to make a dent in solving this problem right off the bat.

Also, most great companies didn't set out to solve a big problem per se. Google didn't solve a big problem. Search engines were perfectly fine. Google saw an opportunity to do search better. Apple didn't solve a big problem. It didn't invent the smartphone. Again, it just came up with a better version of the smartphone solution. These companies capitalized on the opportunity by pulling together some novel technologies that the other guys had not pulled together yet, then cleverly packaged and marketed them and got out to market quickly via robust distribution channels. There's a difference between solving a problem and capitalizing on an opportunity. Most great companies are successful because they capitalize on an opportunity, not because they solve a problem.

Occasionally, an entrepreneur may indeed uncover a not-so-obvious problem or highlight a stark data point that's not commonly known that reveals a massive but overlooked problem. In this case, they can briefly describe the problem and its implications in their pitch deck. More often, that's not the case. Generally speaking, you're much better off jumping straight into talking about your solution, and even giving it as a short elevator pitch right from the start. Tell VCs what your solution is. Tell them what the compelling benefit to your customers is. Tell them how you are different from everyone else. Then tell them why they should believe you. You should be able to deliver an elevator pitch in 30 seconds at most. Do this in the beginning, before you go into your pitch. That way, VCs know exactly where you're heading. This is "communication 101": essentially, tell them what you are going to tell them, tell them, and then tell them what you just told them.

Demonstrate that Your Team is Capable of Addressing Company Challenges

By Bill Reichert, Venture Partner at Pegasus Tech Ventures

Obviously, a strong team is one of the critical factors for success in any startup. Many entrepreneurs, however, think of building a business as having some people at the top who are leaders and then hiring a bunch of people who are followers, because that's our sort of general definition of what leadership means. The reality is that investors are more impressed by a founder who can assemble a team of leaders for every function and at every level.

Many entrepreneurs do a terrible job of showing how their team is able to address the key challenges that are facing the company now. Almost every team slide out there has a bunch of pretty pictures and a bunch of logos that show the companies those people worked for and the schools they went to. So what if you have Google, Amazon, Facebook, or Netflix logos in your deck? If someone was a senior engineer at Google or has a post-graduate degree from Stanford, it implies that they're smart, which is fine. However, that doesn't tell investors whether this is the right person for the right job in your company right now.

There are challenges that you need to address in your deck, and certainly in your business. You need to link your team to the specific piece they're tackling. For example, "This is Bob. He has the background and experience in this area to make sure that we address this specific challenge and overcome it. This is Mary, she has the background and experience in this other area to addresses this second challenge that we need to overcome," and so forth. That's the way you should present your team, not schools and company logos. That's an entirely different approach that tells investors that you're well positioned and have the right team members to build the business, and that your team is well organized and capable.

A corollary to that is you need to define where the gaps are in your team. Who do you need to hire for which area? Many entrepreneurs skip that critical piece. You need to spell out to VCs how do you plan to grow your team and which positions and functions you plan on filling, and for which milestones and challenges. You need to make it clear to investors that you understand what it takes to scale up a company. Conversely, many entrepreneurs say that they have a world-class team and imply, in effect, that that they have sufficient people when they should demonstrate clarity of vision on their human resources needs and plans.

Acknowledge Your Team's Current Limitations and Future Needs

By Uzma Choudry, Investor at Octopus Ventures

One of the fundraising mistakes that founders and management teams should avoid when presenting to investors is to not recognize or proactively address their team's current limitations. For early-stage businesses, investors don't typically expect you to have a fully formed team, but it's very important to communicate where the gaps are in your team. They want to make sure you understand where you need to hire talent to fill those gaps, and how the team structure may change over time.

When you're pitching to investors, you need to be able to sell a story that includes, "Here are the areas we need to strengthen, and this is the caliber of people that we want to bring on board." It shows self-awareness of your own limitations, which can be quite reassuring for investors. It can be a bit of a red flag when VCs don't see this, and can point to the potential for problems later on.

Team building and talent is crucial to the success of any startup, and investors are looking for the founding team's or management's awareness of their blind spots on something as critical as this. It also demonstrates an ability to think beyond product road maps and commercial targets, since the reality is that you will need people to execute on these properly. The founders can't do everything.

For example, in an early-stage deep tech or biotech businesses, the founders end up doing everything from heading product development and R&D, to seeding the commercial and go-to-market strategy, to sales, marketing, and fundraising. They may be great on the product or technology side, but will likely have their limitations on other functions, such as sales and business development. While at seed stage, they may be able to head the sales and business development areas to get traction on those fronts, but as the business matures, these functions need to be super-powered. This will require you to attract and acquire the best sales and business development talent you can find in your industry to own this function. One of the measures of a good CEO is their ability to hire top talent into each function of the business, and the chief business officer (CBO) must be better than the CEO at business development and sales, for example.

The best founders understand this and build a hiring plan that addresses those weaknesses. They will also demonstrate an understanding of how to attract and retain these critical hires. Investors will also want to know there is an appropriately sized option pool set aside for these people with incentives in place to keep them motivated, although good VCs can also help with this. A seasoned executive leaving a huge compensation package at a big tech or pharma company to join a startup is a big validation of the technology, business, and vision of that startup and its team. It's also worth keeping in mind that there is a right time to bring this talent in. For example, if your business is focused on product development and R&D for the next 24 months with no proof of concept, it is probably too early to hire in a seasoned business development executive.

It's important for investors to know that you have clearly defined roles and job descriptions. Founders should be aware of the differences between chief technical, operating, marketing, and business officers and heads of technology, operations, marketing, and business development, for instance. This is because it doesn't always make sense to make C-suite hires at the early-stage level. First, you need someone willing to roll their sleeves up and get things done, and C-suite hires may be used to having a team to support them. Second, they will be expensive and potentially overqualified for the role as it stands. Finally, it doesn't leave any room to hire someone above them when the business reaches the next stage of growth. The business development or sales requirements and output of a seed-stage business will vary greatly from these requirements for a Series B- or Series C-stage business, and the person best placed to lead this will also be very different.

All of this is why it's worth spending some time on your hiring plan before going into a pitch, so that you can communicate it very clearly to investors. It will pay off in spades.

Showcase Your Product in Your Deck's Product Slide

By Jenny Fielding, General Partner at The Fund

In the context of the pitch deck, most investors, particularly early-stages ones, love seeing a product slide that captures a clear, high-level illustration of how it works. Not so much in terms of its features or the technology behind it, but rather in terms of the various touch points that collectively make up the main user experience. Such a slide is often missing in pitch decks. Entrepreneurs often describe the product, but don't actually show it.

At a minimum, have a link to a product demo in your deck, or at least show the user journey. Make sure to include this in the first third of the deck to paint the picture for investors of how your unique selling proposition (USP) translates in real life. You want to demonstrate to prospective investors how much work and thought went into making your product, as well as how intricate and robust your product is. Granted, investors know that your product is far from complete (particularly in early stages) and might in fact be a stripped beta or MVP version. Still, they expect to see that it works in its most basic format.

Showcasing products to prospective investors as a great way to engage them, and therefore a great selling tool. Think through exactly how you want to capture this opportunity to further move the investor along the fundraising sales cycle. Whether there's a link to a video, some wireframes, or even just some mockups or images, never skip this powerful part of the deck. Describing your problem and solution is not enough; you must bring it to life as much as possible. This is the case irrespective of whether you have a consumer or B2C product or an enterprise or B2B product. There's a misconception out there that if you have a consumer product, investors need to see the product, whereas if it's a SaaS or software product, that's not necessary. Investors still want to see screenshots and a dashboard, and the view on both desktop and mobile. Be careful not to get technical, especially in the initial meeting with investors, or get into the weeds by describing too much detail. You don't need multiple slides of all the functionality of the product, for example. Nor do you need to break down your roadmap. You're better off framing how the product works through the customer lens, rather than the developer lens, stressing the benefits of the design to the customer. You also need to hint at your mid-term and long-term vision for the product.

Don't Just Sell Your Product, Sell Your Distribution Advantage

By Yinglan Tan, CEO at Insignia Ventures Partners

We live in a world where digital products can be built and go bust due to competition in a matter of days. With the historically low barriers to entry for tech solutions, it is difficult for you to be able to completely differentiate your value proposition based on your product alone. Even your background or experience, or that of your team, may not be enough, especially in venture-backed, tech-enabled sectors that are flush with money.

Most products and business models that are "leading the way" (or at least versions of them) have already been seen elsewhere in the world. So how do you build a competitive advantage? One word:

distribution. Distribution encompasses channels a company uses to bring products or services from a source—for example, suppliers like fast-moving consumer goods companies or financial institutions with lending capital—to customers.

Over the past decades, distribution has become a critical, if not the most critical, alpha for any company, be it a B2C or B2B business. It is all about answering the question, "How will you be able to sell faster and on a wider scale than the rest of the market?" Having a long-term answer to this question is especially relevant for startups in emerging markets, because they are often solving issues or pain points around distribution, such as the fragmentation of supply chains causing compounding costs for the consumer. There are several forms of distribution, including online-to-offline (O2O) networks, licenses, and regulatory moats that give certain companies an advantage. Being able to sell your current or planned distribution advantage to investors in fundraising is all the more important at a time when the barriers to entry for most tech-enabled sectors are low and there is capital inflation (i.e., more supply than demand, such that competitors are likely to find investors and even potentially raise at a higher-than-expected valuation). A distribution advantage, especially when it is unique to your target market and requires localization, is harder to replicate for new entrants and foreign players.

Investors, especially VCs, place a premium on this ability to stay ahead of the competition, because the economics of their investment strategy incentivize outsized returns, and these can be achieved only if your company has rapid, massive growth, which requires a strong distribution advantage.

This does not discount the value of selling your product as well. But having that distribution advantage can lead to a more compelling product–market fit proposition, which a lot of early-stage investors love to see. Obviously, you can only leverage your distribution advantage if your product itself works and there is a strong team behind it.

Describe Your Market Opportunity, Not Just Market Size

By Bill Reichert, Venture Partner at Pegasus Tech Ventures

Almost every entrepreneur skips over market opportunity and instead tells VCs that they have a big market or total addressable market (TAM). Hence, almost every pitch deck has a market slide that doesn't describe the market opportunity; it describes only market size. They typically have the exact same three bubbles: TAM, SAM (serviceable available market), and SOM (serviceable obtainable market). I believe someone at Harvard Business School invented this framework back in the 1960s and somehow it got adopted in the startup world, although it has almost no relevance there. After all, what VCs are looking for is not a big market, but a good market. The size of the market does not necessarily determine how good your market opportunity is.

In fact, I have never seen a company fail because the market was too small. Almost every market you can imagine is big enough to build a successful, profitable company. Still, many entrepreneurs are advised to do this TAM, SAM, and SOM slide. Meanwhile, every VC on the planet knows that the entrepreneur's TAM is fantasy at best or nonsense at worst. Unfortunately, it's one of those check-the-boxes things that every associate and every VC is told: you've got to get the TAM because we need to put that in the investment memo. It has become a standard now. But how in the world is the TAM relevant? What difference does it make if an entrepreneur says, "Our TAM is $56 billion globally, and we project that this market for our product is going have a compound annual growth rate of 17.65 percent." Obviously, these figures have no impact on the current reality and future prospects for your business. The point is, you know that VCs are going to ask you what your TAM is, so you need to come up with your TAM.

It is more important to define your market opportunity. What investors want to see is that you understand the precise personas of the consumer market you are going after: who they are, where they are, how you are going to get to them, how you are going to deliver your message to them, how you are going to convert them into paying customers, how you are going to onboard and upsell them, and ultimately how you are going to scale the business customer by customer. No business is ever built as a percentage of TAM. Many entrepreneurs frame their long-term projections as some percentage of TAM, SAM, or SOM, be it 1, 5, or 10 percent or whatever. In reality, every company is built customer by customer, sale by sale, license by license. Investors want to see that you understand that, and you understand the process and the economics behind acquiring customers—one by one by one by one—to scale your business. Showing investors a big TAM is not going to do it. You need to get more granular than that to paint the big market opportunity.

For many entrepreneurs, as granular as they will get is to say, "We are targeting Gen Z and millennials aged 18 to 36." That's 20 percent or so of the world. Are you telling VCs that every millennial has this need and wants to buy your product? Surely you can limit it to a particular geography, and still that's not enough. You need to characterize and segment your ideal target customer profile. You then need to spell out specifically who you're going after and how you are going to convert them into paying customers.

Don't Tell Investors You Don't Have Any Competition

By Gary Rieschel, Managing Partner at Qiming Venture Partners

Many entrepreneurs are naive about where their competition will come from. When you talk to VCs, you have to realize that the VC community is funding 12,000 new companies globally on annual basis.

Of these, 45 percent are in the US, 40 percent are in China, and the rest are now global. Understanding where competition is likely to come from is far more important today than it used to be. Before, the early warning system of competition was usually constrained to Silicon Valley. Now, ideally, you would look at New York, Austin, and Boston. But even more importantly, you need to look at China, India, and Southeast Asia. Constantly refreshing the competitive context for your business is very important.

This is something that you can do with fairly minimal resources. You can have your finance team look at the financings that occur globally. There are very good databases today that cover new funded companies, like Pitch Book, Zero to IPO, Crunchbase, and others. It's an exercise that's worth spending a few hours a week on to ensure you always have a fresh context for the competitive environment you are operating in.

One absolute turnoff for investors is when they hear entrepreneurs claim that they don't have any competition. They know that's just lunacy. The startup is claiming that somehow they have a business that's so attractive they want me to put millions of dollars into it, but they don't have any competition. The way you should think about it, and present competition, is by imagining you put $1 into your target market and then asking, who's going to want that dollar? Suddenly, you realize there are multiple players who would jump on the space to capture that dollar. Look at all those adjacent spaces, and you'd better have a very good answer as to why someone who is in an adjacent space isn't going to want the same dollar you are going after.

You also cannot have your cake and eat it too by saying, "I have no direct competitors, only indirect ones." Ninety-nine percent of the time that's also not true. Even if that were true when you started your business, by month six you will have about five competitors if you're doing anything interesting and promising at all.

In terms of presenting your competitive analysis and competitive advantage in your pitch deck, you want to avoid the classic mistake of presenting a grid where you tick all the boxes, while your competitors have gaps. This is particularly true for most early-stage companies, where you couldn't have possibly ticked all the boxes yet, and if you did it begs the question why you need the money. Instead, what you want to say is, "Here are the eight attributes that we need to have to be successful in this business. For this competitor, they are either ahead of us or behind us in each attribute." Talk about why you have a better story or position on a specific attribute. Also, cover a handful of competitors and talk about their strengths, but present a good argument for how you will compete with them. Your argument cannot be simply that you will execute faster than the other guys. It's naive to assume that you're the only one who can execute fast.

If you think you have a lead and you're basing your competitive advantage on it, remember that lead can disappear very quickly. So when you talk about differentiation from your competition, if you have a feature that someone else doesn't have, that difference is likely going to be gone very quickly. If you have intellectual property that protects a particular element of your business, that can be valuable in terms of additional defensibility. If you have a business partner or a channel partner that gives you specialized access to an area or exclusivity, that also can valuable. Think about all the unique advantages you have that might raise the barriers to entry for others, or at least give you a higher probability of success than your competition, and talk about those to investors.

Frame Your Competitive Advantage in Terms of Defensibility, Not Unique Features

By Brad Feld, Co-Founder of Foundry Group and Techstars

When it comes to competition, you should be obsessed with knowing your competitor's product inside and out, but then try to pay little to no attention to them. By product, I'm referring not just to their customer offering, but also their go-to-market strategy and any competitive advantage they have. Then, as you are positioning your company on your pitch deck against the backdrop of your competitive landscape, you want to identify where and why you are different from your competition. Most pitch decks have some version of a two-by-two graph that shows your company in the upper right quadrant and shows everybody else in the other three quadrants. That's OK, as long as you talk substantively about what is truly unique about your business relative to your competition.

It's also useful to talk about what you are doing that's fundamentally disruptive to any of your current or prospective competitors. By disruptive, I'm referring to something that's not simply unique, but more dramatic. Disruption is less about a feature or a function and more about how you are approaching the business, what you are doing for your customer, and how customers are buying from you.

You won't have perfect information about your competitors. Your potential investor probably doesn't either. Therefore, it's a chance for you to frame your aspirational narrative about where you are going versus just what's going on today in the market. You need to have some clarity about where you are today with regard to your competitors, but you also want to talk about where you aspire to get to, especially relative to where you think your competitors are going. You need to explain why you think it will be difficult for your competitors to replicate what you're doing.

The mistake a lot of entrepreneurs make is they say, "We are going to do A and B and our competition is not doing A and B," when the reality is that it's not that difficult for a competitor to do A and B. The entrepreneur doesn't explain what they are doing with A and B that is defensible, which might have something to do with their product or their go-to-market strategy, or how they deal with data. It might also have to do with how they engage their customers, in terms of how sticky their offering is, which they can demonstrate through evidence from historical customer dynamics. Trying to develop that competitive story rather than just feature and function positioning is critical to convincing investors that you indeed have a leg up over your competition in the space, whether you have one competitor or a dozen.

Validate Your Sales Pipeline as Much as Possible

By Elisa Miller-Out, Managing Partner at Chloe Capital

If you're operating a B2B startup, for example, to the extent that you have big contracts in the works, it's worthwhile to demonstrate the potential of the business to investors through your sales pipeline. Granted, investors typically look at a sales pipeline with a grain of salt, because it's not real until it is. Every investor knows that a deal is never complete until there's a signed contract and the money is in the bank. Even advanced discussions and verbal agreements can drag on indefinitely or even fall off entirely. Still, it's good for investors to see how active you are on the sales side, and that you're well versed on how to craft a good sales pipeline, and well organized overall in your approach. It will also help them understand where you are on the sales and business development front, in terms of who you're talking with, where they sit in the different stages of the funnel, and what's happening with each in the different stages. All in all, it's further evidence to investors that you're on the right track, if not entirely a proof point. On the other hand, if you can validate those discussions with letters of intent (LOIs) with prospective clients and partners—whether they have agreed to basic terms, a general relationship framework, launching a pilot, or whatever—then that will help build your business case to investors. Even if those LOIs or any informal equivalents showcased in emails or other communications, personal endorsements, testimonials, or customer references are non-binding, they can still help the investor gain more confidence and get more excited about your business and the progress you're making.

Of course, these supplemental materials will never be as good as a signed contract or money in the bank from a client, but they're better than just showing a sales pipeline spreadsheet. Understanding and demonstrating a well-developed sales funnel, and being able to show some evidence and indicators of activity at the different phases of the funnel, can be valuable. All of this will help you demonstrate to investors that you have customer interest that's more serious than just a conversation.

Your data room is a good place to store those documents. You can also allude to them in your deck. For example, you might say, "We have letters of intent from these five major corporate clients in our sector." You could then have a slide with logos of those clients, and mention that additional information on those deals is available in your data room.

Do Your Homework on Your Expansion Plan

By Shane Chesson, Founding Partner at Openspace Ventures

With regard to expansion plans in the context of fundraising—whether you're looking to use the proceeds you raise to tackle a new vertical, geography, or market segment—it's important to show investors that you've done your homework and have a solid execution plan in place. A lot of entrepreneurs brush aside these initiatives as if they were turnkey and automatic, when the reality is that every new expansion of the business will come with its own set of challenges and even competition.

As you tell your story, you also need to be able to say that your baseline is already working, and you are planning to grow the business in the following directions. Expanding prematurely is almost always a sure sign of disaster: it's likely to spread your focus and your resources too thin, and further weaken your proposition to investors. Make sure you conquer what you've divided, so to speak, before you go on to make bigger plans. The exception here, of course, is where you need to make a strategic pivot based on a significant opportunity you've identified based on market feedback, or to an area you're convinced your business is best suited to.

Either way, you need to consider your expansion options very carefully. You need to show investors that there's preliminary work that has already been done, and that you're well positioned to execute on those plans. You also should take into account the background of the investors that you are talking with. If they are well versed in a particular geography or domain you're pursuing, be prepared to get grilled. Don't expect to get off the hook easily; they will naturally ask you for specifics and challenge your assumptions. If you haven't thought about things deeply or prepared enough, you will come across as a bit naive and unready, or even hubristic. On the other hand, if you've done some digging and can back up your plans with insights and data, and speak clearly about the opportunities and challenges involved and your execution plan, they will be all the more impressed and excited about your vision and growth opportunities.

———

8. DEVELOPING YOUR FINANCIALS

Paint Your Story with a Financial Model that Suits Your Business Type

By Fred Destin, General Partner at Stride.VC

There are two core things that matter when it comes to presenting your financial models to investors. The first is that you demonstrate a clear understanding of how your business is going to function. It's not so much about whether the numbers are correct; it's about whether you demonstrate a sophisticated understanding of the levers that you can use when you're building a company and how they translate into financials. You typically want to touch on things like understanding whether you have operating leverage, what portion of your costs are inherently fixed, and what portion of your costs grow as your business scales. It's not necessarily about having the right answers, because quite often in early stages there are too many variables that are unknown. It's highly unlikely that any forecast will be accurate. Still, it's critical you demonstrate to investors that you're approaching your financials using a sound and methodical approach, and that you're thinking about the assumptions and the mechanics of your business in the right way. Step one is therefore demonstrating to investors that you are thinking in a sophisticated way about the nature of your business.

Step two is showing investors that you have absolute clarity on the short-term milestones you're planning to hit and how they translate into a cash flow forecast. Investors are in the business of taking risk, but also in the business of managing risk. One of the things that investors need to understand is when you're going to run out of cash and what will be achieved by that date. Again, it's not necessarily about whether you have the exact figure, but it's about providing reassurance and certainty about how much runway you have to execute your plan.

When presenting your financials, you should exercise a certain degree of freedom in terms of stepping away from accounting rules and practices. Instead, think about the most logical presentation of what your business is about while using numbers. In other words, don't be completely trapped by what your accountant is telling you. Rather, think about your business model and your financials as a way that conveys intelligent information about the business that you're building. Where you account for marketing costs, when and how you account for cost of sales and margin—it is up to you to present all of that in the most intelligible light.

If you are an engineer, a product person, or a marketing person and you don't know much about finance, you have to educate yourself. You don't have to become a financial expert, but you need to force yourself to step outside your comfort zone and master the basics. This is not an area where you can delegate to your CFO or a financial advisor. Make sure that you have a deep understanding of how your business is going to work and how that translates into a business model and a set of financials, because investors will want you to demonstrate a certain level of control or expertise in that department.

Develop a Financial Model That's Suited to Your Business Stage

By Kelly Perdew, Managing Partner at Moonshots Capital

The level of complexity of your financials, your understanding of your assumptions, and your forecasting are truly dependent on the stage of the company. In all cases, you need to have a profit and loss statement (P&L), balance sheet, and cash flow statement. You need to also know your way around them as the founder, as does any financial person on your team. In early-stage startups, those assumptions are going to have lot more volatility to them, including your pricing model. As you evolve, or if you pick a pricing model to show, you need to understand what impact that pricing model will have on the financials, and how upselling and cross-selling will affect the financial model. For most businesses that have evolved their products and services, you also need to know what the cohort analysis looks like and be able to describe the changes. As you grow and move into later-stage growth models, more sophistication is required for an investor to feel comfortable that you know what you're talking about.

Nowadays, private equity firms are venturing into later-stage venture capital, and in many cases trickling down into earlier stages. They have their own financial experts. They have already analyzed the marketplace and they are coming to talk to you about giving you $20 million, $50 million, or $100 million, so you'd better understand cohort analysis. You also need to understand what churn and negative churn look like. It is imperative that you have a good handle on all the elements of your financial model and what it means for your early, middle, and growth stages.

In terms of how you present your financials to investors in your pitch deck, it's like everything else: it's a little bit of a tightrope walk. If you put too much information on the slide people's eyes gloss over it. Too little and they'll think you don't know what you are talking about.

Leading with the critical elements of your business model is important. You need to show the KPIs around your business; that's essentially what investors are looking for at this phase of the process. Obviously, you need to have the backstop of a full model ready for when investors dig deeper into due diligence. Will you be able to answer a question or find the answer quickly and show them if they ask you, or even run different scenarios on the spot and show on your model how they affect outcomes? If you're capable of doing that and you're going to run your business using these three or four KPIs, that will make it easy for investors to follow along and understand your business.

Having just three or four KPIs to base your financial model on can help unpack the business and keep your message simple and focused. You can say something like, "This is how we modeled our financials. This is what headcount looks like. This is where variable costs are. This is where we run out of money, based on these assumptions." You can also show various models, and say something to the effect of, "This $6 million we're looking to raise will carry us for approximately 18 months, and here are the primary assumptions that impact that burnout date. However, I can show you what $8 million looks like, and how that speeds up our revenue growth, but I really believe that $6 million is the minimum to meet our objectives." If investors see that you can run those permutations, they are going have a high level of confidence that you know what you're doing, which is more important than being exactly right on those KPIs.

Pin Down the Key Drivers of Your Financial Model
By David Cohen, Chairman at Techstars

Recognize that investors know that your financial model is wrong. They are not expecting it to be right because you are just not going to get it right. Almost by definition, when you are trying to predict the future, you will rarely be spot on. When you are creating financial models to share with investors, it's very important to make it clear what the drivers of the business are in that financial model. You have to address what two or three things you are going to have to do. What two or three numbers are you going to have to increase that really drive large numbers on one end and success on the other end? Those numbers must be clearly presented so that investors are going to believe in your financial model. So rather than trying to get your financial model to look ideal, make sure you are focused on how the model works when you are presenting it. For example, stop trying to build this hockey stick that says we are going to grow to $10 million and $20 million and $50 million and $200 million in revenue year-over-year without any supporting detail, such as how that revenue is derived or how many customers are needed for it.

The key is to focus on the drivers in the model: number of customers, average sale price, lifetime value, or whatever the right metrics are. An investor can then say, "Well, what if we got 10,000? Well, what if we got 100,000?" Again, it is not because you are going to be correct; it is that you are explaining the way the business works through the financial model, and demonstrating that you have a good understanding of what will drive your business and what needs to be focused on. That is what the investors are really looking for, more than a hockey stick showing hundreds of millions of dollars in revenue without much in the way of a solid rationale to support such extraordinary growth.

Display Your KPIs and Performance to Demonstrate Product–Market Fit and Traction

By Elisa Miller-Out, Managing Partner at Chloe Capital

The KPIs and performance metrics that investors look at to assess your traction don't just include revenue. Depending on the investor, some value users and growth more than revenue. Revenue, however, is a great validator of product–market fit when you have people actually paying for your product or service. Of course, there's also upcoming revenue: contracts, partnerships, and being able to show your sales pipeline can help strengthen your case. There are metrics around growth that are important to look at. There are metrics around retention and churn. How much are you growing your customer base and sales with your customers? Also, how many of your existing customers are staying with you? What percentage of them are you retaining? How many of them are churning out of the business and not staying with your product or service? How sticky is your product or service, essentially? These are some of the questions investors will typically want answers for.

Other common metrics that investors look at are customer acquisition costs (CAC) and LTV of customers. Those metrics are basically designed to help you understand how much it costs you to acquire one customer, then how much that customer is worth to you over the time they will stay with you. How much can you make off that customer in the long term? And that ratio is something that lots of investors like to look at, to see how the ratio changes over time based on how you get better and better at acquiring customers more efficiently.

It also is helpful to show how much funding you are going to need to hit your customer acquisition targets and growth goals. The investor might also be interested in seeing some metrics related to your go-to-market strategy, and demonstrating that you are ready to scale the business. Key partnerships are important as KPIs, especially in the B2B sector. Sometimes there are metrics around that as well. And sometimes there are contracts with partners that also have financial value.

Revenue, retention of customers, repeat customers—metrics like that are all things that show good evidence of product–market fit and help to show traction, which is something that investors are very interested in. So those are a few KPIs to look at.

Identify the Right Unit Economics Set for Your Business

By Seth Levine, Managing Director at Foundry Group

Companies nowadays have access to lots of data. Thus, it's essential to look at unit economics and be clear about what the drivers of your business are. Fully examine things like customer acquisition cost—whether your business is a marketplace, a SaaS, a hardware business, or what have you—and be knowledgeable about the things that matter. If you are a hardware business, you should have a discussion about your margins. Everyone understands why that is very important for hardware businesses. If you are a marketplace business, there are a handful of key marketplace metrics—things like repeat usage, marketplace take rate, and attachments—that are very important to go through. If you are a SaaS business, talk about a different set of unit economics, the net dollar and net revenue retention, which are different. Look at how long it will take to pay back your CAC, not just your LTV to CAC ratio, especially in early-stage businesses where the latter may not be a particularly meaningful metric. It's also very important to understand your business, not just to operate your business, and to present this information to your board members and to potential new investors. It's expected nowadays that you deeply understand and have a good handle on your unit economics. Then as you build out your go-forward plan, understand how they affect it, and then be explicit about changes that you are anticipating in those unit economics in the later years of your plan. All of this helps form the basis for talking about the success and health of your business.

Base Your Financials on Ambitious yet Realistic Assumptions

By David Hornik, Founding Partner at Lobby Capital

Financial projections can be confusing for entrepreneurs. That's because they are, by definition, inaccurate. They are most assuredly inaccurate the day you put them on paper. Rarely, if ever, does a company hit the financial projections they present to investors precisely, especially in the earlier stages—pre-seed, seed, and Series A. So why do venture investors care? And why would a VC want to see your financials? The reason that venture investors want to understand your financials is because they are the key to understanding how you think about your business. They want to see how you derived the assumptions that you built into those financials. First and foremost, they might look at headcount. How do you think your team is going to grow with this financing? You currently have 10 employees. How many are you going to hire in the next year if you raise this $10 million? How many dollars are you going to spend on marketing? That will tell investors a lot about how you think about your business.

How do you think those numbers grow relative to the user base? Is it going to cost you hundreds of thousands of dollars for each 100 customers you add to the platform? Or is it going to be practically free? These assumptions are all built into your financials. By looking at the financials and seeing how your business changes over time, you will be able to understand the underlying assumptions that really drive the likelihood of success of that business.

The biggest mistake you can make with respect to financials is to present baseless, unrealistic assumptions without sound reasoning and forethought behind them. There is a huge difference between putting in front of investors a projected growth rate that's ambitious but possible and one that's impossible. You need to be realistic in those sets of assumptions. You cannot assume that a business that has grown 40 percent year-over-year for the last three years will suddenly grow 140 percent in the next two years without a material cause for it to do so. Likewise, you cannot assume that the LTV of a customer will increase tenfold when it has only increased 1.2 times for the last two years running. Be sure that your financials pass the "sniff test"—that the things you say are changing make sense in the context of your business.

Your assumptions have to make sense in the context of the real world and in the context of your business. If no business in your space has ever grown at the speed you are projecting your business will, then the natural question investors will ask is, "What is different about your business that would cause that extraordinary growth to be true?" If your business has been predictable in the past, and you are anticipating some change that is not predicted from past behavior, the natural question they will ask is, "What is going to be different this time around?" You need to be consistent and be thoughtful about your financials, so that when someone digs into them, they don't seem foolhardy.

Understand Your Traction Expectation per Your Stage

By Fabrice Grinda, Founding Partner at FJ Labs

At all stages, VCs will have a traction expectation commensurate with your investment stage. Obviously, if you're at pre-seed you're typically pre-launch, so there's a lower expectation around revenues than if you were in later stages, such as Series A, B, C, and so forth. Also, there's an expectation that varies depending on whether you're a first-time founder or not. Assuming you're a first-time seed founder and you're raising $1 million at $3 million to $5 million valuation, your expectation will vary depending on your sector and business model. If you're a B2B SaaS business, for example, it will be $20,000-30,000 per month in monthly recurring revenue (MRR). If you're a marketplace, it will be $100,000-$150,000 per month in gross merchandise value (GMV) at a 15 percent take rate, or $15,000-$22,000 per month in net revenues.

On the other hand, if you're in a direct-to-consumer company, it will be $100,000-$150,000 in MRR or GMV. At that level, you can raise your seed round of say $3-4 million at $8-9 million pre-money valuation and $10-12 million post-money valuation. That's the median. The mean is higher than that, however, because you have second-time founders or founders in hot categories who raise very big rounds.

Once you're raising your Series A, the VCs' expectations rise to, say, $100,000 in MRR if you're a B2B SaaS business. If you're a marketplace business, it would be the equivalent of $500,000 in monthly GMV if your take rate is 20 percent, $600,000-$700,000 in monthly GMV if your take rate is 15 percent, or several millions in monthly GMV if your take rate is 3 percent. The amount required varies based on your take rate or net revenue. If you're a direct-to-consumer business, then you're looking at $500,000 in MRR.

Once you raise your Series A, then the VC's expectation is that it will take you 18 months to go to Series B, and another 18 months to go to Series C, and so forth. The median for Series A could be $7 million at $23 million pre-money valuation or $30 million post-money valuation.

Once you're ready for Series B 18 months later, VCs will then expect you to go from $100,000 in MRR to $300,000-$400,000 in MRR if you're a B2B SaaS company. The same applies if you're a marketplace with a 15 percent take rate. If you're a direct-to-consumer business, then it would need to be around $2-3 million in monthly revenues. Many startups nowadays are raising $50 million at pre-money valuation of $150 million. The expectation then is you get to either profitability or your Series C.

If you have a track record, you may skip stages. For example, say you raise a seed of $3 million and that got you to $1 million in MRR. Your Series A is then going look more like a Series B or C. Obviously, if you grow faster than expected, you're more capital efficient and you can ask for more. It will still be termed Series A technically, by PitchBook for instance. The documents will call it an A, but it will look like B or C since it could be in the order of $30 million, $50 million, or even $100 million.

What investors typically need to see is financial information and a level of traction that's commensurate with whatever stage you're in. Investors will also look at your financial model for that next 18 months or two years. They will look at your underlying assumptions about customer acquisition. They need to understand how much you're spending on acquiring these customers, whether your CAC is in line with the story you tell them, and whether there's enough scalability in the acquisition channels that you're going after. Investors don't need five-year pro forma financials at an earlier stage. They care more about the net revenues as well as your burn rate.

At the pre-seed level, when you're raising $1 million, you want to be burning a maximum of $60,000-$70,000 a month. At your seed level, when you've raised $3 million, you need to be burning maximum of $150,000 a month. At Series A level, when you've raised $70 million, you want to burn no more than $300,000-$400,000 a month. Your burn needs to be in line with the amount of money you've raised and the traction that you have. What VCs don't want to see is that you're generating $500,000 a month in revenues or GMV with, say, $100,000 in net revenues and $500,000 a month in losses. That's not a good business. Therefore, while they don't expect five-year pro forma financials, they do want to make sure that the economics work and that they get you to where you need to be in the next 18 months.

At Series B and onwards things are different, because at this point you probably have a CFO. By then, you probably have more controls on your financial metrics and you probably have more predictability in your revenues. You may even be audited now, and as result of that VCs are expecting a lot more granularity. By that point, they're expecting five-year financials.

---

9. REFINING YOUR PITCH DECK

Include a "Why Now" Slide in Your Pitch Deck

By Jenny Fielding, General Partner at The Fund

Less than half of pitch decks have a "why now" slide or something to that effect. This slide is such a gem. Whatever you're building, you're probably not the first person to have thought of your idea or your approach. As such, really thinking about the context of the raise from a timing standpoint can help you convince the investor that you're the right person for this raise at this time. Think about the "why now" slide as a concentric circle where you're in the middle of these overlapping circles, and ask yourself, "What is the confluence of happenings in this very moment that make this the perfect time for me to run this company and to win?"

One of those circles should be about the technology. What's your technical advantage, assuming you're a software or a hardware company? We all have a supercomputer in our pocket today, with all kinds of capabilities, that wasn't around just few years ago when someone else tried to run a company similar to yours. So that's not an advantage. Think of technology as one of those buckets for which you need to define what makes you unique and more viable in your space versus your competition.

Also, think of current socioeconomic issues and trends. What's going on in the world? How has it impacted our work and our lives? Think about what's happening with your team and how you're able to recruit. Figure out what makes the moment, this moment, the right moment for your business, and articulate it to investors on a slide that answers: why now and why you?

Question Your Assertions and Assumptions
By Isabel Fox, General Partner at Outsized Ventures

As you're aware, you have one shot at raising capital, so you certainly want to put your best foot forward. You have to step and ask yourself whether you've touched on all key aspects of your story and your pitch:

- Why did you decide to start the company in the first place?
- What problem are you trying to solve and why?
- What is your USP?
- Why should you and your team be solving this problem?
- What qualifies you and your team to figure out the solution?
- What is your unfair advantage?
- Do you have proof of concept?
- Are you thinking about hiring in the right way?
- Can you attract world-class people?
- What milestones you are going to focus on and how achievable are they?
- Where are you going to put your time and effort to get to the next inflection point and to be able to raise the next round?
- Does the business make sense in terms of unit economics?
- Ultimately, is it scalable and how does that look over two, three, or five years?

It's critical that you address these basic questions in your deck. You will also need to build a coherent financial model, which investors know will likely be wrong. Yet, what they will be looking at, at this stage, is your reasoning and your understanding of your business and your space. Have you identified and can you demonstrate what your key drivers and levers are? Is your model logical and believable, even if it is aspirational by definition? Your vision will need to come through in your business model. Does the story tie together? If you're forecasting a billion dollars of revenue in SaaS contracts, but you haven't budgeted for a sufficient business development or sales team headcount, then surely your planning and expectations are flawed. Investors are well trained to poke holes in your model, so you need to play out every aspect of the business and anticipate what challenges and expenses may come up and budget for them. You cannot afford to leave any stone unturned in your financial model, or you may scare off investors with how unthorough your financial planning is, or worse, with how unsavvy you are about financials.

Constantly question yourself. Play devil's advocate or have someone role-play with you by trying to prove the very opposite of what's you're putting forth in your assertions and assumptions. Try to address their counter points. The more you can do that alone and with your team, the more prepared you will be for anything that investors throw at you, and the more complete and convincing your story will be.

Rehearse and Role-Play Your Pitch Until You Know It Cold

By Bilal Zuberi, Partner at Lux Capital

Prepare, rehearse role-play, and repeat. VCs see a lot of pitches, almost on a daily basis. You usually get an hour at most. You should be prepared to handle anything that comes up in that hour. Nothing in that hour should come as any surprise to you. It's like a stage performance: the audience may be tired or in bad mood, but the performers are trained and rehearsed to put on their best show to engage the audience, no matter what.

You should write down and have answers to every single question that you think you could be asked. It sounds tedious, but it's a worthwhile exercise for you and members of your team who might be presenting with you. That way everyone stays on message, and no one is caught off guard. Winging an answer to a question that you haven't thought about or prepared properly for could signal a lack of preparation or a lack of confidence. Even if you know your material cold, still you want to take the time to think through how to respond most effectively and concisely. Too often, founders answer clarification questions with long-winded explanations that only further confuse investors. Even if you are the best storyteller in the world, don't count on being so smart on your feet. Sometimes VCs even pose concerns and objections just to test you, so those are perfect opportunities to shine and show them that you're indeed well prepared.

You want to get to the point where you can spit out your pitch without having to refer to the slides, and do so in the same order and the same timeframe. Anything short of that, and you've still got some more rehearsing and role-playing to do. You should also practice with different kinds of audiences, from those who are very familiar with your space to those who know nothing about your space, as well as across different sectors and different levels of experience. That way, you can develop a sense of how to tailor your pitch to the different audiences you will encounter.

You also want to keep in mind that different VCs have different interests, even within the same sector. For example, some will be more technical and are more interested in the technology. Others will be more interested in discussing your financials and traction to date. Others will be more interested in your customer data as a validation of product–market fit. Still others will be interested in your network effect and scalability. In each of those cases, you will need to slant your pitch a bit differently to emphasize the area of interest a bit more. The pitch you do for, say, Lux Capital should be different than the pitch you do for Tiger Global, given the different focus of each firm. Rehearse for all of the different kinds of VCs you might encounter.

Another mistake founders make is that they only rehearse before they go to market, and once they have their first investor meetings they stop practicing. They should be constantly updating and simplifying their pitch as they go. You constantly need to think, "What could we have done better or differently in our last pitch?" and practice the new version before the next investor meeting.

Present Investors with Multiple Scenarios and Dependencies

By Gary Rieschel, Managing Partner at Qiming Venture Partners

When you are presenting your business to a venture capitalist, clearly you are going to have a business model and your financials, and you obviously want to be deeply knowledgeable about those financials. What is also important is to admit up front that whatever your base case is, it's wrong. By definition, the business model is always wrong from the outset. The numbers are never going to be exactly what's in the business model, so you should present investors with multiple scenarios. For example, if we land this account or if we achieve this technological breakthrough, this is the upside; if we don't, and we have to delay product launch by six months, or if we have a problem with recruiting, we're looking at this outcome.

That also means that you shouldn't be afraid to talk about the inherent risks in the business with investors, so long as you can also show that you're doing your homework around mitigating those risks. Remember, any good VC that you are talking with will have lost multiples of the money that they are thinking about putting into your business. They have all had the experience of things that didn't work, and more importantly, the awareness of why it didn't work.

If you start having a positive discussion, saying, "OK, you understand. You trust me enough that we are now discussing what the upside would be, or even the downside," you are already having a business discussion with them around running the business. That's the conversation you want to get to with a VC during a fundraising process. It's less about, "Are you going to put money into the company?" It's more like, since we are now on the same side of the table: Here is the upside scenario. Here is the downside scenario. Here is the base case scenario. You want to get to the point where you're having a conversation with the investor as if they are already a partner in the business. Presenting the different scenarios and their dependencies will help engage them in the business.

What investors want you to say is, "OK, here's the base case. What I want to do is pace my spending based on the achievement of these outcomes. So I am planning on spending X to achieve Y. If I don't achieve Y, I don't get to start spending more money unless I have specific reasons why that shortfall occurred, and how additional money will support achieving that milestone."

Too many companies build in the spending plan, rather than make it milestone-based. If an entrepreneur says their milestones are two years out, that's just not realistic unless, maybe, you are running a pharmaceutical or a semiconductor design startup. But generally, for software and anything related to the consumer enterprise software or consumer software, you have specific milestones over time.

It's always better for you to show discipline by telling investors, "This is the spending plan. If we meet this, then we are going to free up some of the additional cash to take us to the next milestone." In that case, there may be an increase in the spending, but it's clearly understood that you needed X to get to a particular milestone. Once you are at that milestone, then you are going to need Y to get to the next milestone. If you have that milestone to reach, you can always go back to the drawing board and say we need to make a change. Having that milestone and having a discussion around upside and downside scenarios around your spending plan are very important.

———————

Develop a Sense of Your Potential Exit
By Greg Moon, Managing Partner at SoftBank Vision Fund

When you engage with VCs, you need to put yourself in their shoes and see things from their perspective. Then you'll ask, "Why do I need to make this investment?" The primary purpose of an investment, by definition, is to make great profits. Ultimately, the greatest profitability can be achieved in the event of an exit, be it an acquisition, or a merger, or an IPO.

The more you can paint the picture to VCs on your path to exit in terms of potential outcome scenarios that involve great returns for the prospective investor, the more likely you will be able to convert them into actual investors in your company. You don't necessarily have to state specifics around your exit, which will be quite premature, especially if you're in an early stage. You wouldn't, for example, say that you intend to sell to Amazon. Leave the specific details out. You simply want to raise the broad possibilities of an exit to, say, a large online retailer or perhaps to a strategic traditional offline retainer who wants to enter e-commerce. By doing so, in effect, you're speaking the language of the VC. The converse of that is that you're ambivalent about investors' interests, and therefore less likely to align with them in regard to the big picture.

Demonstrating to VCs that you have thought about these various scenarios down the road, and that you share the same goals as the VC, can only work in your favor. If you can point to certain historical trends around acquisitions of similar companies to yours and base your scenarios on some sound assumptions about market dynamics you foresee in the next five or seven years, all the better. That way, your exit plans don't come off merely as a wish list. Instead, they are based on a thorough assessment and understanding of the market and where things are heading.

However, you don't want to bring this up too early in the conversation with investors, before they understand and see the value of your business and are essentially sold on the potential of your business. Mentioning it too early comes across a bit awkward and perhaps a little hubristic or even arrogant, especially if you're an early-stage startup or first-time founder, since you have not established with the investors why your suggested potential exit plans are realistic.

Of course, should the investor ask you from the start to talk about who might be a good candidate to buy your company, then you should cover the various scenarios you've thought about. You can also imply certain valuation levels to further paint the picture.

Granted, not every startup has a clear path to an exit from the outset, especially when it comes to mergers and acquisitions (M&A). For instance, if you're developing an e-commerce platform that's targeting a new market segment or a more robust logistics solution, then you can easily identify big players in the space who might want to expand into your new space or leverage your technology in their existing business. On the other hand, if you're developing a completely new, original concept in software or service solutions or an artificial intelligence (AI) product, then it's less likely that you'll be able to identify clearly where it might fit. This is especially the case in new, fluid industries that are constantly changing, such as AI, blockchain, or crypto, for example. Then, your default option, if you can scale the business, might be doing an IPO. All in all, there is never going to be clear exit path from the outset for the vast majority of startups, as we live in an ever-changing world and things are bound to look a lot different in the next few years than they do now. That said, if you continuously think about and investigate the various exit options available to you down the road, this picture will become more and more clear.

Forgo Talking About an Exit Plan in the First Meeting

By Rob Kniaz, Partner at Hoxton Ventures

If you're an early-stage entrepreneur, it's almost always premature for you to be talking to investors about your exit plan in the first meeting or two. Unless you know a potential buyer personally who expressed interest in what you're building, and you know they likely would want to buy you or have tried to buy you already, it's a futile exercise. Most of the time, it's sort of just "garbage in garbage out." For any particular business, Google could buy you out, but do you really know what's going to happen in the next few years? More often than not, it backfires when entrepreneurs put it in their deck that they're expecting company X to acquire them. As an investor, I can often simply pick up the phone and call company X and ask them. Often, they will say that they will never buy the company. In most cases, you shouldn't really be thinking about your specific buyer, especially when you're at the beginning of the road. After all, what investors are more excited about is seeing whether you can build a very big business that doesn't necessarily need a buyer.

While targeting an acquisition for $100 million is great for the founders, investors are looking often for venture scale return potential that is far higher. Don't disclose to investors that you're looking to exit and already eyeing a particular company, which could make them more nervous about the investment. If you think you're going to sell for $100 million in a couple of years, and you know who the acquirers are, it's probably not a great return for VCs in terms of their own cost of capital. If that's the case, they will likely lose interest in engaging with you further and in funding your company.

---

10. SETTING YOUR VALUATION

Resist the Lure of Aiming to Raise Too Much Capital at Too High a Valuation

By Seth Levine, Managing Director at Foundry Group

One of the common mistakes entrepreneurs make is raising too much capital or raising at too high a valuation. This sounds self-serving coming from a VC. It is not just because I think valuations are too high, but I see founders often making this mistake, often pushing valuation as high as they can possibly get it and raising as much money as they possibly can. Meanwhile, they forget about the fact that raising more capital means more preference overhang. You can actually overcapitalize the business for a specific period of time, and you run the risk at too high a valuation of not being able to catch up to that valuation and raise money in the next round. Many times over my career, I have actually watched companies fail, not because the business wasn't going OK, but because they had raised too much too early at too high a valuation. Their business couldn't catch up to it. So while the business might have been on an OK trajectory, they had spent too much to get there. Their valuation was so high that the there was no new financing at a flat up-round valuation, and investors don't like to come in and do down rounds. It essentially created almost a poison pill for the company where they couldn't raise more capital.

For businesses that do raise a lot of money, my advice is always that just because you raised it doesn't mean have to spend it. Your spending amount should be based on the information that you have about your business and essentially your preparedness to spend that money now. Nowadays, there are a lot of businesses that are raising a huge amount of money at seed and Series A. I understand the rationale: the money is there and people want to make sure they have that balance sheet firmed up. But just because you raise $20 million in your seed round doesn't mean you should be spending a million dollars a month.

The general advice is to raise for at least 18 months to two years. That's a good sweet spot. If you want to raise more money for a three-year period, for example, that's OK too. The difference, however, between raising $12 million and $20 million at seed should be how long it takes you to spend it, not how much you spend per month. You should spend based on your preparedness to spend and your understanding of your business. If you don't know enough about your business to spend it wisely, you should be spending based on the knowledge that you have, not how much money you have in the bank. Companies often make that mistake. As a result, they spend too much money too early. In almost every case where I have had a business fail and where I have looked back and said, "This should have been a good business, we should have made this work," we started spending too much money too soon and by the time we realized the right way to spend that money, it was too late. By then, we didn't have enough of it left. So I would offer that advice, especially in these sorts of heady times where companies are raising a lot of money.

———————

Be Cautious of Anchoring Your Valuation Too Heavily on that of Comparable Companies

By Jon Soberg, Managing Partner at MS&AD Ventures

Valuation is always a tricky topic for founders to figure out. There are no hard and fast formulas, so it is a bit more of an art than a science. Founders have expectations and investors have expectations; meanwhile, the market is always in flux. In today's market, investors are willing to pay quite high valuations for growth and for the potential to be a market leader. If you haven't positioned yourself as a market leader or as a potential market winner, it's going to be tougher for you to get great valuations. There's still a high premium for high valuations.

One thing you need to be aware and conscious of in your fundraising journey is that just because a competitor or someone with a similar business model in a different geography has raised at $200 million, $300 million, or $400 million valuation, that doesn't mean that your company will or should get a similar premium valuation. You don't know all the details or what pitch that competitor or comparable company used. It's not particularly accurate or effective to tell investors, "We have three competitors that have all become unicorns, and therefore you should view us in the same league," without having the full picture to make such a claim. Of course, if you have full visibility on your competitor's metrics and milestones, you'll be in a better position to benchmark your company against theirs when it comes to valuation. Most often, founders don't have detailed knowledge of their competition's numbers, so just be cautious about trying to anchor too heavily on what somebody else raised, because the details of exactly what they look like on the inside is might be different from what you expect.

Some founders also say, for instance, "I want a $100 million valuation." Meanwhile, they're raising $10 million. In such a situation, the math typically doesn't work. VC's often look for a minimum of

20 percent or 25 percent ownership, whereas a standard round might dilute a company by around those numbers. So if you go to market with a $10 million ask in exchange for 20 percent equity, then simple math says you are shooting for around a $40 million valuation. If you are going to market looking for $50 million, then obviously you are at a completely different sort of valuation, and investors' analysis will revolve around whether they think your company is at a stage that justifies that valuation. That means that they will either pass or go forward, or in some cases adjust the parameters to fit where the company is.

Ask for Less Capital and Let the Market Determine the Size of the Round

By David Cohen, Chairman of Techstars

Most entrepreneurs have heard of the oversubscribed round and how successful that is. One common error that a lot of entrepreneurs make is they go out to the market and ask for too much money. They know that they could probably raise a million or two, so they go to the market and ask for $5 million or $10 million. Oftentimes, that will lead to no money at all being raised. It is counterintuitive, but if you ask for a lot, and you have commitments for a little, you don't generally close on a little. What generally happens is those investors who committed part of the round begin to realize that you didn't meet the bar that you set for your commitment size, and they get a little bit scared. That's because you didn't meet the expectation that you set and, as a result, they may never invest. At best, they will drive the pricing down, because you did not do what you said you were going to do. Instead, it is much better to ask for a million or two and let the market tell you, how about $5 million or $10 million? Over time, you recognize that the amount of money you are raising can be a moving target. It is always better if that target increases as you get commitments. It is terrible when it decreases because you can't land any investors. There's a reason that no one has ever said, "I raised this amazing, undersubscribed round."

That said, you obviously have to know your audience. You wouldn't want to go into Bessemer and pitch a $100,000 round and hope they offer you more money. That's not what they do. Understand who you are pitching to, but from their perspective trying to get you to take more money is a good dynamic, versus you asking for too much and not having enough subscription and having to backpedal on the round size. With angels and seed investors, it is going to be piecemeal. So if you are raising a million or two, you want to get to the point where you are oversubscribed; then you can continue to take more money. At that point, as long as you haven't established a price yet, you are just taking commitments and you are flexible on pricing based on what is going to happen and how much subscription there will be. The trick is not to ask for so much that the market doesn't meet your demand, and you end up not having a round at all because those investors sense that lack of momentum.

Price Your Current Financing Round with Your Next Round in Mind

By Andrew Romans, CEO at 7BC Capital

When you're setting the pricing and the valuation of your current funding round, it's important that you give consideration to what your next funding round will be, and even the subsequent funding round. You want the next pre-money valuation to be ideally 20 percent to 100 percent higher than the current post-money valuation. If you raise too large of a round or at too high a valuation and the pre-money valuation of the next funding round is equal to the post-money valuation of this round, that's considered flat. If the pre-money valuation of your next funding round is lower than the post-money valuation of this round, that's considered to be a down round. Down rounds are often where founders get fired or get significantly diluted and hurt. Their ultimate position at the exit will be very badly impacted as a result.

Some founders just raise money with the normal kind of auction process and try to raise at the highest valuation they can. That may not always be the best strategy. You definitely need to consider that if you've got 18 months' cash runway, for example, you will be sitting with a pitch deck pitching your company at a much higher valuation just six to nine months from now. You need to ask, "What kind of progress will I have to make with my company in the next six to nine months?" You want to make sure that you are making sufficient progress that it justifies an up round. Meanwhile, there's always that uncertainty that the macroeconomic environment could shift on you, and you will be raising in a down, depressed market compared to the very bullish, optimistic, up market we are currently in.

These are things to think about when deciding how much to raise, and what the valuation should be. Map out on a piece of paper your next couple of funding rounds and the kinds of progress you think you will make—and be realistic. When I look back at some of the companies that have failed, there are quite a few people who lost their money as an investor. Quite a few of them would not have failed had they taken in money at lower valuations, because they were raising money at too high a valuation when they were feeling very confident.

One more thing: remember that when you sell your company, you typically need to pay back the investors one time, like a 1× liquidation preference. If you were able to get to an exit and sell your company for $50 million when you only raised $1 million, and you own two-thirds of it, you are getting two-thirds of $50 million, and the liquidation stack is $1 million. If you raise $300 million, on the other hand, and you can't find anyone to buy your company for more than $200 million, it will be difficult for you to even get to an exit or make money on that.

Pay Attention to M&A Every Time You Raise Capital

By Andrew Romans, CEO at 7BC Capital

Mergers and acquisitions are fundamental to venture capital. As a founder, it's especially important to wrap your head around your future prospects of M&A and keep them in mind when you're fundraising. Given that outcomes such as IPOs are still quite rare—and statistically will probably remain so, especially in the US in terms of getting listed on the NASDAQ or the New York Stock Exchange—the more likely path for the majority of startups is M&A. Therefore, it's important that you understand some general principles of the types of cash-on-cash return a professional VC firm seeks to make when they invest, and that's where M&A ties directly to pricing: how much capital should the startup be raising and at what valuation? Typically, founders are obsessed with dilution and change of control when they should be paying attention to all the terms in a term sheet, especially those that impact governance. By governance, I'm referring to who is running the company, who is in charge of the company, and what decisions require approval from even minority investors.

You need to keep in mind that VCs diversify across a large number of companies in their portfolio when investing early. They are probably seeking 20-fold returns with occasional 50-100-fold returns in their portfolio. So if they can't see a plausible 10-fold return, they are probably not going to approve any given fundraising or acquisition. Each time you contemplate raising a venture capital funding round or angel funding round, or even when you contemplate starting a company, you should have a keen understanding of the M&A environment for this company. Each company is in an industry that will have some sort of multiple of sales or a level of growth that is driving M&A. You have discounted cash flow, where you are really looking at top-line revenue and bottom-line margin. That's where you'd ask, "Am I making a high profit margin or am I a loss-making company, and what is the growth?"

You will also need to be looking at comparables in terms of similar companies' financings in your industry, and possibly benchmark against them or at least learn from them. When you're deciding how much to raise, and at what valuation, it's not only a function of getting it done and minimizing dilution. You also need to also ask, "Did I just decrease my options for an exit?" For example, if a company were to sell for more than $3 billion, there is a very short list of companies that are able to actually buy that company for $3 billion, whereas if you sell the company for $50 million, then there is probably a very long list of companies that might be interested in buying this company.

You need to understand the difference between the types of M&A exits, such as "acquihire" where someone is just buying the team, or if they're buying a product. It's also important to understand the dynamics of getting cash exit consideration up front versus earnouts. If you are Skype and you get acquired by Microsoft, and you have no control over how much Microsoft embeds the Skype into their Outlook email or Microsoft Exchange email, you might be powerless to achieve your earnout. When things are beyond your control, the earnout may become out of reach.

M&A is fundamental to venture capital and fundraising; therefore, it's fundamental to every decision you make, and you should not make a decision about creating a company or raising capital without careful consideration of the impact on future M&A prospects.

———————

11. BUILDING A DATA ROOM

Set Up an Effective Data Room with Its Own Ground Rules

By Manuel Silva Martinez, General Partner at Mouro Capital

When it comes to your data room, you must remember there's no one-size-fits-all approach. There is no standard formula that works for all companies. You must identify what particular information, data points, and supportive material you need to include to help fully inform investors about your business and present the company in the best possible light. The point is not to overwhelm investors with everything under the sun. Instead, create an easy-to-use navigational map and user-friendly material, and guide investors to the parts of your business that you want them to understand the best. You need to make sure you provide both the right quantity and quality of information to be sufficient for decision making, and be ready to address any questions or concerns that investors may raise. You might even assign someone from your team with good organizational and communication skills to help direct investors around the data room, especially when working with several investors at the same time or under a tight timeline. That person can also help assemble requested material and fill any gaps. They don't have to be C-level, as long as they're up to the task. This will obviously help free you up to attend to the business.

Conversely, there's nothing worse than giving an investor access to a remote data room and telling them, "Given our standard process and in fairness to everyone else, that's all the material you're going to get. Everything's in there, so you don't have much room to ask questions." That's a terrible way to handle prospective investors from the start. That sends the wrong signal to an investor, and makes them think, "If that's the way I will be treated in the beginning, I have my doubts about how the relationship will evolve once I'm an investor in the boardroom." I would wonder if I will be kept in the dark and unable to receive the information I need to wrap my head around the business and make informed decisions. I would also wonder how cooperative and transparent the company will be in general. Granted, some standardization makes sense from a process standpoint. There ought to be some room to accommodate for special situations, but you wouldn't want to put everything in the data room. You want to put in only the key items that investors need to reach a decision. However, depending on investors' interest, it's natural that they will make outside-the-box requests. Leave some room for discussion and for tailored information, but only for the parties that get further along in the process and that are really interested.

The flipside is that VCs love to invest in as much certainty as possible at the end of the day, yet there's no such thing as certainty with entrepreneurship and startups. The more data they collect, the closer they think they're getting to certainty. So the same way you should leave the door open to more questions and discussion, and digging into different aspects of the business, you should also have a sense of how much information you're ready to disclose given the tremendous amount of time and bandwidth it consumes when you're running the business.

Thus, there's a moment where you should tell your prospective investors, "Hey guys, we gave you the key information, we spent time with you on the topics that were important to you, now it's up to you to make a call. Based on my judgment as an entrepreneur, I believe that you have enough to make a decision. Now, I'm moving forward and looking for something binary. So, either you want to invest or not, and these are the terms." Just don't be arrogant or dismissive about it. Investors understand that you have a business to run. As much as conversation is good and creates the bond and the relationship, there also needs to be a sufficiency aspect. Otherwise, investors might hammer you indefinitely with information requests, and the deal gets dragged on. You need to draw that line in the sand when the moment comes and ask politely for a decision. It's your right after being forthcoming, transparent, and accommodating.

Check All the Boxes on Investors' Data Room Checklist

By Keet Van Zyl-draft, Partner at Knife Capital

A lot of deals get stuck at the data room stage. Often, entrepreneurs generate excitement around their business and the investment opportunities, and the investor is impressed by the quality of their vision and the cleverness of their solution or approach. At this point, they decide to proceed further and look under the hood, only to lose interest and reconsider their investment when they come across a poorly organized data room full of gaps and inconsistencies.

As founder, you cannot afford to present anything less than a robust and complete data room if you're hoping to keep investors engaged beyond the initial meetings. For many reasons, there is a bit of gamification as well as real office value in the due diligence exercise. Whether it's due diligence for investment, a sell side, or bettering for exits, an investor is able to tell a lot about you just by looking at how you compile information and how easily accessible you make it in your data room. Just from clicking on an online link and looking at how the various folders in the data room are structured, and how information and data is organized, a savvy VC will be able to tell a lot about how well organized your business is, and about your level of maturity. The key to a speedy investment and getting to yes with VCs is to take your time and do your homework when it comes to your data room setup. Make sure it's complete and answers most, if not all, of the anticipated investors' questions.

When an investor is going through their data room checklist, they are assessing the state of the business. (You can easily find a standard version online, which is essentially composed of legal, financial, historical, vision, human resources, and asset documents, as well as a cap table and any intellectual property.) In effect, they're validating everything you told them, or they're getting more confused—or worse, they're reaching the conclusion that your pitch was hyped and the reality and potential of the business is no longer exciting. Clearly, a data room is a make-or-break point as far as fundraising goes.

Implicitly, having a fully organized and complete data room signals to the investor that you may already be talking with other VCs. This obviously creates a bit of competitive tension and urgency, which plays in your favor in terms of negotiation and closing. Additionally, a good repository of information can be very helpful in ensuring investors' due diligence moves quickly and smoothly. Remember to keep the data room updated throughout your fundraising process, since obviously your figures, team, and customers will change. Also, you want to line up your data room in case some corporate comes knocking on your door for a potential acquisition; the last thing you want is to come across as disorganized and have your team in last-minute fire drill mode, scrambling for data.

———

Make Sure to Have a Signed Founder Vesting Agreement Before You Go Fundraising

By Bill Liao, General Partner at SOSV

Make sure that you have a founder vesting agreement signed with your co-founders. You need to have a formal working framework with your co-founders and an agreement as to what happens if things don't go precisely according to plan. The number of startups that I have seen fail because they had difficulties early in the process due to disagreements about who put what effort in, what the expectations were, and pitting one founder against another—all these things get cured if you set a black-and-white contract early on, which is like a "prenup" for a marriage.

The truth is, you are going to have to do more work for your startup than you can possibly imagine. It is therefore a prerequisite of nearly every VC fund that you have a co-founder. VCs know that partnerships are difficult; hence, the clarity that a founder vesting agreement brings to the co-founders' dynamic is critical. If you haven't formalized such a document with your co-founders, it might reflect negatively on you and your business with investors. They might perceive the business as less advanced than it really is, or you and your co-founder as less mature than you really are.

You can find founder vesting agreement templates for free. There are examples of verified ones all over the internet if you search. You can even get one from our wiki on sosv.com. The clarity those agreements bring is enormously beneficial in making sure that your founding team lowers their expectations and knows that they must keep working, no matter how much money is raised, until the company is viable. The founder vesting agreement should typically have a four-year vesting period with a one-year cliff. It doesn't really affect investors' perception of the company if you distribute the equity asymmetrically, although obviously that should depend on the time, effort, and contribution that people are going to put in, and their stature and standing. Make sure that there are very clear and real penalties for co-founders not participating and not giving their time to the startup.

Specifically in the context of fundraising, having a founder vesting agreement helps you to engage with investors, because they see that you have a degree of clarity and maturity in your arrangements as partners. Whether there are two, three, or five partners, all partnerships carry a dissolution risk. The founder vesting agreement takes that dissolution risk and clarifies it. It implies that you're going to do the best for the company.

Have Differential Stakes Between Co-Founders
By Sajith Pai, Director at Blume Ventures

When you have multiple co-founders, especially three or more, it's more encouraging to see founders having differential stakes—for example, one founder having 30 percent, another having 22 percent, another having 15 percent. VCs prefer this kind of split structure versus more uniform or equal shares among the co-founders. The reason is that this shows that the co-founders have already made a difficult discussion about how to split the equity among themselves. It shows that they've identified the senior or lead founder, who is in effect the CEO and who will hold the deciding vote, so decisions won't come down to a deadlock. It also shows that they went through the exercise of figuring out who brings what to the table, weighing out the contributions of each, and reflecting that in terms of their share of the equity.

Even if there are two founders who started the business together and seemingly play equal roles, VCs like to see one founder having a slightly higher share. Ironically enough, companies where there are differential stakes tend to actually have less infighting and less chance of a breakup. The reason is that there is clarity among the founders as to who is the key founder, who will focus on fundraising, who will run the company, who will be the CEO of the company, and who is number two, number three, and so forth.

If you already have equally distributed equity shares with your co-founders, it's worth revisiting and adjusting them according to business needs and contributions. Remember, the fair thing to demonstrate is that each founder is compensated and incentivized according to their specific value to the business, rather than imposing an artificial egalitarian distribution of the equity just to keep everyone happy. You're always better off to go for differential shareholding, not just for the purpose of influence with VCs, but internally as well, in terms of setting the tone within your company that individuals are rewarded based on contribution, not on seniority or other non-relevant factors.

Disclose Troublesome Information in Your Data Room and Be Prepared to Address It

By Gary Rieschel, Managing Partner at Qiming Venture Partners

You should always assume that anything that's particularly troubling will be found out, whether you put it in the data room or not. You are far better off putting it in the data room and telling your story about it to investors. This is much better than having something that is obviously going to come up during due diligence and having the story dictated by someone else or trying to put your spin on it afterward. If you know there's going to be an issue, and you know there is uncertain data around a particular area, put it out there. Then, prepare to have the conversation around why this is your point of view as to why this happened, and whether it matters or doesn't matter a great deal.

For example, some entrepreneurs will still own or even run additional companies on the side. Some even operate a fund where they might have a large number of angel investments. As a result, they may have distractions that take some of their time. All of those things will eventually come out when investors start to do due diligence on the entrepreneurs. In such circumstances, you are always better off stating all the potential time conflicts up front, and then telling your story as to why that's not material in terms of this particular investment.

Depending on the issue at hand, you could create a special folder to include in your personal folder in the data room. The other items to put in there include any prior litigation that you have had, because prior litigation will also always come up; if you've had a sexual harassment settlement, that will certainly come up. Again, you're better off just saying that you have a chance to have a clean start and have a candid, adult conversation with your investor rather than try to conceal things from them.

PART III

IT'S SHOWTIME: CONNECT WITH & ENGAGE INVESTORS

12. GOING TO MARKET

Know Thy Target Investors

By Manuel Silva Martinez, General Partner at Mouro Capital

What a lot of entrepreneurs forget is that delivering a pitch is not a mechanical action. Essentially, when you're pitching investors, you're asking them not only to trust you now, but to trust you over the long term, knowing very well that many aspects of the presentation are going to change significantly. You're asking them to trust that you can handle the challenges that arise and work with them, and that you will present the right facts and the right narrative throughout.

There's also a bit of an emotional journey, whereby you need to also get to know and create an emotional bond with the investor, because you're basically going to be in the same room for a number of years building the company. There will be moments to celebrate, there will be tough conversations, and that is all part of the journey. This long relationship ahead is something that often gets overlooked when pitching. Many entrepreneurs attend pitching events where they have 50 VCs in front of them, hoping that one is going to get them a term sheet. They rarely do. I would hypothesize that the reason they don't really get a lot of attention through those events is because they're not in the right setting to get to know and create that emotional bond with investors.

As an entrepreneur, you need to understand what moves the VC in front of you. And I mean the person, the actual investment professional in front of you, not only the logo he or she represents. What is their sweet spot? What kind of stage do they focus on, more early stage or Series A, B, or C? What kind of risks are they willing to take on and what kind of track record do they have in supporting entrepreneurs like you? Is it the kind of fund that will keep on funding the company in the future? Knowing this will give you insights on who to target and possibly how to tailor your presentation to each.

You also need to select VCs that are excited by your stage and by the acceleration that you're looking to reach through the fundraise, as opposed to earlier-stage VCs who cannot bring a lot of value or later-stage ones who won't be as excited and committed about your company or would be looking for more validation than what you can show at your current stage of development. It's also important that you get an insider view by connecting with other startups within the VC's portfolio and getting their feedback on how the VC interacts and supports their startups, as well as their style both in the boardroom and outside. All in all, think broadly about the human aspects of who you are taking on board as an investor, because you will be working with that group of people for a long while.

Try to Raise from Different Types of Investors

By Anis Uzzaman, CEO at Pegasus Tech Ventures

Many entrepreneurs try to raise money from a single investor. You're better off, especially in your seed or Series A round, to try to raise from different types of investors. The advantage of raising capital from multiple diverse investors is that you add more breadth of experience and a wider network than if you raise from just one investor. You could also raise from a few prominent angel investors, because they individually give you more time, energy, and advice. At the same time, maybe throw a few institutional VCs into the mix. Let's say you're raising $2 million. You should try to raise from two to three angels and maybe from two other VCs. It's not only about getting help to get to the next level, but also having more options in your bucket, so that you can grow smoothly in your lifecycle. So raise from different types of investors. Try to mix together a bunch of angels and VCs from the beginning so that you have more options down the line.

VCs tend to have a bigger check size, so they will not invest very small amounts. They will most likely invest maybe $500,000 at the minimum, so two to three VCs will be the limit, and the rest of the round you can fill out with prominent angel investors. Angel investors will typically invest anywhere between $250,000 and $500,000. You can add and fill up the rest of the bucket with the right number of angel investors when you're at the early stage of the company.

There is no precise order to which type of investors come when. Often, angel investors are investing along with some VCs that they syndicate with. They will call the right VCs who can help you in the areas your startup is doing business in. So approach angels at the same time as you're approaching VCs; there is no order in terms of who you should land first.

Devise a Methodical Approach to Engaging Investors

By Filip Dames, Founding Partner at Cherry Ventures

It's very important that you see fundraising as a project, which means that you have to start in a very methodical way. You need to develop a very good idea of the target funds that you want to raise from, and have a clear understanding of the target amount that you want to raise and the timeline. You need to list the funds that you want to speak with and prioritize which firms you want to start with, and then initially practice a bit with that set and learn from them before you move on to the ones that are probably a little bit higher up on your preferred list. You should save the ones you're more keen on engaging and the ones that are more challenging for later stages. Sequence matters.

It also matters who at the fund you approach. Look at the fund's portfolio companies and even break it down to a partner level. Which partner at a given fund has done which deals? Which can give you a sense of their appetite for a company such as yours? If someone is very active in intech, for example, that's the right person to approach if you have a Fintech company. Once you've identified the person, the next step is to reach out to them, ideally through a warm intro via someone who knows someone. Alternatively, if you're active on social media, especially on LinkedIn and Twitter, reacting to relevant posts can also help you to engage with prospective investors. If they're discussing certain topics on social media, chime in and add useful input. That's certainly an approach worth trying.

Another venue worth a shot is events. All investors go to events, so those can be great places to strike up an interesting conversation with an investor. You have to somewhat temper your enthusiasm; don't be too much in sales mode. Everyone knows that you're pitching and that you're selling, but try and engage in a genuinely interesting conversation that's high level and that you sense would be interesting to other side. You can then, of course, briefly pitch your story and pitch your company. Those events often attract investment firms' associates and principals. They're also looking for info and building their networks, so they are easy to connect with. Even though you're not speaking directly to a partner, they may still give you insights into the firm and its investment approach, and which partner might be best suited for you to approach. They also may help facilitate your company into a deal flow with the right partner, and help you get your foot in the door. By the end of the process, you need to make sure you're speaking with a decision maker.

Try to Secure at Least One Well-Known Investor

By Anis Uzzaman, CEO at Pegasus Tech Ventures

If you have the option, go after at least one well-known investor. That will help you raise in subsequent rounds. You always need to think about building the company. You are not just trying to solve a problem for a certain time period; you need to always think about how your fundraising decision is going to influence the future of the company. As you're raising money, if you have an option between investor A and investor B, it's more useful to raise the capital from the better-known one, if possible. It's human nature to be more impressed with big-name brands and trust them more, so having an investor of that caliber and credibility can make your fundraising journey easier and shorter.

Another benefit of going after well-known investors is you'll be able to attract better talent. Top talent hiring is one of the biggest challenges for most startups. If you're able to collect capital from prominent investors, talent hiring will become easier, and so do any corporate partnerships you engage with, whether strategic or not. All will become easier, because the thinking around you will be, if those big investors bought into your vision, believed in, and trusted you when they're exposed to countless investment opportunities, you must be onto something big.

De-Prioritize Investors Who Haven't Closed Their Fund or Are at the End of a Fund Cycle

By Thomas Sperry, Managing Director at Rogue Venture Partners

When you take venture money, there are a couple things you want to do when you're raising a round. First, you want to understand how big the fund is and where the investors are in their fund cycle. If they're toward the end of the lifecycle of the fund, it means they don't have a lot of investments left to make. They're going to be picking one or two final investments and they're going to be even more discerning than usual on the last two that they pick.

Second, understand how much money they have for follow on. Some funds may keep a reserve of two or three times the original investment, or even more. Other funds don't reserve any. You need to figure out whether they can and will invest in subsequent rounds. Then ask where they play in those subsequent rounds. Do they lead? Do they follow? Is it just their pro rata? How do they look at follow-on investments? Really understand where they think they want to go with this investment.

Don't spend a lot of time with investors who are at the beginning of a fund, because you don't know exactly where they are with their closing. Are they nearing their first fund close? How close are they to their first capital call? Investors that haven't closed their first capital call can't write checks yet. It could take anywhere from a few weeks to a few months for them to be ready. The same applies to investors at the end of their fund cycle. They're going to be very selective. They're also probably not going to invest across funds unless they're allowed to. Just because you can take money from one fund doesn't mean their second fund will be able to follow on. They should always be investing out of that same fund. So don't waste time or get dragged along by anyone who doesn't have readily available cash. You should be able to find the right VCs who want to invest in you for the right reasons at the time that works for your business.

De-Prioritize Approaching VCs Who Have Invested Too Close to Your Space

By Jon Soberg, Managing Partner at MS&AD Ventures

One mistake founders make is that they look at a given VC's portfolio companies and assume that because the VC invested in a company similar to their company, that VC will be equally interested in theirs. They see, for example, that the VC has invested in an Insuretech marketplace that's tailored to small businesses, then get excited if they also focus on providing a similar service to a similar market segment. They think they've found the perfect partner. That's actually usually the wrong approach, because VCs tend not to make multiple bets in the same space. In this example, you'd want to approach an investor who's focused on Insuretech or Fintech, but not necessarily someone who's already made an investment in this particular space. This is true even if the other company is not a direct competitor. VCs typically don't want to make two investments that are close, because from a portfolio perspective it doesn't make sense to concentrate there. Granted, what constitutes "close" is subjective.

There are a few exceptions. For instance, most famously, Andreessen Horowitz indicated that they are willing to make a few bets in the same space in terms of similar products or services, and even within the same geography, if they love that space.

Granted, if a VC invested in a company that's focused on small business insurance in the US, that does not mean that this company will offer the same service in Africa or the Middle East. Those markets are very different. In that case, it might be worthwhile for you to approach such VCs if their particular investment is geographically remote enough to minimize any chance of overlap. Just remember, VCs usually don't want to work with companies that are potentially going to compete directly with their portfolio companies. Even a company that might be providing ancillary services that relate to an investment they made might be a little too close. Generally, you should shy away from approaching such VCs who are too close to your space, or at least de-prioritize them in your outreach campaign.

Tranche Your Fundraising

By Jenny Fielding, General Partner at The Fund

A proven fundraising best practice for engaging investors is to tranche your fundraising. Back in the day, if you were raising a round you needed to find the lead investor who was going to price the round, and then you had to shop around and figure out who would be the first person to commit. Nowadays, funds are much more comfortable with the idea of SAFEs and notes. Founders can take advantage of that, and raising in tranches provides them with more flexibility around the amount and the close. For example, say you want to raise $1.5 million. You'll probably have to find someone who is going to anchor that amount; otherwise, it will take a long time to collect enough $25,000 checks. But if you were to tranche it so that the first tranche was, say, $500,000, you would be able to fill that up incrementally. That's a much easier approach. You could get some small $100,000 checks and really build the momentum from one tranche to the next.

This will also give you flexibility to potentially raise the cap. Start out with a low valuation, really build momentum, and get early people in. Then you can raise the price, change the terms, and expand the round. This idea of raising in chunks is powerful, and founders who embrace it just have an easier time building momentum in their early fundraises, and close on more favorable terms.

---

13. REACHING OUT TO TARGET INVESTORS

Target the Right Partners Within a Firm, Not Just the Right Firms

By Wayne Shiong, Partner at China Growth Capital

Entrepreneurs are often obsessed with landing a big brand-name investor meeting with Sequoia or Kleiner Perkins or Andreessen Horowitz, for example. Ultimately, the purpose of the meeting is to secure funding with the right investor. Regardless of which firms you intend to meet, make sure you're targeting the right partners within those firms—the ones whose background or investment scope align with your company. Oftentimes, entrepreneurs don't take the time to research the partners within a given venture firm to know who might be their best entry point. The risk, of course, is that you waste everyone's time, including yours, pitching someone who's not a good fit for your type of business, and you have to do all over again with another partner. You might not get the meeting in the first place because the investor deems your business to be irrelevant to them. This is particularly the case if you're running a highly specialized or technical business, such as biotech or robotics.

Spend the time and do your homework beforehand, and try to get a sense of who within the firm you have most common ground with, and who you might be able to establish the most connection with, based on your sector or even your personal background. Of course, if you can reach such a person through a warm introduction, all the better.

You can get some insights on the firm's partners on LinkedIn by looking at their backgrounds and any postings they make, as well as companies they were involved with or whose boards they sat on. You can also sometimes find information like this on the firm's website. It may list the partners and provide a bio for each, as well as their portfolio companies and deals they made. You could also search around for interviews they had, for example, on YouTube or via podcasts, or talks at industry conferences or TEDx, or other press coverage that they were featured in. You can also check references through lawyers, investment bankers, accountants, equity research analysts, and anyone who might be involved in such deals. For example, there are law firms like Henderson, Wilson Sonsini, Cooley, and Fenwick & West in Silicon Valley, or DLA Piper in London. Some of these firms operate globally in addition to more local and regional law firms that focus on investments and venture capital. They might be able to give you some insights or direction to help you target the right individuals and firms. Knowing who to target at a given firm is just as critical as knowing which firms to target.

Approach Decision Makers via Warm Channels
By Vinnie Lauria, Founding Partner at Golden Gate Ventures

A lot of entrepreneurs don't optimally approach a VC. They might meet a junior investment team member at an event and feel like they have engaged a particular firm. Your best route to a decision maker at a VC firm is definitely from a credible, warm intro. The best warm intros are from founders in the firm's portfolio or angel investors who the VC works with. You shouldn't ask a VC who passes on your opportunity to introduce you to another VC; there's often overlap in terms of startup size, stage, and sector among VCs, and they often compete with each other at least indirectly. It's unrealistic to expect them to go out of their way to support you on that front.

If they focus on completely different geographies, that might be an exception where you could ask a VC to pass on your opportunity to a fellow VC they know. Granted, in an increasingly connected, global world, it's rarely the case that any geography will operate in a silo. After all, high-growth startups, by definition, aim for world domination. So again, there's too much overlap among VCs even on geographies. In addition, more often than not, even if a VC is open to introducing an opportunity to another VC, they might not want to present an opportunity that is not a good fit or that they deem to be un-investable, because it may not reflect positively on them. Forgo VC-to-VC intros and focus on finding warm channels through trusted partners and founders that VCs work with. That's going to be your best bet for engaging a decision maker at a VC firm.

Optimize for the Best Introduction Channels When You Approach Investors

By David Hornik, Founding Partner at Lobby Capital

Entrepreneurs often ask the question, "How can I meet venture capitalists?" And they are consistently being told to get an introduction, but that only tells half of the story. There is a big difference between a great introduction and an OK introduction. That difference can be characterized by what I call the "transitive property of relationship." If you are going to be introduced to a VC by someone who has a close and trusted advisor base, that is dramatically more valuable than getting introduced by someone who is merely an acquaintance. Similarly, if you can get introduced by someone with whom you are very close, that's dramatically more valuable than being introduced by someone within your network who is merely an acquaintance. The ideal scenario is to get introduced by someone you have a very close relationship with who happens to have a very close relationship with a VC you're targeting. Pay attention to who's making the introduction, because not all introductions are created equal. Find the person you're closest with and the person that the venture investor is closest with to the extent that you can. That's always going to be your strongest bond.

If you don't have and are unable to create that direct warm channel, then you might have no choice but to try an indirect one by connecting to someone who knows someone who knows the VC. It's unlikely that a multiple-jump relationship will get you a very strong connection, however. It might get you an introduction to the VC, but then everything will depend on your ability to wow them with your cover email or executive summary.

There are other ways to create a proxy for a relationship—by finding common ground, for example, through a shared university or similar background or history. Finding commonality can build trust and strengthen a relationship. If you can, you're always better off to try to make real connections with that person based on your shared experience or your shared background, or your shared appreciation for something that they spoke about, did, or are involved with. That demonstrates that you've done your homework and that you understand what their priorities are and what they're looking for, and also that you understand who they are as a person. Those things are valuable as well and can help you stand out among the dozens of potential deals that land in a typical VC's inbox every week.

Mine Fellow Entrepreneurs for Investor Intros

By Jenny Fielding, General Partner at The Fund

One misconception that entrepreneurs have is thinking that investors are a great source for other investor referrals—after all, they must be aware of fellow VCs in their space. While this may be true, what entrepreneurs overlook is that investors compete, so investors will probably not be forthcoming in passing on names or making intros to other VCs.

Instead, you should tap your fellow founders for intros to investors, particularly ones that they work with closely and recommend. Granted, you wouldn't likely get far asking your competitor or someone in a space too adjacent to yours, even in a different geography, since they may be eyeing your market down the road. You also won't likely get what you need by approaching a fellow entrepreneur in a diametrically different and more specialized field. For instance, if you provide a digital Autotech SaaS solution for car dealers, referrals to biotech or Agritech VCs will obviously have no relevance to you. You want to approach other founders who are just remotely close to your space, not too close or too far. Those are clearly the best introductions. If there is an investor who's invested in that founder and that founder can make an introduction to the fund, that's gold. Really build your network among peers, especially ones that are, say, 18 months ahead of you. Those are the best networks to draw introductions from and are more engaging and credible than a pal of the investor or even another investor. That's a simple and obvious practice, yet very underused.

Talking with other entrepreneurs is also a great way to share fundraising best practices and learn from one another about the dos and don'ts of fundraising, especially in terms of dealing with specific VCs. This will give you greater visibility and a better sense of how to approach different investors.

Be Clever and to the Point if You Have to Send Cold Emails

By Fabrice Grinda, Founding Partner at FJ Labs

Most active VCs receive100-200 potential deals every week, of which one-third usually come from other VCs and one-third come from entrepreneurs' referrals in their network. The remainder come through inbound cold emails. Of course, warm intros from trusted sources of the VC are the ideal channel. But if you've exhausted that option and need to default to a cold email, you certainly need to approach it cleverly. Nothing screams "pass" to an investor more than a poorly crafted cold email that hasn't been thought out or positioned intelligently.

For a start, if you have the investor's email, then you can email directly there. Otherwise, LinkedIn is a great plan B (better than Facebook, Instagram, Twitter, and other social media platforms). Even if you have a great LinkedIn profile, email is still preferred because many investors don't check their LinkedIn messages or requests for connections regularly and often hand these off to their assistants to sort through.

If you're going to message someone cold, there are a number of dos and don'ts you should be aware of. The first don't is to say, "Hi, I have a great investment opportunity, can I talk to you about it?" That is not actionable, not interesting, and does not provide enough information to be able to make a decision. You need to remember that VCs are extraordinarily busy. As a result, they need all the necessary information in the message that you send to evaluate whether or not they should take a call. The objective of your email is for them to want to take the call with you. A shallow approach does not work; you will need much more substance than that to trigger an investor's interest.

VCs need to see a blurb about the idea, so include a sentence on you and your team that establishes credibility, explains how you're an expert in the space, and shows that you're making some impressive headway in tackling your project. Include a few bullet points, perhaps on market size, your traction, unit economics, why your startup is compelling, how much you're raising, and you plan to do with it. All that should fit into a couple of sentences or a couple of bullet points, to which you attach a brief deck or send a link to one. Avoid sending vertical documents, one-pagers, and business plans. The majority of investors expect and prefer decks. All those elements need to be there. This will be enough information for a VC to assess whether or not a call is warranted.

You should also try to avoid approaching more than one partner in the firm, at least at the same time. Ideally, you should do your research and find the right person for you, depending on your sector or business model. If you're a B2B SaaS business, then try to find someone within the VC firm with the same focus or one as adjacent to it as possible. The easiest way to know which partner focuses on what is to visit the VC firm's website and look up each partner's bio or blurb on their profile, which typically will mention which areas they work in and investments they've made. Crunchbase also mentions which partner of the firm sits on which boards. There's no shortcut to doing your homework and being targeted and precise in your investor outreach. You can even show that you've done your homework by further personalizing your message to the investor, and saying something to the effect of, "Congrats on investing in company XYZ. What a great success story. I would like to let you know about what we're doing, which is similar business model."

———————

Play to Your Strengths with Your Cover Email

By Isabel Fox, General Partner at Outsized Ventures

Keep your cover email as concise as possible: short and sweet is the way to go. There's no "one size fits all" in terms of the content of the email, however. You have to play to your strengths and your sense of what the specific VC you're approaching is most likely to connect with. For example, you might highlight a couple of key points around the problem that you're solving, especially if it's one that's massive yet overlooked and not obvious. You can highlight your own and your team's experience if your profiles are impressive and relevant to your business. You may also quickly highlight any significant traction you have under your belt.

Also, include a link to a teaser presentation that investors can download. It may be a DocSend link, for example, so you can track who viewed it, when, and for how long. This will give you a lot of insights as to who is engaging with your material and who isn't. This will also give you a sense of what level of interest you're generating, in which areas, and with whom to double down in terms of follow-up. Obviously, your teaser should not include any confidential information or data points. Just make sure that what you're holding back is truly confidential. Oftentimes, entrepreneurs are paranoid about disclosing certain key aspects of their story, and they hurt themselves more than anything.

Pay Attention to Key Details in the Deck You Send Out to Investors

Nathan Lustig, Managing Partner at Magma Partners

You need to understand what your pitch deck is for. The initial purpose of a deck is to get you the first meeting with an investor. That's it. Its purpose is not to get an investor to write you a check. So you shouldn't be giving investors a ton of information at that stage. You want to give investors just enough information so that they get interested enough to want to get on a phone call or a Zoom call with you or meet you in person. One error that entrepreneurs make is having too many slides in the deck that they send by email. Ideally, send 10-12 slides, 15 slides at most. Don't try to tell them everything possible about your company from the start. Anything above 15 slides is likely to be overkill. Most VCs only look at decks for three to five minutes, if that. Some may only skim through for 30 seconds.

This means you should never send the appendix or supplemental material in the initial outreach; save those for later stages. You can save the appendix for the actual meeting, for instance, so that if an investor asks a question, you can simply pull a slide from there. You may want to create two sets of decks: an abbreviated version you send before the meeting and a slightly longer one you walk investors through during your meeting.

You also want to have one big idea per slide, and make sure that it's very well designed. Spend the money on a designer. It's well worth it. You can likely find a good designer for $500 to $2,000 to make your deck look professional. Don't give investors a reason to say no, especially on optics you could easily fix beforehand.

One thing you might also want to consider is replacing your typical one-word generic headers—such as problem, solution, product, financials, and so forth—with more descriptive titles or sentences that convey a central idea of that slide. Or you could do both. The problem with having a one-word generic label per slide is that you're wasting your best real estate on the deck, and investors' attention, without making any substantive point.

Another thing to avoid in your pitch deck is the curse of knowledge, which can creep in and make your deck less comprehensible. You obviously know more about your business than any potential investor you approach. Thus, it's natural for you to take for granted certain knowledge, whereas an investor might not be as familiar with your context. Your context can be your space or your geography, or even your technology, especially if it's proprietary or a highly specialized application. So it's always best to err on the side of simplicity, provide background information when needed, and avoid jargon or technical language. As much as possible, try to minimize text, especially smaller text. It's always better to present something visually rather than through text, which makes it easier for investors to understand and follow along. A mixture of visuals with some descriptive text is ideal. Remember, the worst decks are the ones that have too much in them, not too little. So err on the side of simplicity, especially in the earlier stages of investor discussions.

You should also consider dropping any mention in the deck of a specific dollar amount for how much you're raising or the valuation you're seeking, for two reasons. First, especially in a market like today's, where the most funds are ownership sensitive and not valuation sensitive, you don't want to put a specific dollar amount because they may be willing to give you more. Second, you might put too high a dollar amount and you say, "I'm going to raise $10 million," and you raise $8 million. Raising $8 million is an awesome achievement, but if you wrote $10 million it could potentially be taken as a bad narrative, because you didn't hit your $10 million.

Entrepreneurs often get it wrong when they name the file that they send. Whatever format you decide to send file in—PDF, PowerPoint, or Google Slides—make sure that it's labeled with your company name. Ideally, it should be called "your company name" followed by "deck" and then the month and year. Don't put any additional unnecessary information, like "version 4," "final," or "Series A." Don't put anything else in there because it becomes difficult for an investor to search for and find it. Some entrepreneurs will use a DocSend, which works fine. If you do, just make sure you set the file as downloadable, because it's difficult to read on the DocSend screen, let alone print it if the investor wants to. Also, the investor can then put it into their own customer relationship management (CRM) system and circulate it internally to other partners.

Evangelize the VC Firm's Associates and Analysts to Get You in Front of Partners if Needed

By Caio Bolognesi, Partner at Monashees

Most VC firms have associates and analysts. It varies from one VC to another, and usually depends on their size and style. The main role of associates and analysts is to play gatekeeper for the partners at the firm. While they're typically not the decision makers, you shouldn't refuse an opportunity to win them over if you get the chance. You might reach a firm partner, for example, only to get handed off to coordinate with a more junior person in the firm. Deflecting them or dismissing the discussion altogether is a mistake that founders sometimes make, thinking that they're wasting their time with a non-decision maker. While it's not the ideal scenario, getting passed to an associate or an analyst doesn't necessarily mean that the partner isn't interested. The partner might be tied up with closing their fund, closing a transaction, or dealing with M&A or an IPO. Occasionally, they might be on vacation and are actually very interested in your company, and therefore want to get the ball rolling with their associate or analyst even in their absence. Having to work with associates or analysts is by no means a death sentence to the deal.

You want to always treat them well and make them feel important. Take the time to walk them through the business, as well as you would if you were interacting directly with the higher-up partner. Assess how much they know about your space and adjust your pitch accordingly; you may need to do some hand-holding in terms of getting them up to speed on your sector. Make sure they grasp the basic elements of your pitch. You also want to give them enough information to share your pitch with the partner easily. You can even send them a short email summary with the key points of your pitch, which will help them formulate their brief. Follow up to make sure they received it and ask if they have any additional questions. Another approach is to send them a short (say, three minutes or so) voice-over summary of the pitch on WhatsApp, so they can refer to it when they're drafting their brief. Once they confirm that they have what they need and any issues are addressed, you should ask them to refer you to the partner or advise on whatever next step they designate.

If you're unable to secure a meeting with the partner or the junior person you've been communicating with is unresponsive, then you're better off to go back to the drawing board and try to nudge the partner through a warm channel, or through one of their portfolio companies' founders. Simply introduce yourself and your company to the contact, and explain how far along you got in the process with the firm's associate or analyst and your interest in speaking with the partner. Try to get them on your side to either pass on your message, nudge the partner, or even make a direct intro to the partner. Trying to bypass the associate or the analyst and go directly to the partner is likely be a futile exercise, or worse, may cause unnecessary collateral damage to the relationship. Be sure to handle the situation delicately and creatively at such a juncture.

Skip Asking for Non-Disclosure and Non-Compete Agreements

By Vinnie Lauria, Founding Partner at Golden Gate Ventures

Some founders think that VCs are going to steal an idea, and therefore they need to protect their company by having VCs sign a non-disclosure agreement (NDA). The reality is that ideas are a dime a dozen. There's little value in having an NDA, so it really comes down to whether or not you're dealing with a professional and reputable individual or firm that you can trust. The NDA itself doesn't necessarily protect you. Furthermore, it can actually give the wrong impression about you to investors, because it means you look different than 99 percent of the other entrepreneurs they come across, especially if you're asking for NDA right from the start. It could flag to investors that this is your first time around the block and you're new to the startup game, and that you're inexperienced with fundraising and you haven't interacted with many VCs. It may also indicate that you probably don't have many investors already at the cap table. You might seem skeptical of VCs and appear to see them as untrusted adversaries rather than potential partners. All of those things are quickly going to send to the wrong signal to investors and hurt your chances of securing funds. I'm not necessarily saying that NDAs are deal-breakers, but they often do more harm than good in terms of making an impression and building momentum.

Brad Feld has a great blog that goes into detail as to why VCs don't sign NDAs. He makes the point that whatever you're pitching, although you think it is special and unique, any experienced VC will have seen many similar ideas, business models, and products. Granted, you may have a leg up on those comparables in terms of a significant improvement or tweak, or a new application. Still, that doesn't make your business idea one of a kind or confidential. It's also very difficult to enforce legally, because there's so much overlap between what VCs see and what you might tell them, so it will be almost impossible to prove that you provided them with some kind of secret sauce that they ran with. After all, Google didn't have a secret sauce. Neither did Amazon, Facebook, Uber, or Airbnb. If you've indeed developed a proprietary technology, you need to protect with a patent. But even then, the patent falls under public filing. No NDA or non-compete documentation will be necessary or useful.

On the other hand, you may choose to keep your company in stealth mode so as to not be on your competition's radar. You may want to forgo talking to particular VCs that you don't trust, or initially conceal certain information or data points from them, especially if they have invested in indirect or potential competitors. That's perfectly OK. But that's different than approaching a professional and reputable investor (who you're trying to excite about funding your business) and, in effect, telling them, "You can't talk about or work on anything related to anything we tell you about." A lot of what you will disclose is probably already public anyway or information the investor has come across or knows about.

---

14. PITCHING PROSPECTIVE INVESTORS

Demonstrate Professionalism in Your Investor Meetings

By James Currier, General Partner at NFX

Demonstrate professionalism in in your investor meetings. You want to avoid minor, amateurish mistakes that don't put you in the best possible light and may send the wrong message to investors and possibly spoil your hard work. For example, when you speak, try to include a number in almost every claim that you make. Don't say we're growing very fast; that's not helpful to the VC. Say we've grown 20 percent month over month for the last six months. Speak in numbers; that's one way to be precise. The other way to be precise is to not exaggerate, don't say we've generated $20 million when you've generated $19.4 million. Show VCs that you have good attention to detail and you're careful about being truthful.

Show up to your investor meeting early, ideally 15 minutes before in-person meetings and 5 minutes before virtual meetings. Don't make investors wait online for you for even a minute or two, wondering if you're joining or if they got the time right. If you're meeting an investor through Zoom, put your head at the top of the screen and don't sit so far back that they can't see you. Actually, lean into the screen and be animated and engaging and show enthusiasm in your voice. Don't narrate in boring monotone like you're reading a script. Position your camera and body properly on the screen. Make sure you have proper lighting and a non-distracting, pleasant background, or blur your background if you have to.

Have your deck and slides ready to go on your desktop, because you don't want to waste time looking for the right file during your meetings. You also want to keep an eye on the time to make sure you're keeping the right cadence and not spending too much time on any given area. When you're presenting your slides, move your cursor to areas you're addressing, so the audience can follow along. Customize a deck for every VC, ideally. If you're presenting to NFX, for example, you should know that they're big on network effects. So at least one of your slides should be titled something about network effect and include a diagram about that. Show them that you've been thinking about them and your business is in line with what they're looking for. If you're presenting to a Fintech investor, read their blogs and understand their mindset regarding which trends they're buying into. Read their brochure and include similar language in your pitch.

Look the part: wear something nice, sharp, and crisp. That shows you're serious about being a professional. Bring a pen and take notes in an actual notebook. Don't take notes on your phone or iPad. Jot down key info VCs mention in a concise and abbreviated way. You don't want to spend the entire time the VC is talking taking notes, nor do you want to skip capturing their feedback or nuggets of wisdom. You need a good balance. Show the VC that you're listening attentively, you value her input, and you're collaborative and easy to work with.

Bring only your best presenters. Don't bring your co-founder just because they want to be in the room. If your co-founder is not a great presenter, bring someone else who will do a better job and can address an important part of the presentation better than you can.

Follow up right after the meeting. If you promised to get back to the VC on an answer you didn't have, or provide a piece of info or material she requested, send it right away after the meeting. Get back to her within an hour. Demonstrate speed—it speaks loudly about your readiness and shows that you're on top of things, and it keeps your momentum going.

Finally, show don't tell. Don't just say you're passionate, be passionate—show your passion. Bring high energy and enthusiasm to the meeting, be friendly, and smile. A simple smile is the easiest way to break the ice and create a connection. Look the part, especially according to your industry, to avoid subconscious bias. If you're in the entertainment industry, for example, you want to play to that persona and look like you belong in it. The look is different if you are in the fashion industry, which is a lot different than if you're in Fintech, and so on. VCs are aware that different personality types excel in different industries. Certain types of people do better in media, while others may do better in enterprise sales, and some people are more suited for product development, manufacturing, or whatever. So you have to look the part and exude the qualities that are suited to your business. It's almost like you're an extension of your brand.

Avoid Buzzwords Like the Plague

By Sajith Pai, Director at India-based Blume Ventures

Investors, especially at seed and Series A stages, get a lot of pitch decks. When you get a dozen pitch decks a day, you struggle to mentally file the pitch into a particular construct. So it's important that you structure your deck as if you are trying to explain your business to your very smart 17-year-old nephew or cousin. Make it as non-abstract as possible. For example, don't describe your ride share business as a mobility platform. Instead describe it as an app for anyone to call a taxi. Instead of calling it a senior citizens' platform or a senior citizens' marketplace, describe it as a shopping site for seniors. Describe it very narrowly in terms of the problem that you are solving. Make it as easy as possible for investors to quickly understand exactly you do.

Similarly, you want to clearly explain the problem you are solving and the broad economic model that you are using. A lot of founders get worried that if they pitch too concretely, the VCs will think it's a very narrow business. Instead, they revert to using too many buzzwords in an attempt to impress investors with how developed their vision is. Actually, VCs understand very well that many businesses start narrow and become broad. In general, they actually like very narrow businesses, because they know that there is a playbook for solving a problem in a narrow business, building a strong economic model around it, and expanding into wider areas later. Forgo the buzzwords and focus on explaining your business in the least abstract and simplest way possible. This will ensure that your business is better understood by the VC, which will help you secure the initial meeting and ultimately close your fundraising.

Get Personal in Your Pitch

By Daniel Rosen, General Partner at Commerce Ventures

In your first meeting with an investor, make sure you carefully introduce your background and your team's. Entrepreneurs sometimes think they're walking resumes, but when you are presenting yourself for investment consideration, you have to present yourself as a human and show investors what kind of person you are.

Try to answer these questions: Why are you relevant to the business at hand? Why are you somebody that the investor would like to work with? What about your journey is relevant to this specific problem you're solving or opportunity you're tackling, as well as entrepreneurship in general? How do investors know that you're willing to learn from your mistakes and adjust quickly and frequently based on what you learn from current and potential customers, partners, and employees? Are you somebody who has high ethical standards, can be a good partner, and will work well with the investor?

You want to make sure that your narrative is relevant to the mission at hand, both in terms of the industry and type of technology that you're pursuing. Convey your background in a way that tells a story about you as a person, first and foremost, along with your relevant professional experience. This sets the foundation for any effective discussion with an investor. You may have to repeat this if you're meeting additional partners at the firm in subsequent meetings in order to establish that same connection and credibility with them.

Like any good story, yours needs to have an arc and a narrative. It shouldn't jump all over the place. Nor should it be exhaustive and cover everything you've ever done or achieved. Rather, it needs to engage the investor in your journey and help them relate to you and build a human connection with you. No more and no less.

You will likely want to write out and practice this introduction, much like your elevator pitch. Think of it as your personal elevator pitch or personal statement. Your investor meetings are not the time to practice your background story or wing it; you need to know it by heart and make sure it comes out fluidly. Nor is this the time to get side-tracked on an irrelevant tangent. Your story needs to be engaging, concise, and very relevant to what you're doing. It needs to hit all the key marks and be crisp. That's why you should think it through and rehearse it.

Remember, investors need to buy into you and your management team well before they buy into your business. No matter how great your product or your traction is, if they're unsure that you make a great leader or they aren't impressed by you, they will have their doubts about making an investment. You never want to leave any stone unturned when it comes to presenting yourself to investors, so make sure you check all their boxes for what a good investment looks like, beginning with their assessment of you.

Credential Yourself and Your Team Before You Start Your Pitch

By Jenny Rooke, Managing Director at Genoa Ventures

Credential yourself and your team. Do it objectively and quantitatively, particularly if you don't conform to the stereotypes of a successful entrepreneur. You may be younger or older. You may be a different gender, race, or color than what's widely perceived more favorably in your industry. As a way to combat these biases, use facts and figures. For example, rather than saying you worked in a particular field, say "I worked for X years at this leading company where I led or delivered the following outcome." As much as possible, incorporate facts and figures into your team slides as well. It may help to use logos of companies and universities where your people have worked or trained. When introducing yourself, or having your team introduce themselves, encourage everyone to use facts and figures that objectively demonstrate the team's relevant experience and expertise to get the job done.

Don't combine the collective experience of your management team into a sum total, as in: "Twelve years of combined sales and marketing experience." Keep it individualized to minimize any risk of being perceived as trying to inflate your team's experience or sidestep any glaring gaps in your team.

It's also important to be clear about your team's roles and titles. These are often presented ambiguously in investor material, and leave investors confused about who's doing what. Make sure you distinguish between roles and functions; for instance, product development is not a role, it's a function. When you are pitching, an investor needs to know who is going to be accountable for each function, who is the CEO, who is the chief technical officer (CTO), who is vice-president of product development? Titles matter because they convey who is accountable for each function in the company. You are not doing anyone any favors by being ambiguous about roles and accountability as you build the company. You also want to present any key advisors, who are in effect an important part of your extended team. They can certainly bring additional credibility to the business, to the plan, to the team's ability to execute, and so forth, provided, of course, that their experience is relevant to your business. It doesn't matter how successful they might have been in another sector, or how prominent and renowned they are. The criteria by which investors will process the value-add of such advisors is simply, what do they bring to the table and how can they help the company execute on its targets? That's all that matters in this context, apart from certain PR opportunities. Having a well-known and well-respected figure on board could draw more media opportunities or bring more public awareness to the company in general.

Pitch, Don't Present (Big Difference!)

By Bill Reichert, Venture Partner at Pegasus Tech Ventures

As an entrepreneur, it's important that you understand that a pitch is not a presentation. Almost every entrepreneur is coached in presentation skills or believes that they need to present their company in front of investors. Almost every pitch coach, accelerator, and mentor is teaching presentation skills, not pitching skills. So what's the difference between a pitch and a presentation? Well, if you have ever seen a TED talk, you know what a presentation is. TED does a phenomenal job of coaching presenters on how to create an arc in their story over 18 minutes or so. They have this incredible formula for coaching presenters on creating this narrative. That's presentation. On the other hand, as an entrepreneur, you will rarely get the opportunity to present. You will get many opportunities to pitch—and the difference between a pitch and a presentation is that a pitch is an interactive process. A pitch is a two-way interaction, whereas a presentation is a one-way communication. A pitch is more like playing tennis, whereas a presentation is more like delivering a monologue. In a pitch, if you hit the ball over the net, so to speak, and they don't hit it back, you are in trouble. Now, it's possible that you hit the ball over the net and all they do is nod. Or you ask them, "Is that clear?" and they respond "Yes," or give you some kind of body language to indicate that they're following along. Generally, if you are talking to anybody who is engaged with what you are saying, when you hit the ball over the net, they are going to hit it back in the form of a comment or a question.

If you are not getting an interactive dynamic when you're pitching, then you are just presenting. More often than not that means you're losing the audience and they're not into what you're saying. A proper pitch has a high degree of back-and-forth interaction compared with a memorized monologue. Clearly, if they're distracted or checking their phones—which is one of the challenges of Zoom, where it's easier to hide the fact that someone is not paying attention—then you need to quickly read the situation and try to re-engage your audience. One way to day to do this is by asking a question. And had you done your homework about the VC firm, then you'd already know quite a bit about the person or team you're speaking with, the firm, and their portfolio companies. So you could throw something out there and ask, "How does that compare with your investment in XYZ company?"

If you sense a minimum threshold level of engagement, you could just ask, "Does that make sense?" That can also get them back to listening to you. But fundamentally, if you discover that you are pitching someone who is not engaged, then it means either (1) you are doing a poor job and you need to go rework your pitch; or (2) you're wasting your time, because this is not the right person to invest in your company or likely to invest. You may not be able to solve this problem in the moment, but if you're cognizant of what's happening in these meetings, you will develop a sense of how to troubleshoot situations as well as refine your message and approach for future pitches. You'll know, for example, where you got more engagement on a particular aspect or section of the pitch, and where you didn't. You can then emphasize the stronger portion and either rework or eliminate the weaker portion. You'll be in a good position to diagnose your performance after the fact and make the necessary changes for the next pitch.

Tailor Your Pitch to Your Audience
By Jason Chapman, Managing Partner at Konvoy Ventures

Obviously, different investors have different backgrounds and different interests. While you could dig up some of that intelligence before your pitch call by researching the individuals attending, the other way to do this is by asking directly and trying to tailor your pitch to them early in your call. For example, you could ask, "Did you have a chance to peek through the deck I shared with you before the call, and are there particular areas you're more interested in and would like me to focus on?" You may also ask, "What do you want to dive into most in my presentation?" Granted, they may indicate that nothing in particular jumps out at them, or they've merely skimmed at the deck, or they will save their questions until the end. On the other hand, they may point out that they were fascinated with a certain application of the technology or your customer acquisition and engagement. This might allow you to tweak your story a bit to make it more personalized.

This also gives you the opportunity to mention at the end of the call something along the lines of, "At the start of the call, you said you were interested to know about these three areas. Do you feel like I've covered them or do you have any questions?" This shows investors that you were listening to them and made a special effort to accommodate their requests, further signaling that you will be easy to work with. It's also a gesture of respect and courtesy, which investors will likely appreciate and reciprocate. You should follow the same approach regardless of who you're addressing during the pitch and where they sit in the chain of command—whether they're a general partner, a partner, or an associate at the firm. Their decision-making capabilities should not factor into how you approach and pitch them.

Delay any Questions Until 15 Minutes into Your Pitch

By Gary Rieschel, Managing Partner at Qiming Venture Partners

You should always be prepared to do the first 15 minutes of your first meeting with a VC in a structured way, because otherwise many meetings go off the rails. You go to a venture firm with two or more partners, and each has their own questions. If you immediately ask what questions they have, you may end up all over the place in reactive mode, addressing whatever is getting thrown at you. One partner's question may take you here and another will take you there, and before you know it, it's difficult to get back on track.

You cannot afford to lose control of the narrative in the first meeting. You absolutely cannot do that. You should dedicate the first 15 minutes to walking the investor through your deck before you open to questions. You absolutely must steer the discussion in the first 15 minutes.

If after 15 minutes there is an uncomfortable silence because the investors have nothing to ask, you are in trouble. It's good to break up the meeting into 15-minute blocks. The first 15 minutes is your pitch, where you introduce yourself and the business. The next 15 minutes is focused on covering questions and having an open discussion. You could also use the second 15 minutes to provide more details on the strategy, on timing, on who the potential business partners are, and your revenue forecast. That gets you to 30 minutes.

If they still don't have any questions, this might be a sign that this is probably not going to be a great fit. At some point, you could simply say, "If you don't have any questions, that's what we wanted to present today," and move on. If an investor is even remotely interested, they will surely have some questions.

Forgo Giving Your Elevator Pitch in Your Pitch Meeting

By Gary Rieschel, Managing Partner at Qiming Venture Partners

You should avoid giving your short elevator pitch at the start of your pitch meeting. Once you are in the meeting and you have your hour or half-hour scheduled, you don't want to give a three-minute to five-minute elevator pitch, because the elevator pitch is quick to end. You don't want to race to the punchline and be unable to keep the investor's attention after the elevator pitch.

After all, the purpose of an elevator pitch is to quickly hook someone you meet randomly in public, in the taxi, at the airport, in a restaurant, over a quick phone call, or even over an introduction email. That's the right context for it, and you should have one prepared and even memorized to quickly engage someone, typically for the purpose of proposing a follow-up action in the form of a call or meeting, or to request an introduction. An investor pitch meeting, on the other hand, is not the right place for an elevator pitch.

Many entrepreneurs make the mistake of using their elevator pitch as the opening of the pitch meeting. How to use the first couple of minutes of the opening is totally dependent on you and your business. The idea is to put your best foot forward and try to engage the investor immediately. You can talk about your traction to date if that's impressive. You can explain your business model if it's unique. You can also describe the problem you're trying to solve if it's massive and not so obvious. If you're particularly seasoned and accomplished in any given space that's relevant to your business, you can leverage your track record and credibility to engage your prospective investors from the outset.

Another tactic that works in certain contexts, where the space where you're operating in is a bit vague, is to spend the first couple of minutes simply telling the investor what your business is and what it's not. Oftentimes, entrepreneurs make the mistake of taking for granted that the investor is familiar with their industry. They jump into explaining the nuances of their business without providing sufficient context and positioning to begin with, and consequently the investor is lost from the start their pitch. This is particularly the case if your domain is very technical, cutting edge, or niche, in which case you cannot assume that your prospective investor has the necessary specialized knowledge to follow along right away. In such cases, spending a few minutes providing a framework, or giving some background on the industry or historical perspective on the space, can help your audience better absorb what's to come.

Use Reflective Listening with Investors When it Really Matters

By David Cohen, Chairman at Techstars

When you feel like there is a big moment in the conversation with an investor—such as a commitment from a VC, an angel investor, or a seed fund, or a very important piece of information that they're explaining about the next step in the process—you can use a skill called reflective listening. You play it back in your own words, restating what you just heard the investors say. For example, you'd say, "What you are saying is you are in for a million dollars on this round. Do I have that right?" The reason you use reflective listening is to make sure there are no misunderstandings, because when there is a misunderstanding, it can make you look like a liar. Someone might not have committed, and you may end up telling someone else that they did. That type of news travels quickly and can give you a bad reputation. Reflective listening in the moment can help you make sure that you are hearing what you think you are hearing.

The second part of the skill of reflective listening is not only to play it back and say, "Do I have that right?" But then to say, "Is there anything else?" For example, "Thanks for the commitment of a million dollars that you made here today. I want to be sure I heard that right. Do I have that right?" At which point, if the investor confirms, you'd follow with "Great, are there any other conditions to the commitment that you just made that I need to understand now?" Then you confirm by saying, "I really understand your commitment now, thank you."

Reflective listening can save you a lot of heartache when it is used in the big moments. Don't use it in the small moments. For example, "Hi, you said your name is Amir. Do I have that right?" That will just make you sound like a lunatic. Save it for the big moments, once in a while, to make sure there is no misunderstanding about a big thing that is happening. After that, follow up with reflective listening via email so that you also have in writing what you heard. Investors can then confirm by replying, "Yes, that's what we talked about."

Another example of how important and subtle this practice can be is if an investor were to say something to the effect of, "We're thinking of putting in $5 million. I just have to run it by my partners." You might then say something like, "I just want to be sure I understand, you are saying you are in for $5 million, but you need to confirm that with your partners. Do I have that right?" And the investor might say, "No, I can't commit yet. I need to talk to my partners first." By using reflective listening, you have clarified what is being said and gotten rid of any potential for vagueness or misunderstanding. In effect, you have not allowed yourself to leave the conversation with a lack of clarity. When you allow yourself to do that, because you don't use reflective listening, you can get yourself in trouble. You might go and say, "Great news, this group just committed $5 million." And if somebody checks on that, they might say, "No, we are just interested. We haven't even had our committee meeting yet." That then makes you look like a bad listener or presumptuous at best, or a liar at worst. Obviously, it's not your intent to be a liar, you simply misunderstood. Still, it is your fault as an entrepreneur if you allow yourself to leave the conversation with a misunderstanding about something big.

Synchronize with Your Team on Pitch Meetings

By Jason Chapman, Managing Partner at Konvoy Ventures

A common mistake co-founders make that undermines the effectiveness of their pitch is to interrupt each other on the pitch call. Interruption between two founders is not just distracting to the investor, it raises a huge red flag because they don't fully trust one another. If you're caught up in this dynamic, where your co-founder or team member states something to investors that's not entirely 100 percent correct, it's better just to wait and correct it later over email versus trying to correct it on the spot, unless it is paramount.

Investors often try to read between the lines and assess the health of the relationship between the co-founders. They're looking to see how the founding team treats each other. If they spot that they don't treat each other very well, they might take that as an indication of how they're going treat investors. Therefore, when you go into those pitches with your co-founder, it's important to attentively listen to what they have to say, and make sure to not speak over them.

Another aspect investors may pick up on is the extent of respect and warmth exuded between the founders. If you're on a pitch call, and you compliment your co-founder or insinuate some positive quality, or if you defer to them to handle a question by saying, for example, "I'll let James answer that, that's an area he knows quite well," this can leave a positive impression on the investor. It not only reflects well on your co-founder and empowers them by acknowledging their expertise or work ethic, for instance, it also reflects well on you as a gracious, positive leader.

Of course, some of this can be planned out prior to your call with investors, where you and your co-founder agree on who covers what. You wouldn't necessarily want to break up the core pitch itself, which is ideally presented by a single voice in one shot. But you can divide and conquer follow-up questions or any additional areas that need clarification. You can hand off a particular aspect of the discussion by saying something lighthearted like, "I defer to Jackson, who's a marketing genius." Obviously, this also depends on the length of the meeting, whether it's a short pitch or one that leaves room for follow-up discussion and questions.

Talk Up Your Team During the Pitch

By Shane Chesson, Founding Partner at Openspace Ventures

One of the most important aspects of VCs' assessment metrics or their scoring mechanism of any startup is the quality of the team. Most of the time, you as the founder, along with maybe your co-founder, are the ones who are actually in the room with the VC. It's difficult for you to bring in five people and give them all enough airtime; however, you will always have time to present your team.

There are two ways to present the team page. One approach is to quickly breeze through, emphasize some of their previous roles, and describe their functional roles. This gives investors a high-level picture of the team in terms of team size, how the team is structured from an organizational chart standpoint, and a sense of the focus areas and skill sets of the team. It does not, however, sell the investor on why your team is the right team to take your company forward to great success. It does not pull your investor in and engage them on a personal level, excite them, and build their confidence in the personnel you've assembled.

The second approach, which is more powerful, or at least supplementary to the first approach, is to tell stories while you're on the team slide in your deck about how individuals on your team have already contributed to the company. Briefly share some anecdotes about some of their more tangible contributions and creative solutions they've generated, especially in the face of roadblocks. For example, someone who is looking after external relations may have solved a regulatory problem or managed to knock out a particular aspect of a marketing channel. Maybe there is someone who managed to create the tightest control system; you could perhaps tell a story about why that control system has already helped to deliver cost advantages. Tell these stories with passion. Speak to your team members' commitment and work ethic. Exuding a sense of pride and admiration in how you present your team will further intrigue investors and even fill them with enthusiasm about your company. Even small body language gestures, like smiling as you're talking about your team members and sharing their heroic stories, will bring a bit of warmth and life to what might otherwise be a static, dull team slide. Much like a parent talking about their children with excitement, it will illustrate how much you enjoy working with your team, and indicate a great internal chemistry as you share this collective journey of innovation and building your company. These little tidbits of embracing your team in your pitch go a long way in adding color to your story and building investors' confidence in you and your team.

Don't Just Know Your Numbers, Show Mastery of Metrics

By Byron Deeter, Partner at Bessemer Venture Partners

Even for early stage businesses, it's important that you show mastery of metrics, because that demonstrates that you have mastery of your business model over time. Often, early-stage discussions with founders and investors involve a healthy discussion of key metrics when you track your KPIs (both financial and product) and user base. In many ways, the actual quantitative answer isn't as important as demonstrating that you know what you want to measure and what's important for the future. Any investor coming on in the early stages is underwriting the future. They don't really care where you are at today; they care about the slope of the line—how fast this thing is going to take off. They're interested in how big your company can get. From your standpoint when pitching, what you want to be able to show is that you know what's important to the business, you know the measures of success, and the early signs of metric mastery are there. But more importantly, you want to show that you have a plan to scale to meaningful metrics and to measure them on an ongoing basis.

For example, in the enterprise cloud computing world, at Bessemer we published the *10 Laws of Cloud Computing*. We have what we refer to as the "six Cs of cloud finance," which we believe are metrics that everyone should show in their board meetings and track internally, and that you definitely should master when pitching outsiders. Those are just core metrics that we think are applicable to just about every cloud business and many other businesses more broadly. We publish this externally. If you are coming to pitch us, it certainly is important that you understand those, since we are going to ask you about all of them. If you have done your homework, you will actually know them. Thus, a meaningful majority of the companies that pitch us will have these metrics in their deck, because they are already tracking many of them. They understand that this is a framework that Bessemer has shared out to the cloud world, and therefore they have started to internalize some of it themselves.

While there are a few firms that have their own nuanced metrics that they prefer, the vast majority use standard metrics. Showing mastery of metrics signals to investors that you're an experienced entrepreneur: that you have a good read and sense of your business and know how to run a business.

Present the Right Metrics Based on Your Business and Fundraising Stage

By Sajith Pai, Director at India-based Blume Ventures

When you are at the seed and Series A stages, product metrics are more important than financial metrics. Financial metrics are past-facing metrics; they were invented for analog companies, not digital companies. Analog or traditional companies are meant to be profitable from the start, unlike fast-growing tech startups. For example, if you are a product company and you approach a VC, they will need to understand such metrics as usage and engagement more than your financials. Usage may refer to the number of downloads, time spent on the site or the app, and cohort behavior.

The most critical metrics to a VC at an early stage are not financial metrics, they are product metrics; specifically, your cohort metrics or how the cohort is behaving is probably the single most important metric if you are a consumer app. Cohort metrics have become even more important recently. If you are a consumer app, no good VC will fund you without looking at your cohort metrics to understand whether engagement is dropping or stable on say day 10, 15, or 30, to gauge your retention curves. Such product metrics are therefore very critical. If you are a SaaS business, clearly churn matters but, again, it depends on your stage. At a very early stage, it's fine to have a higher churn because you're still pre-product–market fit, so naturally you still haven't got your retention curve under control. If you are B2B, you can also use cohort metrics, but they are less useful.

Founders rarely present cohort metrics, because they don't have the confidence to do so. There is, in fact, a hierarchy of metrics. The most important metric is stickiness behavior, which means people are not leaving your product. When someone presents your cohort metrics, they are designed to show that retention curves are not coming down after, say, 10 weeks. If it's still 30 percent, and it's flat, that's very impressive.

A lot of founders show growth metrics, but most VCs are typically not excited by growth, per se, because they may feel that founders are buying growth. For example, if they tell an investor, I have 100 users the first week, 200 the second week, 400 the third week, it sounds like impressive growth at face value. But then if investors ask founders, "How much are you spending on customer acquisition?" and the founder hesitates, that means they are buying growth simply by spending more on marketing, which is not sustainable. At the early stage, investors don't want you to buy growth, because it may not be sustainable in the long run. Investors are not interested in that kind of growth. When the hierarchy of metrics is at the early stage, you don't want to show growth unless it's only organic. Investors want to see stick metrics, which indicate stickiness or retention. Those metrics are rarely shown.

Your product metrics never become less important as you move up the ladder of rounds from pre-seed, to seed, to Series A, B, and so on. They continue to matter. But then your financial metrics also start becoming important, because by Series B you have revenue coming in. Collections and churn become critical. In SaaS companies, for example, existing account landing and expansion metrics, such as net dollar retention rate, become critical. Financial metrics, such LTV and CAC, become very important. As you get to Series C, then financial compound metrics (CMs) start becoming important. As you move from the super-early stages to the late stages, the importance of metrics starts with product being 100 percent, while financials are 0 percent; as you hit your Series A and B, product is 50 to 60 percent, and financials are 30 to 40 percent; then, as you move into your Series C, D, and beyond in your growth stage, product is 25, 30, or 40 percent, and financials are 60 to 75 percent important. That's how every VC thinks about metrics: it really depends on your fundraising stage.

Identify What Kinds of Risks Are Inherent in Your Business and Communicate Accordingly

By Brad Feld, Co-Founder of Foundry Group and Techstars

It's important to separate any risks associated with your business into two categories. The first is general business risks, which covers any issues around your business that you need to touch on with your potential investors. This can take the form of a simple conversation rather than a formal disclosure, and it can be folded into your discussion with your potential investors around the strengths and weaknesses of your business. Every time you start a company, you are going to have lots of risks and challenges, and every stage along the lifecycle of the company has risks and challenges. That's the nature of startups. You shouldn't shy away from letting your potential investors know about those risks, but do it in a way that lets you address their potential implications on your business and what you are doing to mitigate them.

This is a separate class from legal risks, which you should disclose formally to your investors. Do you have any litigation pending? Do you have any regulatory or other compliance-related issues? Are there any founder contractual issues? Do you have any issues with customers that are potential legal threats? Do you have any lawsuits with other companies or intellectual property issues? Those kinds of issues should be disclosed formally as part of a disclosure schedule in your formal legal agreements. Your legal counsel should help you disclose all those risks in appropriate detail.

The key is to ensure that the investor has had a chance to look at these risks and is fully aware of them. Ninety-nine percent of time, the investor may have a question or two about something that you brought up in that disclosure statement, but that's it. Most often, they will just want to understand or clarify an issue. Every now and then, you will have a serious legal risk that's going to scare off a potential investor and potentially cause a financing to fall apart. If you have something like that looming that you are very concerned about, it's better to bring that up casually in conversation with the investor earlier in the process than to wait until that disclosure schedule drops and surprises the investor at the last minute. If you wait until that moment, it's difficult to regain enough trust from the investor to work through the issue. As a result, it can spoil everything at the 11th hour, and sour the relationship with the investor.

Never Put a Difficult Person in Front of a VC
By Bill Liao, General Partner at SOSV

If there is a difficult person on your team, make sure to never put in them front of investors, or better still, fire them. Startups cannot afford difficult or deceitful people to be involved in fundraising in any capacity. Even the smallest amount of deceit can completely derail capital raising.

There are plenty of people in your life already that you know you really don't want to hang out with much. They are the takers. They are the ones who are always penny pinching and nit-picking. They are the ones who gaslight you. They are the ones who borrow money or waste your time, and you know you are never getting it back. You cannot afford such people in your startup. Most of all, you cannot risk involving them in your fundraising efforts, and especially in any high-stakes startup process. I recently had a company that hired a difficult CFO, and that CFO destroyed the fundraising efforts of that company for a good six months. That CFO is now out of that process.

Difficult people will take their moment. They will show up, you will ask them to meet an investor to talk about their subject expertise, and they won't be able to resist showing off, or they won't be able to resist telling a little lie, or they won't be able to resist trying to gain some leverage. They will mess up your fundraising and they will mess up your company. I can tell you, as an investor, don't bring difficult people in front of me and don't be a difficult person to an investor. We have not got the time to spend with difficult people, thank you very much.

You need to be a humble and kind person. You need to instill kindness in your startup. You do not need difficult people. Sometimes, people might consider a hardcore engineer to be a difficult person. That's not the kind of difficult I'm referring to; I mean the kind of person who always has their own secret agenda ahead of that of the company, and they will manipulate their way to the best outcome for them and sacrifice the company in the process. They really don't care whether you raise money or not.

––––––––––––

15. ADDRESSING INVESTORS' OBJECTIONS

Learn to Break Through Investors Bias

By Elisa Miller-Out, Managing Partner at Chloe Capital

Investors sometimes pose different questions to male and female founders, as a recent Harvard Business School study by Dana Kanze found. The study analyzed questions that men and women were asked by investors. One of the key findings was the idea of a "promotion" versus "prevention" orientation. In other words, men might get asked more promotion-oriented questions, such as, "What's your vision for sales over the next three years?" or something big and forward-looking. In contrast, women often got a question with a prevention orientation, which might look at the past, such as, "What were your actual sales for the past three years? And can you tell me more about your track record?"

If you find yourself in a situation where you're confronted with gender role biases and you pick up on that, you can actually flip the orientation of the question. For example, if you're being posed a prevention-oriented question, which is what women often get asked, then instead you flip that bias by answering in a promotion-oriented way. For example, if you're asked a question about your sales for the past three years, you can address the question but also add a promotion angle by describing your vision of where your sales are going to go over the next three years. You can incorporate something that's more vision- and promotion-oriented. That can actually get a more favorable response from the investors in some cases, and help flip any bias you may be encountering.

Unconscious bias in fundraising and in business exists. Understand what kinds of biases exist and why, and how to spot them and work around them. There are actually all kinds of biases out there—from gender, to race, to age, and many more—and they can be studied as a field. The more you learn about them, the more useful tools you'll have in your fundraising toolkit with investors, and in business in general. That will also help you to neutralize and flip them to your advantage, which can be quite powerful.

Have a Backup Handy to Address Investors' Anticipated Objections

By Shane Chesson, Founding Partner at Openspace Ventures

Investors will be impressed when they ask you a question to try to dig down on a key metric or some aspect of your competitive differentiation related to the technology landscape or the technology implementation, for example, and you are well prepared to address it. This is especially the case if you can bring up a backup document or slide that touches on the specific point they've raised. This can easily be facilitated during online meetings, because you can quickly, without pausing your flow or flipping pages, bring up that supplementary document. Perhaps it's one you've included in the appendix section of your deck, or one that you simply had in your back pocket that is not part of your deck, given the specificity of the topic. This will add further depth to your story and substantiate some of the smaller yet critical fine points and assumptions that you have alluded to in your pitch. If you can bring up that document, and it's well formatted and well structured, and quickly get to the punch line—be it a conclusion section, a comparison table, or a cost analysis—then you'll manage to gain further credibility with the investor. They will have additional confidence in your claims and assertions, knowing that these critical questions are being carefully considered and that there is a process in place for proving the market opportunity, delivery, and execution in the company's performance.

The other advantage with this approach is that it validates to the investor that their questions are so reasonable that you've already carefully considered them. This will further help you establish a connection with that investor that may just turn into a propensity to do the deal.

Separate Different Kinds of Objections Investors Throw at You, and Handle Accordingly

By Brad Feld, Co-Founder of Foundry Group and Techstars

There are two layers to dealing with investors' objections to your business. The first is in the process, when you are trying to convince a VC to invest in you: you are still in that evaluation cycle, where the investor is really exploring what you are doing. The second is after the investor has said no, and you're trying to understand what you can learn from the investor. It's important to separate those two layers.

In the first scenario, which is the most salvageable and the one where you should put most of your energy, many investors will ask questions or play devil's advocate just to see how you answer them. Some investors ask the same generic questions, while other investors can quickly go deep on your business and start poking holes in things they find. This is a process of exploration—some investors are trying to learn how you react to questions, while others are just trying to decide whether they want to spend more time with you. Being responsive to investors' questions and concerns is critical.

When you are confronted with a question from the investor and you don't know the answer, admit that you don't know the answer. Then, instead of trying to bluff your way through the question, go figure out the answer. When investors realize that you don't have any idea what you're talking about, or your answers are generic and do not go deep in terms of what you are trying to get across, it's a turnoff. If an investor realizes that you don't know what the answer is and yet you're trying to pretend that you do, rather than being candid and forthright, that hurts your credibility. In this situation, acknowledge that you don't know the answer and ask the investors for advice from their experience. You could simply say, "Is there somebody in your portfolio I can talk with who you feel has mastered this area, or has solved this particular problem in their business, and might have some insights for me about how to address this issue?" You aren't simply saying, "I don't know the answer," but instead showing that you are humble about what you don't know and proactive about looking for help to learn about it.

Say "I Don't Know"

By David Hornik, Founding Partner at Lobby Capital

There is an assumption by entrepreneurs, and it is a false assumption, that to say "I don't know" in a conversation or a pitch with a venture investor is a failure. Quite the opposite is true. The failure is never acknowledging that there is something you don't know. Great entrepreneurs not only know what they know, but they also know what they don't know. When you're engaged in a conversation with a potential investor and someone asks you a question, when you truly don't know the answer, it is absolutely advantageous to say, "I don't know." If you fail to say "I don't know" to something that either can't be known, or that the investor knows that you don't know, it will make you lose credibility instantly. All too often, entrepreneurs try to use the first seemingly plausible answer that comes to mind and look worse in front of the VC as a result.

The other advantage of saying "I don't know" is that it gives you the opportunity to explain what you do know. Don't simply say "I don't know" and leave it at that. Say, "I don't know, but what I do know is X, Y, and Z, and therefore I suspect the following," and go on explaining your speculation, if you have any. It gives you the launching point to essentially say, "I understand what I don't know, but I have gathered all the necessary information to come to rational choices in the face of this lack of knowledge." Not knowing can be an opportunity, not a failing. Actually, if you never get to "I don't know," you're probably not having a deep enough conversation.

Saying "I don't know" also demonstrates to investors that you have self-awareness and you are candid in your responses. It demonstrates humility and a certain level of confidence. Entrepreneurship, by definition, is about novelty. As such, every investor knows that you can't possibly have all the answers up front. If everyone knew everything about the business you're building, then everybody would be doing it and be successful at it. Entrepreneurship is about taking what you do know and extending it into the unknown, and having the ability to understand the challenges and opportunities that can come from those risks and uncertainties. That's what great entrepreneurship is about.

There are some instances where the answer "I don't know" indicates that you are missing certain facts. For example, an investor might ask you a factual question for which you don't have the details. In that instance, you should absolutely always come back with an answer to the question. Venture investors will often ask you about your metrics. They may ask, "What is your app's conversion rate? What is your worst churn rate? What is your customer lifetime value?" You should always know the answer to internal questions about your business, but if you don't or don't recall, just be sure to return with an answer to that question right after the meeting. It's a great way to follow up with VCs and say, "You asked about this particular statistic, here's the chart that shows the answer." It also shows that you're on the ball and resourceful enough to dig up information and come up with answers quickly.

They may also ask you questions for which the answers to are unknowable; for example, the future likelihood of a given prospect or event. Say you're Uber in the early days, and an investor asks, "How will the regulators and the taxi companies react to your service?" Or, in other niches, "How will Amazon react to you going in their space?" or "What will Intuit's reaction be when you take on their QuickBooks business?" Since these are future-oriented questions that are predicated on a given event taking place and the likely outcomes that will take place as a result, there's no way for you to answer these questions with any level of accuracy. Granted, once you've done your homework and identified certain historical patterns, you might speculate on likely outcomes.

Your best bet is to say, "I will follow up with the answer after our call." You should only follow up when you've done more research and given it some thought and are able to come up with your best answer to the question. It's perfectly reasonable to say, "Let me give it some thought and revert back to you with an answer."

Listen Closely to Investors' Feedback

By Izhar Shay, Venture Partner at DisruptAI

Listen closely to investors' feedback. Try to learn and be open-minded while standing by your fundamental beliefs. It's important that you get as much feedback from investors as you can, especially if it's contrary to your own views. Oftentimes, entrepreneurs stop listening to the naysayers, and even become emotionally defensive about any criticism or opposing opinions. You should hear out the feedback, both good and bad; weigh it out carefully and never take it personally. You need to learn to deal with feedback politely and professionally, no matter how harsh it is. After all, you have nothing to lose by listening to investor's feedback, while you have a lot to gain in terms of refining your pitch or, even more importantly, in terms of helping you build the business.

Investors are experienced in detecting hidden risks, while entrepreneurs are wired to see opportunities. Naturally, investors might see blind spots that entrepreneurs don't see or unconsciously dismiss. You should remain open at all times to their feedback, comments, and questioning. Investors may even throw negative feedback at you as a test, to see how prepared you are, how mature you are, and how you handle it in general. See it as an opportunity to demonstrate your professionalism by listening carefully and trying to learn from contrarian opinions, and remaining cool in the face of tough and even annoying questions.

That said, you have to weigh out the feedback and the opposing arguments carefully, and not automatically change your mind regardless of who or how many people share the same view. You also need to have the courage to stick to your guns if, after careful analysis, you're not convinced of the merits of the feedback given. On the other hand, if you arrive at the conclusion that the feedback is valid, by all means change your mind. This doesn't imply that you're a weak, undecisive entrepreneur. On the contrary, if there is a logical reason for it, in many instances changing your mind is a sign of self-confidence, business maturity, and good management skills.

Handle a Pass from Investors Tactfully and Gracefully

By Brad Feld, Co-Founder of Foundry Group and Techstars

Many entrepreneurs fall victim to the classic sales mantra, which is to never accept no as an answer. In this situation, you endlessly try to convince an investor to invest in you, even after the investor has said, "No, I am passing."

Many investors invest in multiple stages. Rather than trying to press the investor to keep exploring and investing in you at your current stage, get some constructive feedback from them and stay in touch as you make progress as a business.

If an investor has passed, you are generally better off going with the flow rather than trying to reverse the investors' decision by showing them where they might have overlooked some aspect of your business or misunderstood you. Usually, when an investor passes on an opportunity, they won't disclose all the reasons for their decision. Even if they do, they will likely not give you too much detail around their decision. In cases where they indicate that they're passing because of A and B reasons, there are probably C, D, E, and F reasons as well, which they don't mention. If they were truly interested in investing, or if there were actually only one or two reasons, they would have said something along the lines of, "I am concerned about A and B." Investors are not very precise when they pass, and they usually just want to give you a reason (rather than saying nothing) and then move on.

On the other hand, if you think the investor truly misinterpreted what you are doing, then you want to handle it in a tactful way. In this instance, you could say, "Regarding reason A that you're concerned about, that's not actually how it works in our business. Here's how it's working in our business." The key is to be graceful, because a lot of times you might think they didn't understand when they actually did.

So when you come back and say, "Well Mrs. VC, you didn't understand this," her response could be, "Actually, I did understand." As a result, you may end up in a defensive position. It's just easier to be gracious, view the relationship as a long-term one rather than a transactional one, and accept that many investors are not going to want to invest in your business.

Sometimes, investors will give you an opening to be connected into their world rather than just dismissing you, especially if they like you and what you're doing. These are investors who may potentially want to invest in your business the future. They might say, "If anything changes in your business, please feel free to give me a call sometime in the future when you're ready for your next round," or "You are too early for us, so we are not ready to invest, but please get in touch when you're further along." This keeps the door open, especially if you can figure out how to engage with one or more companies in their portfolio, either as a vendor or a customer. Similarly, if there's another entrepreneur in their portfolio—maybe not a super successful or famous one, but somebody that you think is doing something similar to you, and who might be a couple of funding rounds ahead of you—ask them for an introduction. Finding touchpoints that create connectivity with the investor who turned you down can position you to be more attractive to them for your next round.

Ask VCs the Right Questions

By James Currier, General Partner at NFX

Always take the opportunity to learn from VCs when you can. Understand that you might have to meet with 15 or more investors to raise the capital you're looking for. Since 90 percent of them are going to say no to you, make sure that you spend at least 50 percent of the time asking them questions about your business. Ask them open-ended questions: What does my business remind you of? What patterns do you see in my business that remind you of similar companies that succeeded or failed? What would it take for your partners to decide this is a good deal? You need to come up with creative ways of asking them to reveal what they really thought of your presentation, and how they perceive you and your business? Think of them as free, experienced consultants who you can tap for key insights that you're unaware of or that may be a blind spot of yours.

To accomplish this, there are many questions you can ask VCs you meet with, including: How do you think I could grow this business faster? What do you think I would need to do to make this more of a success? Do you see this potentially being a multibillion-dollar company? How do you think we could make this a multibillion-dollar company from where we're starting today? There are lots of open-ended questions like that, which allow the VC to actually share their knowledge with you in a safe space. Most founders are just there for the money, so they miss out on taking advantage of the learning opportunity. It's actually refreshing for VCs to come across founders who ask the right questions and are very keen to learn, and who are open to feedback from investors.

You can also ask them questions about you and your team: How much do you think we have founder–market fit? Or founder–product fit? Just meeting me, do I seem like the kind of person who can make this business work? When you look at the team I have assembled here, how would you compare them to other teams that you've invested in? What are the pros and cons of the team I've built so far? Who would you like to see me add to this team in the next year? What areas do you think we need to excel in to make this business work? What are the skill sets and expertise we need to be world-class in to succeed?

Another good set of questions to ask, which are even more likely to solicit real and potentially harsh feedback (which you want) includes: What's the one thing you think I'm underestimating or being naive about? What are the main barriers that you see to our success? What are the main concerns you have that would cause you not to invest? Can you see your partners investing in this company? If not, what might be their objections? This allows them to speculate on what their partners might be concerned about and tell you what they're really thinking without being on the spot for delivering bad news.

The order of these questions is also important: start with the more general ones and, depending on the answer, try to focus on the more specific issues and dig several layers deeper to get to the bottom of any given issue. If you are disciplined about turning every interaction with a VC into an opportunity to ask questions and learn, this will go a long way in shaping how you think about your business and your own understanding of how VCs think. It will ultimately help you be more successful in your fundraise and in building your business as a whole. As such, you cannot afford to be the only one on the receiving end of questions in a VC meeting.

Remember, VCs are a lot more exposed to entrepreneurs and startups than you are. They typically see six pitches a day, five days a week, 52 weeks a year. Meanwhile, you're very focused on your customer and your product. They have knowledge that you need. This is why a lot of people who work in venture capital go on to be very successful CEOs—because they've seen so much, they understand the patterns, and then they can pick the business approaches and the patterns that are going to work. Leverage them as free advisors, so that after every meeting you have with a VC, your deck and your pitch get better and your awareness of what you need to do to make your business better improves. Eventually, you'll have answers to all those questions, the pitch meeting will go very well, and you'll end up raising money.

---

16. FOLLOWING UP AFTER PITCH MEETINGS

Remember Pitching Investors Is a Multi-Course Event

By Seth Levine, Managing Director at Foundry Group

The most common fundraising mistake I see is that people try to do too much in each meeting. Fundraising is a multi-step path; it's a journey; it is not a single meeting. The goal of early meetings is simply to get to the next meeting, not to convince someone to invest. That is the biggest mistake that many companies make. As they try to put together their pitch deck and they have those early meetings, they mistake the purpose of that meeting and believe that the right outcome from that meeting is that they have convinced someone to invest. That is not at all the case. If you are doing that, you are trying to bite off too much too soon. You want to design a process that allows you to get to multiple meetings. I understand things are moving very fast and you might have, for example, Sequoia Capital or Tiger Global there and two days later they tell you they are going to invest and they give you a term sheet. But that is still the exception and not the rule. So yes, of course, you want people to leave that first meeting excited and leaning in, and you want to leave them wanting more, but don't try to oversell in that first meeting. If you do, you often lose the chance to really get people excited about the business itself.

Save Some Ammunition for Your Second Investor Meeting

By Gary Rieschel, Managing Partner at Qiming Venture Partners

Everyone talks about the first pitch meeting with investors, but rarely do you hear about what goes on in the second meeting. All too often, entrepreneurs prepare and put on their best show for their first meeting with investors, and then deflate for the second meeting. That's because they didn't take the second meeting as seriously as the first, or they went in not knowing how to optimize for that step. It's important that you avoid this in order to maintain momentum and keep the ball moving down the field.

When you have had your first meeting with, say, six firms, and two firms call you with a list of questions, you should immediately focus on answering the questions from those two firms. Be very careful to remember and record every piece of communication that you have with them. You could then go to the four other firms and say, "We are in discussions with a couple of folks, and these are some of the questions that we anticipate you might have." You can use the questions from the first two firms that contacted you to proactively go back to the other firms, answering those questions as part of the reason to stay in touch. If you don't hear back from them, or if you are constantly having to push them as opposed to them reaching out to you or "pulling," then you need to divert all your resources to anyone who is pulling on you, as opposed to assuming that you are going to be able to push your way into a term sheet.

The other trick, and this depends very much on your situation, is if there is something happening in the background that makes it unlikely that you will generate a term sheet in the seed or Series A round, hold something back. Don't tell the entire story right off the bat in your first meeting. Tell the story that makes your first meeting with an investor end on a very positive note. Go in, tell them what you have to say to generate interest, but hold something back. It could be that you didn't talk about an exciting market segment you've started tapping into, an additional application for your product or service, a new senior hire you're recruiting, or a big account you just landed. Whatever it is, just make sure it will be something interesting to the investor. When you do have that second meeting, you're able to generate one of those, "Oh, I hadn't thought of that" or "Wow, that makes things more interesting" moments for the VC. When you can provide things that they haven't thought about, you will have a trajectory of increasing engagement. All too often, entrepreneurs are so excited they just can't stop talking during their first meeting, and they fail to reserve anything and plan ahead for their second meeting. Just like in courtship, the second meeting needs to generate even more interest than the first.

Don't Disclose the Names of Interested Investors Too Early

By Ahmad AlNaimi, General Partner at STV

When you're running a fundraising process and simultaneously talking to multiple investors, there is no need to disclose the names of the investors that you're speaking with, at least until you sign a term sheet. You can allude to them by saying, "We're speaking to three tier one investors, one in the Valley, another on the East Coast, and one in Europe, and they're all interested. So we expect to receive some term sheets in the coming month or so." If some offers have already come through and you don't like the terms or the valuation, you could say, "They offered a term sheet, which we're negotiating as we speak."

Again, you don't have to disclose the names of those potential investors. Sometimes it does not reflect well on you if you do. Regardless, it does not serve you well to mention the specific names.

It might even harm you by putting you in a weaker negotiating position. For instance, if the investor you're already speaking with and the new one you just started speaking with know each other, they may team up and lower their valuation in sync. In that scenario, it's better to keep them separated as opposed to them working together and owning the dynamic, and ultimately controlling the syndicate. You're trying to avoid one VC calling another and saying, "I heard that you were speaking to this company. You were planning to extend the pre-money valuation of $90 million. We already offered them $70 million, and they didn't say no. How do you think we should design this investment and the rights?" This could put you in a less favorable position, especially if you start to negotiate board-reserved matters. Don't put yourself in a situation where VCs can gang up on you.

Be Careful Not to Oversell or Be Too Pushy with Investors

By Tim Draper, Founder at Draper Associates and DFJ

You have to balance substance with style when you're dealing with investors. Great style is no substitute for substance. In fact, entrepreneurs who have a great and differentiated business don't have to create a dog and pony show for investors. They don't need to be super salespeople. In fact, super salespeople can actually turn off a VC, because they get sold all the time. They're looking for people who are super committed and deep down want to make this thing happen, and that's not something you can fake.

Be careful not to oversell. There are some great, strong personalities among entrepreneurs. Sometimes that can be exciting and investors can be impressed by them because it sounds like they can make things happen. But if they oversell to VCs, it almost sends a message that something may be wrong. The enthusiasm starts to look like neediness or desperation, or lack of tact or courtesy. That is where entrepreneurs often get it wrong: they think they have to constantly sell. What they really need to do is sell and then hold back and respond to questions and concerns, and generally carry on a normal conversation.

There are many cases where an entrepreneur did a great job of engaging investors, holding their attention, and getting them excited about their business, but then pushed or tried to rush the investors too much, only to lose the deal altogether. Whenever an entrepreneur puts too much pressure on the investor to close quickly, it can actually undermine their position of strength and almost always backfires. It even brings into question how lined up the entrepreneur is with other investors. The investor might think, for example, that if the entrepreneur is indeed oversubscribed like they claim they are, or if they have multiple advanced investor conversations going on and standby term sheets, then why are they so pushy about making this one go through? Be careful to handle this dynamic delicately, especially as you get closer and closer to the finish line.

Write Up a Mock Investment Memo
By Rob Kniaz, Partner at Hoxton Ventures

One of things I have learned in life is that the best way to get something from people is to try to do their work for them. This is especially true in the context of fundraising. The more you can figure out what investors need to make a funding decision and then spell it out for them and, in effect, make their job easier, the more likely it is that you will raise capital. VCs typically finalize their investment recommendation process by writing an investment memo and circulating it internally just before they agree to write a check. So the more you can frame your communication with an investment memo in mind, the better.

The most effective founders that I've seen with fundraising are ones that come in and basically have a partial investment memo already prepared. They are essentially answering the questions that may not have come up in the first meeting. If your goal is to get someone to invest in your company, they will be thinking about what to put in their investment memo, and how they will answer all the related questions. So why not take the opportunity to do their homework for them and give them ready answers. Take a PR approach where, for example, founders often try to write the story on the journalist's behalf to get them up to speed. Equally for investors, you need to put yourself in their shoes. Think about all your weak and strong spots from an investment opportunity standpoint, and present them in a comprehensive way that properly addresses any potential concerns. This document will particularly come in handy, and could materially speed up due diligence, if your business is complex in nature and involves lots of science. You need to approach it from the standpoint of, "How can I make someone very smart about my business very quickly? What materials and documents do I need to provide for them without overwhelming them?" That's an underused tactic among founders that you should use in your fundraising.

In terms of what goes into that memo, it varies from startup to startup and from VC to VC. You can find Sequoia's YouTube investment memo by searching online, and you can borrow its structure and format and customize it to your situation. Typically, you'd want to include a framework of how to think about a deal and provide some background around market size and characteristics. It should make a clear case for why this is a big market opportunity and how your company is going to tap into it and be very profitable. It should also explain why your team is particularly suitable to execute in this space, describe the landscape and other players in the space from small startups to large corporates, and so forth. Also, state why and how you're going to win against or in spite of them. Finally, it should outline the risks associated with this investment, and your strategy to mitigate these risks. It needs to spell out all those aspects as clearly and concisely as possible, in logical order, using bullet-point style. You should make it super easy for investors to wrap their head around your business and the investment opportunity presented, as well as clarify what would be expected from them.

Leverage Unwanted Acquisition Offers Toward Fundraising

By Byron Deeter, Partner at Bessemer Venture Partners

If you have a great company, you might get wonderful acquisition offers. Having a trusting relationship with your prospective investors means that it will be your and your team's choice if and when to sell. Your job as a CEO and a founder is to always create the best alternatives possible, so that you raise the bar for what it would take for someone to divert you from your goal. If you are always building value and always more excited about the goal and path, then the buy price will always go up aggressively and keep building value that way.

Should an acquisition opportunity arise while you're fundraising, you should have open and direct conversations with your investors around it. Whenever you encounter an acquisition offer and people are poking you, you should always have those conversations right off the bat. Those could turn out to be massive opportunities, so you want to invest in those relationships and have good dialogues with potential suitors. At the same time, usually you are going to be confident saying no, and you are going to play it from a position of strength to say no. The added benefit of the current market environment is that you can pick middle positions where you have your cake and eat it too. If someone walks up to you with a big, frothy valuation offer to acquire you and you don't want to sell, but there is some appeal to the liquidity and the ability to offer your team a chance to cash out, then that creates another fundraising opportunity for you.

It's highly likely you could go out to the investing market and say, "Hey, we got pitched an acquisition. I don't want to sell 100 percent of the company, but I would be open to selling 20 percent of the company, and maybe half of that as secondary or doing a tender for my employees so that some of them can choose to sell." That is tremendously liberating. To be able to tell investors, "We turned down an acquisition offer, but for those who want to take some cash off the table, you still can." It's the best of all scenarios. Often, you will be surprised how few investors end up selling, and because they have made that decision their trust and faith goes way up. And you have forever given them the opportunity to determine their own fate. So even if the company goes belly-up and doesn't succeed five years later, they will know it was their choice, not yours, to resist taking the liquidity. That's a great offer for a CEO to be able to present to investors and employees along the way. More and more investors are comfortable with meaningful liquidity pre-IPO and without needing to sell the company on the journey to becoming a great business. That's a very positive development for the market.

Do Your Best to Maintain Engagement with Prospective VCs at All Times

By Simon Cant, Managing Partner at Reinventure Group

Early on in your pitch to investors, and even before in your initial email cover note, you want to hook the investor with an interesting data point related to the problem you're solving or an impressive traction performance metric. It might be customer conversion or retention. It might be your GMV, client LTV, or whatever. Obviously, you need to decide which info and data points showcase your business in the best possible light and demonstrate its strengths. Without a hook early on, it will become increasingly difficult for you to keep a VC engaged.

When it comes to actual pitching, there is no formulaic model for the pitch. There are tried and tested best practices, but even those have exceptions. One is that you should give a short overview or elevator pitch at the beginning of the pitch to give investors a heads-up on what's to come. The pitch itself should be covered in 10 to 15 minutes maximum unless, of course, the investor is engaged and asking questions as you go. If this happens, that's a good sign that they're paying attention and are likely to be interested.

The best pitches are more of a conversation. If you're interrupted with a question, try to sufficiently address it as concisely as possible without going on tangents or spending too much time on details. You can also simply defer the question to a later point in the pitch if you feel it will derail the discussion and break your story. In that case, you could politely ask, "Do you mind if we cover this a bit later? I think it will be much more clear then when I explain X." It's clearly a judgment call, and you have to be quick on your feet and read the room, so to speak. That's when a pre-pitch practice session will come in handy. You need to be rehearsing your pitch with your co-founders, team, partners, clients, and even your existing investors, well in advance of the investor meeting. This will give you both the feedback and confidence you need to go into your pitch strong. Although you'll be showing your deck slides during your pitch, the last thing you want is to come across to investors as though you're simply reading off the deck. You want to know your pitch cold, without having to refer to slides. It will come across more naturally and more as commentary, and less canned.

One thing to keep in mind is that your main goal in that initial meeting with the investor is to get to the next meeting. The next meeting will be the opportunity for the investor to do a deep dive into particular aspects of the business, such as the financial model, product demo, sales pipeline, and so forth. Obviously, when investors bring other partners, analysts, or experts to the second meeting, that's a good sign that they're interested in looking under hood and further understanding your business and evaluating the investment opportunity. You may, of course, invite the right person from your team to the second meeting for additional support, such as the CFO, product manager, or head of business development and sales. It's important to ask for the second meeting, and even suggest an agenda. Then, properly follow up to try to schedule it as soon as possible. You want to build up any excitement and momentum you've managed to create in the first meeting, and not let too much time pass in between. Don't expect VCs to outline what the next steps are. If they have a process they're following, they will be explicit about what comes next. Otherwise, you need to take the lead and propose the theme of the next meeting.

If they have gone silent after the first meeting and are unresponsive regarding scheduling the next meeting, you definitely need to follow up. You need to be relentless without being annoying, so space and vary your follow-up notes. Don't assume they've lost interest if you don't hear from them right away. Remember, VCs are very busy and are often overwhelmed with thousands of pitches they review each year, so they may not have the bandwidth to give you attention at that particular moment. If you continue to not hear from them, you could simply ask, "Just checking to see whether you had a chance to think about next steps. Could we talk through any questions you might have sometime next week?" If you don't hear from them after the second meeting, you can frame your follow-up as an inquiry and further probe where they stand. For example, you can ask, "We were wondering what you thought of the product demo and if you had a chance to download the app and play with it?" The main thing is to pose an open-ended question that will re-engage them. Another tactic is to update them on reaching an important milestone or securing a key customer account or a new product launch. It's a bit of an art, so you need to get a sense of the person you're dealing with and decide how best to approach them at every touchpoint of the interaction cycle.

Rebuild Your Case to Re-engage Disinterested Investors

By Oliver Holle, Managing Partner at Speedinvest

When it comes to pitching investors, one of the biggest mistakes entrepreneurs make is to oversell whenever they face VC resistance. Oftentimes, they keep trying to persuade investors of their point of view when it's clear that the investors aren't buying into it. They simply keep reiterating their argument without providing very specific proof points. It then becomes this kind of one-sided dialogue, where they keep pushing and trying to convince without really addressing investors' concerns or objections. In such situations, their chances of bringing a skeptical VC back to the table are probably very low.

Typically, if your engagement with a particular VC has cooled down, there are two things you can do. First, learn and understand very specifically the issues at hand and why they were raised in the first place, and then try to address them head on while backing up your case with data points and figures the best you can. The better you can do that, the more likely it is that you will be able to overcome investors' concerns and objections. You will also be prepared if similar issues arise with future investors. Second, try to create a dynamic of fear of missing out (FOMO) with investors, whether through leveraging a lead investor, demonstrating progress, or setting a deadline. If you don't develop FOMO, it will be increasingly difficult to re-engage VCs you spoke with who likely have turned their attention to other opportunities.

Obviously, your point of disagreement with the investor may be unverifiable—for example, if an investor is concerned that Amazon will move into your space and eat your lunch but you don't think they will. Short of gaining an insight into Amazon's playbook, which itself might change, there's no way to know for sure whether this concern will play out. You could, however, try to build a case for why your business will succeed, even in the event of Amazon entering the space, through a first-mover advantage, various barriers to entry you set, certain exclusive key relationships or partnerships you've created, and so forth. Or you could simply demonstrate that the market size is large enough to absorb more than one player, and even reference other markets with a similar scenario and present the right data points to strengthen your argument. Again, the point is that you need to address investors' objections and concerns and help mitigate the risks they would be undertaking. Simply restating that you don't think Amazon will enter the market, when investor's view is to the contrary, isn't sufficient to convince them otherwise.

Granted, sometimes you have to simply accept that you cannot see eye to eye with a particular VC, and that you're better off to direct your attention to someone who shares your vision. I also wouldn't recommend trying to re-engage with a VC firm through a colleague partner of a given partner you've been speaking with. That typically doesn't work and may rub the VC the wrong way and hurt any potential for collaboration on future rounds. Of course, should a material event take place where you've reached a major milestone or signed a massive deal down the road, and you're back in the driver's seat with some leverage to re-engage investors, then by all means go for it. You can simply update the investor on progress and any exciting new developments since you last spoke with them and try to segue into bringing them back to the table.

———————

17. BUILDING INVESTOR RELATIONSHIPS

Don't Ask Anyone to be Your Lead Investor

By David Cohen, Chairman at Techstars

One piece of advice that I give to entrepreneurs is to not to ask anyone to be their lead investor. It's a bit controversial, because many entrepreneurs feel like they need a lead investor in order to bring their early-stage round together. The reason I say this is to provoke a bit of thought. If you are working with a VC, and you ask them to invest and they say "yes," they commit to invest—they will be your lead investor. You don't need to ask them that question at that point. Instead, you simply ask them to invest. When you go to an angel investor and say, "Will you be my lead investor?" what they hear is, "Will you do extra work and take on extra responsibility?" What you really want is for them to commit to invest. By asking them to invest rather than to be your lead investor, you let that next step happen more naturally. If they are indeed willing to provide terms and write a big check, they will emerge as your lead investor once they are committed. You don't need to ask them to be your lead, you need to ask them to invest, regardless of whether they are an angel, a seed fund, or a VC.

Coupled with that, what you will find is that as you get more and more commitments, even if there is not a clear lead investor, one will typically emerge. It is one who feels like they may not be getting the amount of money they want, or the round is becoming oversubscribed, and they will emerge and quite often offer terms. Let the lead investor come to you rather than starting by asking them to be a lead investor. The reason entrepreneurs ask for lead investors is because other investors often tell them to come back when they have a lead investor. Many entrepreneurs will recognize that phenomenon: they ask someone to invest, and the investor says come back to me when you have a lead. That is simply a way for that investor to learn more and keep the option open for later without having to commit today.

Remember, if you're asking a VC who is leading a large venture financing to be your lead investor, that is the same as asking them to commit. Again, you don't need to use that language. Just try to get them in and they will be your lead investor. If you are talking to a smaller investor, on the other hand, it is just extra work for them when you put the "lead" label on it. It forces them to take responsibility for your success very early in the round. It is asking them to do more, rather than asking them to commit, which is what you really want. Don't let the fact that other investors who aren't ready to commit are using the lack of a lead investor as a way to buy more time to make their decision. Ask them to commit and ask other investors to commit—that's the momentum you need to cause others to want to come in and to drive toward the lead investor emerging over time.

The other thing to keep in mind is that for early-stage companies— for example, the thousands of companies we work with at Techstars— about half of their seed rounds have not had a lead investor: they have been what are known as "party rounds." Those are all committed investors with no one clearly identified as the lead. That is a very common way that startups raise money.

Talk to Investors About Difficult Business Decisions You Had to Make

By Gary Rieschel, Managing Partner at Qiming Venture Partners

Entrepreneurs like to talk about their hiring, and they generally will give themselves great marks for hiring. What they rarely discuss is situations where they had to fire someone. It can be a bit of red flag to some investors if you've never had to fire anybody, since it can be a difficult decision. Investors are often wary of entrepreneurs who are not able to have those difficult conversations and make those difficult decisions. They want in invest in someone who is charismatic, has a great idea, and can bring people together, but they also want someone who doesn't become so enamored with the people on the team that when presented with very clear evidence, they can't make a difficult change. They don't want someone who puts their personal sentiments above the needs of the business.

This doesn't have to happen in a precipitous way, but you have to realize that every single person who is spending a day in the company not producing is costing you something meaningful. The other thing that entrepreneurs don't realize, especially founding CEOs, is that when someone is not performing, everyone else in the company knows that they are not performing. Somehow, the CEO thinks they are the only one who sees it. That's nonsense. Everyone else in the company knows, probably before the CEO, when someone is not performing. So a CEO and founder who steps in and shows that they can handle it and are not afraid of making those tough decisions echoes very well throughout the organization in terms of the culture.

When you are fundraising, you can tell the investor about a tough situation where you had to terminate some people. For example, "I was building out this group at Cisco. In the sales organization, we had some people who were not performing. They had been there a long time. I stepped in and I was able to find them other positions or move them in a different direction." You're showing that you had control, and you were willing to take a risk to move the business in the right direction. You wouldn't want to tell this story at the first meeting. The first meeting is about sharing the vision and what you want to build. However, the second meeting is along the lines of "Here are your likely concerns regarding how we are going to get there. Let me give you some examples of things that I have addressed along the way when I ran into speed bumps, and how I removed those speed bumps to succeed in prior organizations." Save that story for the second meeting, not the first meeting when you're covering the most essential elements of your story.

You also shouldn't proactively say, "By the way, I walked into work one day and fired 20 people," and then smile about it. Investors are not looking for ruthless founders who lack empathy. Again, it's about the control of the business. This gives the VC sitting across from you when you are raising money the feeling that "this is an entrepreneur who is going to engage me in the process when they have problems with people, so that we can be beneficial to them and make sure the team always operates at a high level." That's one of the things that is often underestimated when entrepreneurs go forward. They hide the fact that they have problems on their team because of a sense of loyalty. They are trying to protect people. It's exactly the wrong thing to do if you are trying to build a hypergrowth business.

Have Those Difficult Conversations with Prospective Investors Early On

By Jenny Rooke, Managing Director at Genoa Ventures

Don't shy away from addressing bad news with your potential investors. Instead, step up and show the candidness and courage to bring it up as early as possible. Avoid withholding any information that may be pertinent to any stakeholder, current or potential. You want to open a dialogue around these issues, no matter how disappointing such news may be, and explore potential solutions and paths forward together. These can be difficult conversations, but it's often precisely those difficult conversations that are most productive and insightful for identifying breakthroughs that you would not have considered alone. Whether a lead investor has dropped out of the round, you've lost a key executive or a key hire, you're experiencing problems with your co-founder, a major client has terminated their contract, a significant product flaw emerged that's driving high user churn, or whatever—no issue is too big to bring up with your prospective investors. This is true irrespective of which stage of investor dialogue you're in, whether it's during pitching, due diligence, negotiations, or closing. If the issue is significant enough, it merits a discussion.

The mistake that entrepreneurs make is that while they may be forthcoming about whatever issue they're encountering, often they will downplay or deflect it by stressing other aspects of the business that are working well. Their reasoning is that the business as a whole is heading in the right direction. While that may be true, it's not a reason to hide a critical issue or give it less than the attention it deserves. So avoid any kind of packaging or spinning of the issue. You want to be as objective as possible by sharing all of the facts—planned and unplanned, good and bad—that are affecting the journey of the company. I'd even go so far as to say that, if you find yourself tempted to withhold information from your key investors, that's a sign that you are in a difficult situation, and it's time to step up and say it first and show leadership.

That said, you certainly want to be tactful about when and how you bring up such issues, depending on the specific information and its significance. It also depends on the overall context; often, there is a lot of nuance around what constitutes appropriate communication. There's not going to be one prescriptive answer for every situation. You need to weigh out your options and think through who to tell, in what order, and when and how to say it. Generally speaking, difficult or complicated news should not be shared by email or messaging apps. It should ideally be shared in person, or at least by phone or during an online meeting, in order to ensure that you meet the objectives of the communication: clarity about what's happening and alignment on how to proceed next. You cannot do that effectively through a text-based channel, and there's a much greater risk of being misunderstood. The exception is if the communication is intended only as a heads-up before a further discussion. For example, you might send an email stating, "This is something we are going to talk about at our next board meeting. I am going to fold it into the board meeting agenda." You don't necessarily need to set a separate session around the issue, although sometimes you will have to when it's a serious and urgent situation. But in general, it's best to fold the issue into an agenda for other meetings, so long as issue gets addressed in a timely manner.

Always Anticipate and Be Ready for Due Diligence Requests

By Manuel Silva Martinez, General Partner at Mouro Capital

You need to be due diligence-ready. Oftentimes, entrepreneurs pitch a VC, then the VC gets interested and comes back with a list questions or requests particular information or data points. Then the entrepreneur replies with, "OK, please give me a week to prepare the materials." This slows down momentum and may undermine investor's perception of the entrepreneur's organization and preparedness in general, or worse, her ability to manage complexity and keep her finger on the pulse of the company. There's a fine line between being early-stage, agile, and flexible, and being disorganized and improvising. The latter may portray the entrepreneur as not having investor-ready material and even cool off investors' interest or hurt the prospect of reaching a deal. Granted, if the requested material is from left field, then it's expected that researching and gathering the information will require time. More often than not, most investors' requests are likely to be routine questions that you should be able to anticipate and therefore be able to prepare for in advance. You should have the answers ready to provide on request beforehand. That way you're never caught off guard or required to freeze the process midway through.

You should anticipate, for instance, that you might get a question about particular features of the product, or an inquiry about the team's skills and capabilities, or a concern around financials and projections; there are five or six items that you're likely to get follow-up questions on. There is no reason why you should not have the answers handy or even address them in the appendix section of your pitch deck. It will also help to think about the "make it or break it" pillars of your business and remember what questions you got in past rounds. That should give you a good sense of what you need to prepare.

This preparation will also make you come across as more confident and ready, and help bring your story together all at once, not in bits and pieces with time lapses in between. It will make your story more consistent and complete. There's nothing worse than having a high-level deck and a prospective investor who decides to deep dive and ask a question or two, and because you haven't really dug into the topic, you provide a half-baked and unsatisfactory answer. Take the time to anticipate follow-up requests or curve balls that may get thrown your way by investors—requests that are meant to validate your story or even to test you—and be fully prepared to step up to the plate and hit them out of the park. Doing so will leave a lasting positive impression on investors and will bring you that much closer to securing the funding, assuming that your fundamentals are sound and you've presented a compelling investment opportunity to the right target investor in the first place.

Leverage Transparency to Build Long-Term Investors' Trust

By Jimmy Fussing Nielsen, Co-Founder of Heartcore Capital

Transparency is the key to building trust. As a founder, you cannot afford to withhold critical information or data points from the very investor partner you're trying to build a long-term relationship with. Every time you do, you're taking a chance on harming that relationship and potentially undermining all the effort that went into developing and nurturing it. Trust is ultimately something you earn over time with your investor; it's not something you can talk someone into. Entrepreneurs are often too worried about presenting bad news to their investors at any given stage—during pre-fundraising or after—so they conceal weak performance and poor results or a critical product flaw, for example. This creates the wrong ynamic with their investors from the start. They should instead be candid about their challenges and try to elicit as much support as possible from their investors to tackle those challenges.

No VC is impervious to the fact that every startup, by definition, is struggling to take on a myriad of challenges. There is no shame in sharing your problems and where you're stuck with your investors. If they're the right partners to begin with and are committed to the business, then only good can come from involving them at such junctures. Furthermore, it's exactly such experiences that will further strengthen your trust and bond with your investors. Every investor knows that building a startup is an iterative process of trial and error, and there will be many bumps along the road. No investor is expecting a straight path to success. One of the worst things you can do as an entrepreneur to hurt your investor relationships and maybe even your future financing is to hide critical information and consequently present investors with surprises.

PART IV

WHEN THE RUBBER HITS THE ROAD: NEGOTIATE, CLOSE & BEYOND

18. SELECTING THE RIGHT INVESTORS

Always Aim for More than One Term Sheet

By Jenny Fielding, General Partner at The Fund

One big mistake founders make when it comes to fundraising is that they don't run a process. Oftentimes, the word gets around that they're fundraising, then they get contacted by an interested investor or have some beginner's luck and get a verbal commitment from an investor early on. Then, before they know it, there's a term sheet in their inbox. At this point, they may make the classic mistake of settling for the first investor they encounter; or worse, in the heat of the moment they skip over important terms that may come back to haunt them later. Notwithstanding a thorough review of term sheets, the biggest problem with this scenario is that they haven't actually warmed up other investors. They have a term sheet and are stuck with the terms because they have no leverage.

What you should be doing is to run a tight process where you always have 7 to 10 investors on the go who you're speaking with. The moment you get a term sheet, go out to the other investors and say, "Hello folks, I have a term sheet, are you stepping up or not?" This puts you in the driver's seat in terms of building urgency, negotiating, and ultimately commanding great valuation and terms.

Get to Know Your Investor Partner on a Personal Level

By Gary Rieschel, Managing Partner at Qiming Venture Partners

When it comes to doing due diligence on a venture capital firm, entrepreneurs often search the firm and prepare for a meeting. They will typically look up at basic statistics on the firm in terms of their portfolio companies and success stories. They might also talk to founders within their portfolio. But what they also need to do is put the VC firm in the context of its peer group. You really need to look at the culture and the reputation of the firm, not just among entrepreneurs but in the industry as a whole.

Many VC firms are purely financial institutions that are completely oriented around financial results. That's one type of culture. Others have partners who are more interested in fame: being on CNBC and doing a lot of press coverage and public speaking. That's another type of culture. Looking at these aspects will give you a sense of how the firm is going to be focused on or distracted from their investment in you, and what they hope to get out of that investment.

Entrepreneurs also rarely do a detailed review of the partners. You have to remember that raising money is what is referred to as a major account exercise. It's millions and millions of dollars invested over a long period of time. As with major account selling, you need to look at cultural and personality matches. You want to form some kind of relationship with this person.

It's surprising how few entrepreneurs ask VCs questions. They are very excited about telling their story, which is great, but they don't really take the time to get to know the person or the firm they're going to partner with. Then, when they do ask questions, they tend to only scratch the surface. You need to dig deeper. If you're talking to a VC, for example, and they are describing this difficult situation with one of their startups, often people are not specific enough in their description.

They may frame the situation as a classic case where the business model didn't work and the company didn't pivot quickly enough, for example. In this instance, you shouldn't take that explanation at face value. You should try to get more granular by asking, "How soon did you realize that it wasn't working? Did you just run out of money or was it the reason you ran out of money? Was it because you didn't have enough time? You didn't see the problem soon enough? Was it tied to having the wrong people trying to execute a different strategy?" Really try to understand the why that failure occurred and not just stop at their answer of, "Well, we lost money and we made a mistake with the business model." The more substantiative discussions you can have, the more you can shed light on their style and build a bond with them, and engage with them both professionally and personally.

Also, take the time to understand the history of the person and the history of the firm across from you throughout the process. Showing genuine interest in someone who might be your investor partner for many years will make a lasting impression on them, and make you stand out as being people- and relationship-oriented compared with the more transactional entrepreneurs out there.

Have Uncomfortable Discussions with Prospective Investors to Test the Waters

By Fred Destin, General Partner at Stride.VC

A lead investor is not someone you can fire. When they come on board, they are likely to be on your boat for 5, 7, or 10 years. There's a set of checklist questions you should run through before you commit to such a relationship. You need to ask, is this someone who demonstrates insight and passion for my business? Do they deeply understand what it is that I am doing? Will they have my back through this unpredictable and chaotic startup journey, which is full of ups and downs and might involve moments of underperformance or even near failure? You want a lead investor who is going to support you every step of the way and work together on finding solutions, rather than someone who freaks out when you start missing your numbers or brings their fear or pessimism into the boardroom.

You should also have uncomfortable discussions before they invest. You could pick any topic of disagreement with your prospective investors. You can almost engineer them. Having those uncomfortable discussions or disagreements will help you to assess whether you can have a real dialogue and resolve conflicts together. Conversely, you may sense that you're going to find yourself in a power play situation or one where they will shut down when presented with opinions they don't agree with. Bring up these situations to test the waters.

Don't be afraid to lose the deal. The risk and potential damage of having the wrong member on your board for the long haul is much greater than an investor already sold on the business walking away because they don't see eye to eye with you on all issues. On the other hand, if you don't have these intentional disagreements and discussions, you may never find out your investor's true colors. What happens all too often is everyone is in a sort of "seduction" mode during the investment process, and everyone is excited and getting along great, only to encounter some unpleasant surprises afterward. Whatever you can do to spend time with the lead investor and get to know and understand their management style and how they behave in certain contexts, the more likely you are to end up with someone who can bring real value to the company. Make sure they pass your bar before you bring them on board. It's perfectly OK to make trade-offs where you favor a more aligned lead investor who's coming at lower valuation and greater dilution over one who is not the right fit for your company. In extreme situations, be prepared to walk away from money instead of involving the wrong investors, even a big brand firm.

Selecting the Right Investors Goes Well Beyond Valuation and Dilution

By Rob Kniaz, Partner at Hoxton Ventures

Early-stage founders often try to overoptimize their valuation when they're fundraising. This often manifests in the form of chasing valuation versus chasing quality. Instead, what you should be looking at is who you want to be on your cap table. Maybe it's a situation where you don't have much choice and you only have one or very few term sheets on the table, but when there are several, you sometimes need to balance the highest paying deal against the highest quality investor. You need to look at which investor is going to be there for you in the long term, and think about follow-on rounds and signaling. If you are doing a round and you are trying to split it three ways among investors, that sounds great because you have three people who can theoretically help. The reality is that you often encounter the tragedy of the commons: when you need something specific, or when things go wrong, no one steps up to take the lead. If you need to rely on your investors and there are three investors, it's probably a small check for each of them. Frankly, not one of them has enough skin in the game that they will be willing to go the extra mile for you.

Some founders don't want one person bossing them around or don't want a board. But you should be thinking about who you want to build the tightest relationship with, find them and lead your round with them. In a world where reputation matters, the VCs with the best reputation don't always pay the highest prices. Conversely, those who have no reputation or a bad reputation tend to pay higher prices. Optimizing solely around valuation often doesn't lead to the best outcome. It's great if you have someone willing to pay a fair amount even if it's not the highest. All in all, you need to optimize for who's going to be your best long-term partner and firm to work with.

Making a good choice is a function of performing thorough due diligence on your prospective investors, doing reference checks, and figuring out how they have acted in good times and bad. It sounds great to optimize and get the absolute lowest dilution you possibly can, but when it means you are working with someone who's going to be difficult down the road it's not worth it. It's a case of short-term versus long-term thinking, and you'd be much better off having someone in your corner in a slightly more diluted situation. You need someone you can trust to be around and be able to write additional checks, as in the case of a bridge, and who will be useful in the next round of funding.

The natural question is, what makes a great investor partner? First and foremost, you need to be introspective about what you really need from an investor. As a founder, you might think you need nothing outside of cash, but if you sit down and really think about it you are probably going to need fundraising help in the next round. You might need domain expertise, help with hiring, help with certain parts of the company, or help with high-level business development and access to particular government channels or politicians, for example. You will need to look at the investor and think about (1) what they're promising, and (2) how realistic their promises are. For example, if you think that you're facing difficulty in hiring, then you might want to find a VC that has a lot of experience in this area or an extensive network. You have to figure out what you specifically need the most from an investor and assess the quality of your potential investors from that perspective.

Some founders just want investors to leave them alone and let them get on with the business. For example, Travis Kalanick at Uber, who was quite self-sufficient, had the view, "I want my investors to mostly just let me do the driving. I know what I'm going to do and how I'm going to do it." And he found investors that were generally helpful in that way, who let him run the show. Most of the time, however, founders can benefit tremendously from finding and involving the right investor partner.

There are no shortcuts around doing reference checks to figure out what a particular individual investor or investment firm is really like. You need to spend some time with them and get a feel for them. At the end of the day, this relationship is being formed as you go. You also have to talk to people who have been in longer relationships with this investor, both with the firm and with this partner, to see what they are like when things go well and when things go poorly. When the company fails to hit a milestone or faces money problems, which often happens during the early stage, how do they behave? Do they step up and become useful? Do they help figure out the problem? Or do they wash their hands or walk away?

These are a few of the different factors you need to be looking at in addition to whether they have the capital to keep funding your company. There will always be a lot of lovely people with good intentions, but unfortunately many have very small funds or funds that aren't growing for whatever reason (such as bad performance or a lack of LP base), and who may be a mismatch for your business. This is especially the case if you expect to need more capital from them because you don't have an additional outside funder. In that case, you should aim to secure a bigger fund, particularly if you're doing something very capital intensive. You can choose to go with a small fund if it's not capital that you really need; for example, if you're seeking more of a strategic partner or someone with domain expertise or credibility in the sector you're focused on.

Sometimes investors exaggerate their fund size, or at least their liquidity. Nevertheless, you can get a sense of whether they are a $20 million, $100 million, or $1 billion fund. You should also look at how active they are on Crunchbase or Pitchbook. There are plenty of free resources that will tell you how active they are in deploying capital. You can also figure out, at a high level, how successful have they been in the past. Those are all good indicators. From there you can figure out whether they have more capital available. If you see a firm that's doing three or four deals a year, or their pace is noticeably slowing, that's probably a signal that they're nearly out of capital or can't raise more. Likewise, if they've been around for 10 years and don't have much of a track record, at some point they're going to have a hard time raising more capital themselves. There is no perfect heuristic, since there's no real database except for the Crunchbase articles and what investors and startups announce and publicize they've raised.

Finally, talk with other founders within the fund's portfolio companies. Figure out who in your network has worked with them directly. Put the question to them, is this firm flush with cash or are they tapped out? Most of the founders will have a good sense of liquidity of a given investor they've worked with. This will give you extra assurance that you will be working with a well-capitalized firm if you foresee a need for subsequent funding form existing investors. There are a lot of firms out there that are very undercapitalized and sometimes out of money, especially when you're outside Silicon Valley. If it's been five years since an investor's last raise, that's a red flag that they're probably out of capital.

Pick the Right Angels for Round Syndication

By Filip Dames, Founding Partner at Cherry Ventures

When it comes to round syndication and adding relevant angel investors, you can start with friends and family and the various sources you know before speaking to funds. That said, you need to think hard about selecting the right angels for your company—those who complement your round. You need to be doing this across all rounds, not just for your seed round. You need to make sure you pick the ones who will add value to the company, well beyond cash, by spending time with you and providing ongoing support. Be very specific and explicit about what you expect from them. Meanwhile, be careful with people who do a lot of deals (say, 100 deals) and thus don't have the bandwidth to provide meaningful attention to you.

You need to be thinking, can I leverage this person to help me build the business? Can they help me with recruiting, business development, and connecting me with other prospective investors? Do they have specialized expertise or experience that's germane to my business? Think about the different areas where you need help or someone to learn from. Angels can also help open the door to other angels in their network who could potentially bring value to the company. You need to directly ask them what kind of support they're committed to providing.

You need to always ensure that you're pursuing smart money, irrespective of ticket size—whether it's $10 million from a VC or $100,000 from an angel. Similarly, you always need to ensure you avoid so-called angels from hell, or the wrong type of angels, who typically ask for very low valuations and want to invest at a different price than some of the other investors. They will often ask for free shares or request advisor shares. Their advice should come with the privilege of investing in your company and shouldn't be something that they get additionally compensated for. Watch out for those investors and do not involve them in your company. Good VCs typically have strong networks of angels that they can also bring to the table, so they can also be a great resource on that front and can help you pick the right ones.

Thoroughly Background and Reference Check Your Prospective Investor

By Simon Cant, Managing Partner at Reinventure Group

When it comes to doing due diligence and reference checking your investor, you need to make it super clear to the founders you're surveying, who work closely with a given investor you're performing due diligence on, that everything they say will remain confidential. They need the assurance that what they say won't get back to the VC. These founders already have those VCs sitting on the board, so the last thing they want is to hurt those investor relationships.

To pick the founders that you want to speak to, it's useful to get a list directly from the VC that includes all the investments they've made. Then ask them if you can pick some of those portfolio companies at random, because you would like to get an interview with them. Otherwise, as always happens with reference checking, you will be fed only the success stories and the ones they know are going to tell you positive things. That's OK, you need to hear what the good version of their behavior is, but you shouldn't stop there.

You need to also interview founders who didn't have such a positive experience with the investor and ones who hit rock bottom. Remember, you need to ask for the list of investments that the individual partner has made, not the VC firm, because ultimately when you are dealing with VCs, you are really dealing with the individual partner. In difficult situations, it's often unclear who did what. Fingers can easily be pointed regarding who's to blame and every side has their own version of the story. You may never get to the bottom of it. It's therefore important to hear multiple founders' experiences with the investor to attain a representative sample and a sense of how the investor operates, and their strengths and weaknesses.

It's a good idea to ask founders specific questions, such as: How has the VC actually helped? What concrete support have they provided you with? What role did the VC play? Assuming they took a board seat, did they help solve problems, bring about resolutions, and bring alignment to the board? Were they a productive and positive contributor to the board? Or were they an adversarial and negative contributor to the board? It's also worth asking, what's the most stressful situation you have been in with your investors? And how did that investor operate in that stressful situation? It's important that you try to connect with the founder and build a good rapport, get them to sympathize with your situation, open up about your concerns and fears. Overall, you want to create a relaxed conversational tone that invites them to be open and transparent. The last thing you want to do is come across as interrogative and transactional.

Hit Up Your Attorney and Co-Investors for Intelligence on VC Firms

By Gary Rieschel, Managing Partner at Qiming Venture Partners

There is one very interesting group that almost never gets questioned during the due diligence process: your attorneys. The attorneys representing you should have worked with virtually every VC firm out there, yet entrepreneurs almost never ask the partners in law firms about what is it like to work with these VC firms. The attorneys will have a pretty good sense of the culture and the working style of the firm. Before you dive into the minutiae of the term sheet, the lead investor, and so on, you should take the time to ask the attorneys, "What's your experience working with these firms? What are they most concerned about? How responsive are they?"

The assumption here is that your attorney is experienced in raising traditional or institutional venture capital money. If your attorney doesn't have any experience with that, they shouldn't be your attorney.

Another overlooked element of the due diligence of a VC partner is speaking with the co-investors who sit with them on the board. That can be very useful for you, because if the investors were all in alignment, then you get a very consistent response. If the investors were not in alignment, then you understand more granularity as to what that particular VC might have been looking for, compared with some of the other investors on the board. You will also be able to also tell whether or not some of the other investors on the board felt that the person you are talking to was taking them down the wrong path. When talking with co-investors, try to dig up any past misalignments with the VC firm to understand whether any problems that arose were because they couldn't agree on additional financing or pushing the business in a new direction, or some personal issue. All of this intelligence will help you understand the pros and cons of different VC firms, and ultimately help you make a more informed decision on which investor is right for you, and how best to manage that relationship going forward.

---

19. UNDERSTANDING THE TERM SHEET

Know Thy Term Sheet

By Bill Liao, General Partner at SOSV

Make sure that the term sheet is explicit and matches what you're after with your fundraising, in terms of your business needs and what you can live with. You need to be clear on what is right for you. Do you want a convertible note? Have you already got a convertible note? Are you stacking the deck with another convertible note? Should you price a round? Are you going for a super-high valuation; and if so, will you be able to deliver on that valuation in the next round? If not, that's a very dangerous thing to do. Because when you disappoint investors, the next valuation can be very low, or non-existent.

You must understand the terms. You must know what drag-along and tag-along rights mean. It's easy to find out by checking Brad Feld's website; he explains every term in detail. You must know what your cap table looks like in every iteration, whether you are giving out preference shares, what your liquidation preference is, and why it matters. You must know how many classes of stock you are selling. You must know, if you are pricing a round, not only the price of the round and the number of shares issued, but also the price per share and how that differs from the last round.

You also need to look through your term sheet, especially if it's a strategic investor, for clauses like exclusivity, specific market performance, or sales targets that you must achieve. You need to look at whether you have milestones and assess whether you can deliver them. You need to see what the penalties are, if any, in that investment term sheet. If that term sheet expires, you need to know what day it expires on—what day you are going to move the dots. Finally, when you test that term sheet, it's going to be tested against the actual legal docs. You need to make sure that every term that was agreed on in the term sheet is matched exactly in the final investment documentation.

So many times, I have seen founders not understand the terms they signed up to, despite having them explained, and suddenly realize that they owe a huge amount of debt, for instance. If they have stacked convertible notes, they will also be massively diluted. If they have messed up the cap table, they may discover that they no longer control their own company.

You need to understand literally every term in that document, from the confidentiality clause all the way through to the signing box. It must be just right. If you don't take the time to know the term sheet and the investment docs, you are going to run into trouble, even if you have a lawyer and advisors helping you. Of course, you must get your lawyers to review all the documentation, but don't just read a summary. Actually, go through it line by line. Let's say it takes you six hours to really figure out your term sheets and your docs, and let's say you are raising $2 million—$2 million for six hours work, that's a pretty decent pay, I would say.

Don't Rush Through the Term Sheet

By Ali Karabey, Managing Director at 212 Ventures

Don't rush through the term sheet process. Most entrepreneurs want to get it over with quickly because they're impatient to start the actual shareholders' agreement and the due diligence. But you cannot afford to cut corners with the term sheet. It's the first real face-to-face negotiation with your potential investor partner. Taking the time to be thorough, go line by line, and ask investors questions shows a level of attention to detail, and ultimately maturity, that investors respect. Conversely, if you skim through document, even though it's non-binding, it may signal to an investor that you're lazy or careless.

Investors would rather see someone who asks lots of questions without being afraid of looking dumb than someone who is too timid to raise their voice and bring up questions and concerns they might have.

Entrepreneurs should be looking particularly closely at terms such as rights of first refusal, protective provisions, drag-along clauses, good-leaver and bad-leaver clauses, and employee options.

Another mistake that entrepreneurs make when it comes to term sheets is to hand off the process to their lawyer when they should be at the forefront of it. After all, they're the ones who will be most affected by the terms. Everyone else involved, from the VC partners to the lawyers, the advisors, and even many members of the founding team, will come and go. The founder will most likely remain and stand the greatest chance of winning or losing. You therefore need to make sure you can live with the terms for many years to come. Similarly, you need to ensure your co-founders are also comfortable with every clause that you're signing.

Look Through the Term Sheet with a Fine-Tooth Comb
By Filip Dames, Founding Partner at Cherry Ventures

The term sheet is essential. It provides a framework for the relationship that a founder and investor will share. It's intended to leave no room for interpretation between the two parties, while outlining the key agreed-on terms. Even though the term sheet is technically legally non-binding, it's a critical document and the first step to closing a successful round. As such, you need to examine it very closely before you sign it. Don't skip over the fine print—remember, "the devil is in the detail." That couldn't be more true and crucial than in your term sheets, perhaps the single most important document you will sign and which your company's future is riding on.

First, the valuation, of course, needs to be right for your stage of the business. You need to clarify whether it's a pre-money or post-money valuation: an investor might give you a price that either includes or excludes the amount that they're investing, so be sure to clarify which it is.

Second, you need to look at the option pool. An option pool means the investor wants you to create room for shares to incentivize team members. The question is how big that option pool should be. Should it be 7, 8, or 10 percent? Obviously, the larger that option pool, the greater your dilution will be. On the other hand, if you don't create the right incentive mechanisms, particularly for your key executives, it will be more difficult to attract and retain top talent, especially the earlier stages. Looking at the fine print, clarify whether that option pool is in reference to pre-round or post-round dilution. If it's in reference to pre-round, and the investor wants, for example, a 10 percent, fully diluted option pool, then you're the one paying for it. However, if it's post-round and the investor is already in, you're both paying for it together. So there's a big difference in the impact of the option pool depending on whether it's created pre-round or post-round.

Third, in terms of overall dilution, you need to know how many shares or how much equity you're giving away in the financing round. Typical dilution levels range from 20 to 25 percent. If it gets higher than that, it's usually problematic, because it's most likely not the only funding that you will raise for your company. Just keep your valuation in check and be mindful that your equity is your most valuable currency. Giving away too much equity in a small financing round will mean that at the end you're left with a very low share of your own business if investors and capital pile up in later rounds.

A fourth area to watch out for in the term sheet is proceeds preference. Most investors have either a participating or non-participating liquidation preference. There's a big difference here and you need to familiarize yourself with it. With the proceeds preference on liquidation, my advice would be to accept only a non-participating request, which means that there is a request but there is no double dipping for the investor. A participating preference is particularly dangerous because when there is an exit, the investor subtracts their investment amount first from the exit price, and then still gets the full return. This puts you at risk of a much lower return. Professional investors don't typically add participating preference clauses in their term sheets, but make sure it's out or negotiate to change it to non-participating preference. As soon as you see something to the effect of two- or three-times participating preference, you know this is already a huge red flag. You might even reconsider whether that's an investor you want to engage with.

Fifth, vesting is another aspect to look at. More than anything, it serves as an additional risk mitigation tool for investors, in the sense that they are provided extra assurance that you're unlikely to depart the company. The most important assets, particularly in an early-stage company, are the founder and the management team. Vesting ensures that they are more likely to stay on board for the long haul. Vesting, of course, means that a portion of your shares will vest, or become available to you, in accordance with the amount of time that you stay with the company. You should be looking at the vesting term. Is it three-year or four-year vesting? Market standard, especially in the US and more mature VC markets, is three years.

The other item to look at with respect to vesting is whether it involves a cliff. A "cliff" means that you don't get any shares if you leave before a certain date. You want to be super careful up front about the implications of the vesting propositions in the term sheet. Cliffs are particularly important with respect to early employees, where you want to set some kind of trial period in case they don't work out for whatever reason. In such a case, the employee won't receive shares and end up on your cap table.

Also, you need to be clear on the leaver conditions, as well as all the possibilities that trigger a vesting event. Is it only triggered if you quit, or also if the investor fires you? If the investor fires you, would that be considered a "good leaver," so you receive the shares you have accumulated to that date? Or is it a "bad leaver" and you lose all your shares? If you quit or if an investor fires you, that should be a good leaver. A bad leaver should be reserved for extreme cases, such as a criminal or destructive act that significantly erodes the trust between founder and investors. Occasionally, investors will define good leaver narrowly, making it more likely that you will lose all your shares. So that's another area you should watch out for. Ensure that the definitions of "good leaver" and "bad leaver" in the term sheet are fair and do not throw off the balance of power between the founder and investor in favor of the latter.

Finally, pay attention to investor rights, guarantees that you're giving, or lockup periods during which you're not allowed to sell any of your shares (typically, a 36-month period). You must be crystal clear on all these nuances well before you go into the negotiation of the shareholder agreement. The shareholder agreement is the long form of the term sheet, where all of these term sheet clauses will be spelled out in greater detail and made much more explicit.

Follow Your Own Market Standards When It Comes to Term Sheets

By Rob Kniaz, Partner at Hoxton Ventures

If you're a founder in Silicon Valley, term sheets tend to be pretty standardized. Most term sheets there aren't that variable. For better or worse, Silicon Valley has tried every possible iteration of terms and techniques; there's a reason why things become market standard. Looking at a term sheet from today compared with a term sheet from 25 years ago, there might be quite a few things that have changed. Generally speaking, however, most of the terms stay pretty similar and stand the test of time. Some of the numbers might move, and you might have more onerous terms like higher liquidation preferences, for example. Those standards tend to be geographically market-specific but are increasingly similar in all markets.

As the founder, you should be looking for on-market terms. It cuts both ways. Look at the standard documents for wherever you are—for example, documents from the National Venture Capital Association (NVCA) or Y Combinator in the US have a standard SAFE note posted online. If you are in England, then there's a British Venture Capital Association, and so on. For the most part, at least in Europe and America, this usually that means having a US-resident (specifically Delaware) or UK-resident top company; those are usually quite useful for investors to work with. In the US, you are going to have a Delaware company; outside the US, it's still often Delaware with a local subsidiary, or the UK if you're in Europe.

Use the right documents for the region you are in, and keep things as standard as you can. Some founders try to overoptimize documents. You can spend a lot of time working out the very fine details of certain things that, generally speaking, will change or become irrelevant at the next financing. You can't really predict what's going to happen. Things might go phenomenally well or phenomenally badly, and it's hard to write legally for that in great detail. Likewise, some investors try to get away with non-market terms, so you should be aware of market norms and usual practices.

Find a good lawyer—someone who's done a lot of venture deals. That's the single biggest help in getting a deal closed easily. Find a lawyer who knows how to do venture deals and has extensive experience with them, not your sister-in-law or your buddy who happens to be a lawyer. On the other side, look at the investors' terms and consider whether they are offering on-market versus off-market numbers.

You may choose to fight for some things, but remember that most of those standard terms are there for a reason, and usually for a good reason. They're worth discussing nevertheless. A lot of founders take a long time to close. If you have good legal counsel around you who will figure out what the market terms are, and stick pretty close to them, it will usually work in your favor. It will also help with a speedy close, rather than adding an extra month or two of back-and-forth negotiations. You often see these negotiations drag on for a lot longer than they should, because the founders either have bad counsel or are making things overly complex. It can also indicate that the investors are being difficult, in which case this might be a red flag to the founder, especially if they're asking for all sorts of things that aren't standard market terms.

Optimize for Terms, Not Just Valuation
By Camilla Dolan, Partner at Eka Ventures

Generally speaking, allow the market to set the valuation. Early-stage valuation is an art, not a science. There are many variables that go into valuation, including market size and opportunity. If the market size is extremely large, early-stage investors can take a risk on paying a higher valuation than if the market size is small. Another important criterion is founders' ownership. Many venture capital investors are focused on ensuring that founders retain good ownership in the business. If your business is capital intensive in the early stages, then the valuation might need to be higher to accommodate this and ensure that you and your co-founders don't get overly diluted. Competitive tension in a process is also an important factor: processes with a lot of competition will typically lead to higher valuations than those where there is no or limited competition.

Headline valuation is important, but so are the terms associated with that valuation. Consider the financial terms—such as preference shares, anti-dilution, and priority over dividends—and control terms—such as investor consent rights over strategic decisions or future fundraising, and options to acquire shares in the future.

Consider the following two scenarios. In scenario one, an investor puts in $20 million at an $80 million pre-money and a $100 million post-money valuation; meanwhile, investor ownership is 20 percent with terms at two times participating preference shares. This entitles the investor to two times the amount they have invested before others get their capital back, plus their ownership percentage of the remaining proceeds. If you were to exit the business at $120 million, the investor would get $40 million from the two times participation and then 20 percent of the $40 million, which is $8 million. So, in total they would receive $48 million of the $120 million. In scenario two, an investor puts in $20 million at a $60 million pre-money and $80 million post-money valuation. In this case, the investor's ownership would be 25 percent. If there are no preference shares, then the investor would get $30 million of the $120 million exit valuation. There is a vast difference in investor's exit amount, depending on preference shares.

In terms of how valuations get set, early-stage valuation is much less focused on revenue multiples. It is more focused on the quality of the team, the product, the potential market size, and early commercial traction. For some business models, revenue does impact valuation; but for many business models at an early stage, it is not a relevant factor. For example, if you are developing innovative technology that requires significant upfront capital expenditure and experimentation before it can be commercialized, valuation is unlikely to be linked to revenue and more likely to be linked to technology execution milestones or confidence in reaching those milestones. In other business models, for example app businesses, which often monetize early in their journey, revenue will be an input into the valuation decision, but it will be one of many inputs rather than the guiding input. As companies move from early stage (seed and Series A) to late stage (Series B and onward), financial metrics typically become an increasingly important variable in valuation.

Position Fundraising to Maximize Investor Partner Relationships, Not Just Terms

By Jimmy Fussing Nielsen, Co-Founder of Heartcore Capital

Very often I see founders who are consumed with maximizing their terms, rather than focusing on developing the right investor partnership frameworks. Especially in the earlier stages, it doesn't matter so much what terms you get in a particular round regarding your market rate, level of dilution, and so forth; as long as you are in the relevant range, you should be optimizing for firm and for partner. After all, you're in this for the long haul, perhaps 8 or 10 years, and it's quite painful to have the right valuation but the wrong partner from the start.

Make sure that you pick investor partners that you want to engage with for this long journey. You need to spend some social time with the prospective partner and get to know them, meet more partners in the firm and understand their decision processes, and figure out if there is chemistry.

Always do reference checks with their portfolio startups and their co-investors, for both their successful and not-so-successful undertakings. This will help you get a sense of how collaborative they might be in helping you build the business. Ask for concrete advice on whether those you survey would recommend working with a given investor partner and, if so, for advice on how to structure and manage that relationship. If you've done sufficient homework, you can then trust your gut feeling as far as chemistry and personality go, after interacting with the partners directly. This approach flies in the face of what many founders and founding teams do, where they're typically exclusively focused on financials and neglect the people factor and the big picture in their assessments.

Another trap entrepreneurs fall into is to run a competitive fundraising process and be lured by a great investor firm brand name that they'd like to be associated with. Although they don't have chemistry with the partner, they go for it anyway. In effect, they're optimizing for optics and what looks good on paper, but they totally overlook the prospects of that partnership flourishing in the long haul, since the partner won't add as much value or be as collaborative in helping them scale than a more compatible partner. This is another classic mistake. Often, there is no direct correlation between how collaborative and valuable the partner is and the brand name of the firm. The brand name of the firm is usually something that was built by predecessors, but not necessarily by the partner that you are meeting.

Don't be enamored with a firm brand name, regardless of the clout it has, the wildly successful companies it has in its portfolio, or its outlandish exits. Rather, you need to make sure that you're selecting the right partner to work with, and that he or she is someone you'll be aligned with, who believes in your vision, and who is committed to supporting you for the long haul. Ultimately, it's about the working relationship and longevity of that partnership more than any other factor.

20. NEGOTIATING THE TERM SHEET

Beware of Common Pitfalls when You're Negotiating Term Sheets

By Brad Feld, Co-Founder of Foundry Group and Techstars

When negotiating term sheets, try not to get hung up on minor, unimportant details. Ultimately, there are two categories of terms that matter: economic terms and control terms. Then there are a bunch of other terms, most of which don't matter that much. Every now and then one might matter to you as a founder, for a very particular reason. In this case, you should be clear about why the term matters. For example, negotiating around certain terms like registration rights that would happen in the event of an IPO is generally a waste of energy. It can also be a distraction for you, since if you are worried about irrelevant points, it is harder to focus on the key terms during the negotiation.

Make sure you understand the terms that matter and how they affect each other. For example, if you think about the economic terms, a lot of entrepreneurs are focused only on one economic term: valuation. Recognize that there are several economic terms that are linked together that impact the ultimate valuation. These terms include the size of the unissued option pool and how anti-dilution works for future financings. Sometimes, entrepreneurs argue for a higher valuation but don't recognize that they are trading that off against a one-and-a-half times liquidation preference. They would be better off to argue for a slightly lower valuation but get rid of the liquidation preference.

You also want to avoid entering into a negotiation around a term sheet without capable legal counsel on your side. If you have raised capital before, you will generally have been through it a couple of times, and you will know what you care about. On the other hand, if you are inexperienced with VC fundraising, make sure that your legal counsel understands the negotiating points that are important. There are a lot of lawyers who are extremely good at negotiating and understand how to negotiate a venture capital investment; however, there are many more lawyers who either don't have much experience with venture capital or are only experienced with a very narrow type of deal structure. You are a in much stronger position if you have someone on your team who has real perspective and deep experience on all aspects of VC fundraising. This is especially true if your legal counsel has been on the opposite side of a negotiation with your prospective investor, since they will know what the prospective investor is going to care about or not care about, and they will be able to give you advice on that.

The ultimate legal agreement, which is the shareholder agreement, generally follows the term sheet, so it's important to negotiate whatever is going to be important to you in the term sheet. It's also useful to recognize that whatever you have negotiated in earlier rounds is going to carry through to later rounds, because many deals simply inherit the terms from earlier rounds. That's another reason to try to keep things simple, especially early on, and to make sure that you understand the implications of how different terms interact with each other.

Once you get to the shareholder agreement, the lawyers occasionally will include different minor points that are not necessarily well defined in the term sheet. This underscores the importance of understanding and agreeing to terms in the term sheet. There is a trend toward lighter-weight term sheets in venture financings these days; however, the shareholders' agreements tend not to be lighter. If the terms are not dealt with in the term sheet, you'll have less leverage when you are trying to negotiate all the rest of the terms in the definitive agreement because they weren't specified clearly. That's when the investor starts saying some version of "take it or leave it." You are already far down the path with that investor and will be more inclined to just take it. Although lighter-weight term sheets are easier and allow you to move more quickly, if they aren't explicit that they are inheriting the terms from the previous round, those lighter-weight term sheets can be more difficult to deal with when you are trying to negotiate a long-form, definitive agreement.

Pay Attention to Investors' Negative Controls

By Seth Levine, Managing Director at Foundry Group

It is important to understand term sheets, and especially the difference between positive and negative control. "Positive control" is my ability to vote as a director, which is usually pretty limited. Unless they are control investors (holding more than 50 percent of the equity), which few true venture investors are, VCs don't control the business with positive control: they don't have the majority vote, and they don't have the majority of the board. All of their real power comes from negative control, which is important for founders to understand.

"Negative control" means that you as a business can't do certain things unless you get approval from your venture investors. Those things might include raising more capital, increasing the size of the board, increasing the number of shares, selling or merging the company, taking on debt above a certain amount, etc. Those are called protective provisions, because they protect the preferred investors from the company doing things that they don't approve of.

It's very important to recognize my ability as board director to vote for or against something. That is my negative control as an investor: the list of things that I get the right to block, whether I own 2 percent or 32 percent of the company. I have found that founders are very focused on dilution and on board control. They are not typically as focused on the laundry list of things that they're agreeing they cannot do without their venture investors' agreement.

If someone is investing a large amount of money and owning a meaningful amount of your business, but not a majority, perhaps they have right to little bit more of a say in those decisions. I see companies getting in trouble with this where they raise a smaller amount of money, or they sell a very small portion of their business, yet those investors expect the same amount of control and don't get pushback on that ask. There are cases where that pushback is very appropriate, and where companies should be more cautious about how much negative control they give investors.

Fight for Permanent Information Rights

By Andrew Romans, CEO at 7BC Capital

When it comes to term sheets, you need to know what to pay attention to. You need to decide what to fight for and what not to fight for. Brad Feld's book, *Venture Deals*, is still a great, timeless read on the topic and provides many great lessons for entrepreneurs. At a high level, the terms in the term sheet tend to be on either the economics, such as the valuation, or exit-related items, such as liquidation preferences, participating preferred shared and non-participating preferred shares. The term sheet also covers governance: Who is in charge? Who gets to make a decision? And who is influencing what?

However, some aspects of a term sheet are often overlooked and rarely discussed. The one thing I recommend you do is negotiate permanent information rights. If you get permanent information rights, then even if you voluntarily leave the company and later get kicked off the board of directors, you'll be able to sell your shares because you will have access to financials. If this happens and you're running low on money, for instance, and you want to sell some stock of a previous startup on the secondary market that is now worth hundreds of millions of dollars, you will be able to do so. Without permanent information rights, you won't be in a position to do this. It often comes down to asking for these rights when you're negotiating your Series A financing. You will be in a whole different position then. I am sure anyone can negotiate venture deals and go through all the differences of participating versus non-participating preferred shares, but I'd like to give that advice. For well-known companies like Pinterest, you can just sell shares without showing people the top-line revenue, bottom-line profit, and growth for the business. But having permanent information rights might give you a way to get much-needed cash if you started a company that is extremely valuable, but not a household name.

Avoid Getting Absorbed by Strategics at the Expense of Your Business

By Kelly Perdew, Managing Partner at Moonshots Capital

Strategic investors, or "strategics," typically in the form of large companies, can be a very important ally for you. Besides putting money in, they can bring additional credibility to your young company in the market. Their investment can be first step toward an acquisition and, of course, you can get real operational leverage with certain mutual synergies. However, having a strategic corporate on your cap table may curb the appetite of other large players in the space to work with you, whether they are direct or indirect competitors of the strategic company. That is particularly the case where the strategic investor would have access to others' data or visibility into their operations. Additionally, the strategic investor may also want to limit your right to sell your product or service to their competition, or within your space in general.

Unless they're the number one in the space with a significant share of the market you're after, and that's why you're keen on working with them, you need to be very wary of what rights you give to that strategic investor and what information you share with them. Don't give away too much to that strategic investor and basically chill other potential clients and strategic investors.

You have to weigh the importance and the timing of having that strategic investor with your other group of investors, the momentum that it gives you, the positive marketing that comes from having such an anchor, the type of support the strategic investor will give you, and how big the opportunity is with that strategic investor versus the chilling effect. Having Apple as an investor, for example, would potentially kill any opportunity to work with Samsung, Google, or anyone in the smartphone space.

You will need to think about that, and ensure that you have mechanisms in place to give assurances to other potential strategic investors and clients that your strategic investor will not get any of their confidential information, such as customer data, pricing data, and so forth. It's a dynamic that you need to consider very carefully, because that type of large client investing in you can sometimes take over the trajectory of the company. All too often, founders are totally focused on pleasing that strategic investor, especially where the strategic investor's CEO, who is typically a more senior and credible force within the industry, is playing a mentorship role for the founder. The founder can end up being absorbed by the preferences of the much larger strategic investor and forget about the rest of the business model.

Negotiate Sufficient Employee Options to Incentivize Your Team

By Thomas Sperry, Managing Director at Rogue Venture Partners

You should think about having an employee option pool in your term sheet of between 10 and 20 percent. You're going to get pushback from the VCs to have the pool come from the pre-money, not the post-money. If it's from the pre-money shares, you dilute more than using the post-money; the new money coming in dilutes alongside you. Either way, the reality is you're going to want an option pool that's large enough to cover your incoming employees. You should be thoughtful about how many employees you plan to have during this period before you go on to raise another round. Make sure you have enough options in the pool for that, and a little more just in case, because in the next round you're going to increase that option pool again.

You're going to have that debate about whether it's from the pre-money or post-money valuation. Your lawyer should always push for the post-money. That said, you shouldn't stress out too much about dilution, because it's really about finding the right VCs for the right reasons. Always remember, the employee option pool is critical for hiring the right team members and keeping them incentivized over the long haul.

Entrepreneurs often worry too much about valuation and they create a small option pool. Then they hire too many people and don't have enough options to incentivize the team. If you are raising a round and you're personally getting significantly diluted, good VCs will always look to increase the options for management if they're doing well.

You want to allocate options for different levels of employees, especially early ones and major hires. You can always look at standard options for different levels of employees since there a lot of data available on that.

Focus on the Forest, Not the Trees, When It Comes to Term Sheet Negotiations

By Izhar Shay, Venture Partner at DisruptAI

Entrepreneurs sometimes over-negotiate, and they don't focus on the main issues of the term sheet. In those cases, they run the risk of dragging out the deal and the investors losing interest as a result of time passing and momentum being lost. There is no deterministic decision there, but sometimes investors get concerned. They may think, "This guy is focusing on a minor issue, which is not a real concern. I am concerned that they are going to lose focus on the main issues of their business and focus on nuances, miss seeing the forest for the trees, and lose time." Being perceived by investors as too focused on minutia and so-called fine print is not going to work in your favor. This is entirely different from being detail-oriented and thorough on terms that really matter.

If you have a good corporate law and equity finance lawyer who is experienced with startup fundraising, they will tell you what's a standard term sheet practice and what's not. Around 30 percent of the term sheet is pointless to discuss. For instance, you see entrepreneurs getting hung up on investor's rights for information, which is a fairly standard item whereby investors have the right to get information from the company. Whenever such issues arise and become a negotiation, or even a point of contention, it's often a sign of inexperienced entrepreneurs or lawyers. In such cases, investors may think, "Why am I wasting my time on something that is so trivial and such common practice in the industry? Something is wrong here." In some cases, investors will take the time to educate entrepreneurs and to explain to them the specific term, while in others they will simply say, "Forget it." They typically do this in a polite, professional manner. For example, "We're fond of the you and what you're building, but we don't think we're the optimal fit for each other at this point in time," or something to that effect. Be careful to choose your battles wisely, over-negotiating is the last reason you want to lose a deal.

One a side point, always be on the front lines of the negotiations. While you certainly want to consult with your lawyers and get their advice, never delegate the process to them entirely. Lawyers are not entirely immune to over-negotiating, though a good, experienced lawyer will help keep you in check and address any unwarranted concerns you may have. Actually, you should set the tone for your lawyer. You could tell them, "I reached this agreement with the investors. These are the general terms. We are in agreement on the main points. So now, please go talk to their lawyer and deal with all the fine details. Make sure that all the key terms are covered. Let's take this to the finish line." Similarly, good, experienced investors do not let lawyers negotiate on their behalf. They reach an agreement with the entrepreneurs and the company on the business terms, on the main provisions of the agreements, and then let the lawyers do whatever is needed in order to close the deal.

---

21. ASSEMBLING THE BOARD

Keep Your Board Small and Focused

By Fred Destin, General Partner at Stride.VC

As the founder, the composition of your board is one of the most important things to get right. I urge you to keep the board small. Small startups need small boards. Small boards are more efficient and faster, and they make better decisions. Because you want to be nice to people and you want to get them engaged, there is a tendency to have too many people around the board table. This gets unwieldy and difficult to manage, and the board is likely to underperform.

A pre-seed company should have a board of three people. A seed-stage company should have a board of no more than five. You should try to stay at five for as long as you can. Over time, you might grow to seven, which is the absolute maximum I recommend. Better to set that buffer by staying at five, and not be stretched to maximum capacity, so to speak. Adding board observers is almost always a bad idea. They are not technically board members, yet they are in the room. They might be vocal, and you can get into performative mode where you are presenting to a bunch of people instead of having focused, engaged discussions with people who are close to the business. The aim should be to create a forum for engaged discussions with people involved in the business, not some kind of tribune where you present the progress of the business to a bunch of people you're trying to keep onside.

Pick Your Board Members Strategically

By Byron Deeter, Partner at Bessemer Venture Partners

Your board should be a great resource for you as well as for your co-founders and executives. A well-functioning board is really an extension of your team. You want to select them very purposefully, by the platform they bring to the table and by personality type. Who do you want to work with? Who do you enjoy working with? Who is additive? And think about specific skill sets in terms of what gap they fill that's in line with the company's needs, and what value they add over time.

Obviously, a company's needs change from one stage to the next, and so should its board composition. In later stages, for example, you may need to get ready to go public. In that case, there are specific skills you'll want to prioritize in your board members, including an audit chair, a compensation committee chair, probably a CEO mentor, and some others. In earlier stages, however, you have more flexibility. You will want to mix in those investor seats, which are precious, with outside board members who can bring in skills that round out your skills as the CEO and the skills of your execs.

Look for a couple of value-adding, strategically-minded investor partners to join your board early on. Make sure they're ones who you like working with, who you think are going to work hard for you, and who are culturally additive and have a style consistent with your team. It is a critically important part of the fundraising decision process to decide who you want to work with day in and day out, and add them to your board.

As you get to later stages, and the money becomes less active and more passive, then the being strategic in your board selection certainly still matters. But by then you have more flexibility because people may be observers, board members, or may not even attend board meetings. Obviously, when you get all the way to the public side, most of your investors are unknown to you. Then you want to layer in the skills. So early on, the most important outside board director's skills to seek out address specific pillars of the organization, such as product strategy and or go-to-market strategy, and then a CEO coach and mentor.

The first board seat you should add is a world-class CEO who's going to mentor and support you right off the bat. That person can be any age, but it should be someone who is experienced and has had immense success. This person is often at a stage ahead of you in their career, and a company or two ahead of you in terms of the success they have under their belt. It is equally important that it be someone who is going to invest in you and be an objective, candid source of feedback and development. It's not just someone who is going to say you are great every day, but someone who truly is going to push you to be better, help you develop as a great CEO, and coach you toward that end every step of the way.

The second seat you should add is a world-class head of product, ideally representing the voice of the customer so they understand your market. You can also swap this for a world-class global marketing executive, depending whether the business is mainly product-driven or market-driven. This could be someone who is experienced as a chief revenue officer or chief marketing officer (CMO) who understands the market segment you are selling into. This person can be a coach and advisor to your team on the challenges of building an organization. Those early board members should be the aspirational dream candidate that you would hire if you were planning to hire a CEO or CMO or head of product. Chances are, because they are so good, they are already extremely wealthy or successful or at some other great company. Yet, they are willing to give you part of their time to be involved and really help develop you, your team, and your business as a board member.

Many founding teams totally underestimate the value of great outside board members early on. This an opportunity that they don't take advantage of when they get started. They often think of a board in terms of control or governance; hence, they want to keep a board small and less involved. That's too defensive a position. Instead, they should be thinking of the board offensively in terms of it being a precious opportunity to get more great people around the table, and get outside contributors who are objective and successful to bring their skills to bear for the company.

Recruit a Strong, Independent Board Member
By Federico Antonio, Managing Partner at ALLVP

Recruit a strong, independent board member whenever you can. That's one practice founders often overlook when they're designing their boards. You should do this after your Series A, once you have added a board seat for your lead investor. At this point, you should create a new independent board seat and reserve it for a world-class founder who is further ahead on their journey than you are—someone who is a couple of stages ahead of you, for instance. Such a person has presumably faced or is facing many of the challenges and growing pains you're likely to encounter. Those challenges will still be fresh in their mind, so they will be in a great position to share best practices and help you avoid problems as much as possible. They will also relate to your situation in general.

This practice is of immense value for enriching the board dynamic and more. You should also try to bring in someone with complementary experience and skill sets. If, for example, neither you nor your co-founder come from a strong technology or product background, then find someone with that profile. On the other hand, if you're a technical founder but inexperienced in terms of sales and business development or fundraising, then you'd frame your search around those areas.

Conversely, if you neglect this or are unable to convince such a person to join your board, what typically ends up happening is that your board becomes too homogenous. Your board will consist only of investors, in effect, with investors' mindset and logic. It will lack sufficient diversity and the richness of dialogue that's generated when you get people with several perspectives, backgrounds, and opinions in one room. Investors are typically masters of seeing opportunities and weighing out risks, so they certainly bring an interesting perspective to the board. They are usually well versed in consumer behavior and industry trends, and able to envision the big picture. The outside founder will bring an operational and an execution mindset to the board, coupled with a healthy reality check. They will be more astute and insightful regarding product development, human resources, and outbound marketing, for example. They will also bring a greater level of understanding of, and empathy with, your situation than investors likely will.

The two types of board member, the investors and the outside founder, are more likely to feed off each other to the benefit of the company than if the board comprised solely investors. Find a capable founder who can assume the role of that independent board member as early as possible. They don't necessarily have to come from your industry, so long as there's an element they bring to the table that you lack, which is relevant to the business. For instance, if you are an A round founder, you could bring on board someone who has raised a C round. They would have raised two more rounds than you, and possibly scaled the business from 20 employees to 300 or even 1,000. So never skip this critical piece.

---

22. MANAGING THE BOARD

Set the Right Tone and Format with Your Board

By Fred Destin, General Partner at Stride.VC

Running effective board meetings is critical to the growth of any company, particularly in the early years of a startup where there's less room for strategic missteps, and the overall existential risk is much higher than in an established company. There are some core guidelines that you need to follow.

First, a board is a decision-making body. Hence, you want to focus primarily on making sure that you use the board to make and finalize important decisions. It's not a debate club. It's not an information-sharing exercise. It's a place where you make decisions about your future strategy, about important hires, and about your budget. Treat it as such. The board is expecting you to set the tone and the direction. One mistake that founders make is to go to the board asking them what to do, instead of telling them, "This is the strategy that I want to pursue and please feel free to challenge me on the choices we've made or are about to make. I want to be sure that we're on the right track." This is exactly the right leadership tone you need to take, and which the board expects of you. Ideally, you and your management team will set the strategy and the agenda and propose decisions. Then the board will provide their input on what's in front of them and flag any overlooked aspects or potential problems.

Second, you can use the board for deep, open-ended strategy

discussions—in other words, as a thinking forum. The board is a unique environment where you're going to meet people with a wide variety of experience, and you want to open the floor to wide-ranging discussions about the future of your business. As a founder you are often going to have your head down executing and operating, and the board should be an environment of trust where you can explore your long-term strategy, including difficult decisions you have to make and are having doubts about.

Contrary to common belief, reporting shouldn't be part of the board agenda. This is not the place where you give snapshot updates on performance or whether you hit your numbers or not. Rather, it's a place for deep discussion and critical decisions. Blow up the classic board meeting format and take reporting out of it completely. You might have 10 or 20 minutes at most at the beginning for a quick CEO update, where you can briefly run numbers by the group. Block a set time for these updates and make sure you have a hard stop, after which you delve into either the key decisions or the key strategic topics that you want to discuss.

If your board members are not well suited for deep dive and strategy discussions, it is totally your prerogative to convene a strategy group that may involve some, but not all, of your board members plus external experts, and perhaps some members of your management team. As a founder, you need to use the board in the way you they see fit. It's your tool; you have no obligation to do what the board wants you to do. Design a board experience that you feel is helpful, efficient, and conducive to making the right decisions and devising the right strategy.

Fully Utilize Your Board to Build the Company

By Ahmed El Alfi, Co-Founder and Chairman at Sawari Ventures

As a founder, your job is to utilize your board in the interests of your business, not just for mere reporting. Boards often view themselves in a position where founders should report to them. Instead, you should use them as much as possible to benefit the company. You want to make them work as hard as possible, even push them outside their comfort zone, to help you grow the business. You want to have all their contacts at your disposal. You want to have all their expertise and insights at your disposal, not just their oversight and decision making, to try and guide or control the company. You need to be proactive in mining your board based on the company's needs.

There are multiple ways to get benefits for your company from board members. You can have specific asks for them with accountability to the other board members in board meetings. Don't shy away from taking charge and outlining who's doing what, by what date, similar to any regular team meeting you have. All too often, entrepreneurs, especially early-stage ones, are a bit timid in terms of asking their board for support. They're either too fond of their more senior board members to ask, or they're concerned about admitting they need help or are struggling in specific areas of the business. That said, you want to keep them focused on supporting you where it matters most; don't overwhelm with so many tasks that they're unable to give proper attention to any. You also want to build the case for why they should support you in any given area, in terms of its impact on the business. Don't be afraid to outline specific deliverables to your board member; for example, board member X will do tasks one, two, and three by the next meeting. Your board is meant to be your all-around partner in your entrepreneurial journey, for both strategy and execution. Granted, you want to focus their support on areas that you and your team are unable to crack or have already exhausted your efforts on. You should also work with each member, or assign someone from your team to with them, to offload as much legwork related to your ask as possible.

Other than serving on committees, which have different types of formal rules, informal asks are the norm in any board dynamic. Hence, it's fair game to ask for support on business development, fundraising, strategic input, domain expertise, or whatever else you need that they have access to. For example, they many have financial relationships with commercial banks, governments, or other large corporations that can benefit your company. You want to utilize your board in all those areas. You should never be bashful about pushing those priorities. The only thing to bear in mind is that most board members are very busy, so be cognizant of their time and availability, and be as precise as possible with your requests.

Delegate to Your Board Members

By Shane Chesson, Founding Partner at Openspace Ventures

Don't be afraid to delegate to board members. Obviously, this a case-by-case situation, but most board members will want to help you on an extended basis. They may have specific expertise that doesn't come up or cannot be fully utilized during a board meeting. They may also have access to teams that can execute in areas you can't, either because you don't have feet on the ground in a particular market or you lack the resources or expertise in a particular functions or domains. These areas might include environmental, social, and governance issues; product development; data science; marketing; and so forth.

Get to know your investors and their capabilities. They may very well offer their services, but if they don't, feel free to ask them or delegate tasks to them. This can be done in various ways. You can invite them to your stand-up meetings, for example. You can also set up additional committees or subcommittees of the board. Or you can just schedule regular calls with both board members and their teams. This gives you an additional opportunity to learn from their broad experience. Some entrepreneurs feel that this sort of poking into their business is intrusive, but the reality is that if you don't ask you won't know what is doable and what is not. If you choose to avoid asking, you may be missing out on some ideas, input, and assistance that the investors are ready to give that could contribute to your execution.

Set Ground Rules and Performance Reviews with Independent Board Members

By Kelly Perdew, Managing Partner at Moonshots Capital

With independent board members, it's critical that you set expectations up front in writing. You need to document your understanding of what the expectations are of that board member, and they agree that "I'm going to have X number of board meetings. I'm going to have X number of phone calls directly with the founder. As a sales expert, I'm going to have X number of meetings per quarter with the sales team and be able to report back on that. As the company gets bigger, I'm going to meet the compensation committee's or the audit committee's expectations." All that stuff needs to be clearly defined, articulated, and agreed on by both sides on the front end. That allows you to hold that board member's feet to the fire. It also allows that board member to push back when you're asking for a lot of stuff that they didn't agree to. They may ask for additional compensation, or to cut back on the agreed tasks that they're not doing as much because you wanted something else from them instead. You don't want to be in the position where you don't really know what a board member is doing other than showing up to meetings and talking about what they think might be interesting based on what you presented during the board call. You want them adding explicit value.

To effectively manage independent board members, or advisory board members for that matter, everybody must be aware of what the deliverables are and understand them. That review should occur regularly, depending on how fast the company is moving and what that independent board member or advisory board member is supposed to do. Quarterly is a good timeframe for having independent calls with those advisors and or independent members anyway, to get input and get their help, especially in companies in the early stages. Checking in quarterly and saying, "You made all your calls, you made all your board meetings, you're providing good input, you've made X business development introductions," or whatever those expectations are, is key. If you walk through it, you can see what's missing, if anything. This way there is not some performance surprise. Everyone is clear on where they stand against their deliverables. If someone is not performing and you don't address it, it's your fault.

Set Up Specialized Board Subcommittees to Focus on Specific Areas

By Shane Chesson, Founding Partner at Openspace Ventures

One tactic you can try to complement your board meetings is to set up a follow-up board meeting or subcommittee that's composed of some, but not all, of your board members. The subcommittee will be focused on driving action points raised in the more strategically focused board meetings. Obviously, the function of such a subcommittee is separate from that of the board, which is focused mainly on core strategy, financial performance, fundraising, and M&A. You can also set up a more specialized subcommittee—for example, a risk subcommittee or a public policy subcommittee, or whatever big area is most pressing in your business. You may want to set up a remuneration subcommittee, an audit subcommittee, or even an M&A subcommittee.

Another advantage of the subcommittee is that its structure is more flexible than that of the board, in the sense you can swap folks around, and even bring in select team members or outside experts as needed. These types of subcommittees may also help free up space in the actual board sessions, because you can avoid getting distracted from the high-level issues and digging too much into any given issue. They can be scheduled on a quarterly basis, or even a monthly basis if you're dealing with a more urgent and consuming issue. They can also happen on an ad-hoc basis. This strategy is predicated on the fact that the world is moving fast, and you can tip the business one way or another between quarters. You might literally wake up one day and find out the dynamics of your market have changed quite significantly and you need to adapt immediately. Waiting until your next quarterly board meeting to address those changes may prove to be too late; this is where the subcommittees could prove to be a great glue between your quarterly board meetings.

Nominate a Lead Director for Fundraising
By Bilal Zuberi, Partner at Lux Capital

When you go out to the market to fundraise, it's a very dynamic process. You learn new things on a daily basis, but you also have to be quick to respond. There is often little time to go back and forth with your entire board and get everybody's agreement on things. You're answering certain questions, you're making certain assumptions, you're doing backchanneling, and so on. You need to have a single director nominated as a fundraising leader by the board, who is available to you on a daily basis to provide that coaching and backchanneling. That way, you can remain focused on what the next set of investors bring to the table, while the board member helps you with all the questions about what the previous set of investors will or will not do.

That lead director on fundraising will also help you get buy-in from other members of the board in a timely manner. The last thing you want in a fast-moving fundraising is to have to go to each director one by one to fill them in and get their alignment, and end up having multiple conversations going at once. Ideally, that lead board member will speak with you on behalf of the board and advise you throughout the process. They can then go back to the board if need be and do bit of backchanneling on your behalf.

23. SETTING BOARD MEETINGS

Orient Your Board Meetings Around Discussion, Feedback, and Interaction

By Seth Levine, Managing Director at Foundry Group

There is a real art to running board meetings and a lot of companies get it wrong. The more the board meeting is oriented around discussion, feedback, and interaction—and the less it's oriented around the management team providing information to the board—the better. The mistake that many companies make is to essentially have an executive team-like meeting and let the board listen in: each of the executives comes in and talks about what's going on with their part of the business. A lot of the reporting function can and should happen outside the board meeting. CEOs should be more thoughtful about how they prepare information and what information they prepare to present to boards. The board meeting should be focused much less around the "what" and much more around the "why." Board members want to hear the team's *interpretation* of what is going on. They don't need to use board meeting time to hear what is going on.

There is often a misperception or a misunderstanding among boards about whether they are making a decision or providing input. When you start talking about a topic at the board meeting, you should clarify whether it is a decision topic or a discussion topic. The vast majority of topics should actually be discussion topics, where the board provides input to the CEO and the management team; then the management team makes a decision about what they want to do. There are relatively few topics that are true decision-type topics, where the board actually is going to discuss something and have to reach some sort of conclusion and decide what to do. Understanding the difference between those and setting them up properly is key. A lot of board members, in the course of meeting about a discussion topic, mistakenly believe they're making a decision. That, in turn, causes all sorts of issues and challenges in businesses.

Add Fundraising and M&A to Your Board Agenda

By Shane Chesson, Founding Partner at Openspace Ventures

Always have fundraising and M&A as agenda items for your board meetings. These items should always be part of your ongoing strategic discussions with your board members. Make sure that in every single board session that you hold, you touch on which investors and M&A partners who have shown interest, whether or not you're fundraising or looking to exit. If you've identified potential opportunities, you need to also break down to your board the upside and downside of each, and any trade-offs associated with raising more money or commencing a new round, or maybe selling secondary. Also, on the M&A side, even if you're not in the mood to sell, and even it's too early, it's a good practice to describe some of the strategic interest out there and get a sense of who is eyeing your space and the rough value they're placing on your company.

This gives your board members one indication of progress, in the sense that you're getting big enough to have some people interested in financing or strategic partnerships as well as buying. Those internal discussions with your board may revolve around asking questions like these: Who are those parties? What are their strengths and weakness? What are the advantages and disadvantages of working with each? How do we get to know them better and explore potential synergies? How do we keep them warm for the future? How do we create a relationship with them, so if we are in the mood to sell a few years down the track, we can build on that relationship?

Then the flipside of the coin is your own board's assessment of the situation in terms of evaluating your readiness to fundraise, merge, or get acquired. Different members may have different perspectives on the topic and different incentives, so it's good to hear their positions as well, and weigh out the various opinions. Some may have the view that it's too early to sell, and you're better off building the business and commanding a higher price down the road. Another may question the strategic or cultural alignment with a given potential partner; if it's an established corporation, for example, they might question how much of a fit the company will have with the larger organization. Will you be able to position to scale or will the new structure bog down your decision making and speed of execution? These are all natural and valid concerns around these issues, so the sooner you can get a framework for discussing these opportunities and align with your board on criteria by which to assess them, the better. You don't want to wait and bring these topics up only when you're ready to sell. You're always better off keeping fundraising and M&A on the radar and part of the discussion on a regular basis, and keeping your board alert to those opportunities.

Delicately Manage Emergency Board Meetings

By Shane Chesson, Founding Partner at Openspace Ventures

You will need to call an emergency board meeting if an urgent material situation arises that requires you to make strategic decisions with the board's participation, and the situation is so time-sensitive that it can't wait until your next board meeting. You will have to try to pull the board together on short notice, ideally in person, or partially virtually through Zoom if some members are geographically remote or have tight schedules. Obviously, an emergency board meeting has to be about something impactful enough to merit such an event—a determinative issue, where a key decision that can drive the business up or down needs to be made urgently. It could be, for example, that a regulatory action has been initiated and the company needs to formulate a quick strategy to respond to it. Or it could be in response to an investigation or something serious of that nature. On the flipside, maybe you just received an M&A proposal or (a little bit more mundane, but still important) maybe there is a renegotiation happening on an ongoing fundraise. It should be something time-sensitive and very relevant to a valuation outcome.

As soon as you call the meeting, you need to contextualize the situation for each board member. You should contact each by email or on WhatsApp and ask, "Can we catch up later today? I just want to let you know what's going on before our meeting." Each board member should get a 10-15-minute (or more if needed), one-on-one chat. That way, they all know what is coming and have a chance process the situation and prepare to discuss it. You want to give them as much lead time as possible and a chance to understand the issue and consider it from their perspective, and the chance to discuss it with others they trust. This puts them in a better position to make a decision during the meeting.

---

24. DEVELOPING LONG-TERM BOARD RELATIONSHIPS

Keep Your Investors and Board in the Know with Regular Communication and Updates

By Vinnie Lauria, Founding Partner at Golden Gate Ventures

You should prepare for board meetings well in advance. Good reporting is essential to effective board meetings and is something you should start planning at least one month prior to your meeting if it is quarterly. It also helps to have frequent communication with the board between board meetings, and the simplest way to do this is with a monthly newsletter that provides a good snapshot of the business and an update on overall progress. The newsletter will essentially need to cover how the business is doing against whatever performance metrics are important and reflective of progress and directly related to KPIs and key milestones. They may include downloads, users, revenue, and so forth. Obviously, this varies from one type of business to another.

The other key item you need to include in this newsletter is your financial vitals: how much cash you have left, your runway at the bank, and your burn rate. One major benefit of such a tool is that it frees up space in board meetings for substantive discussion around priorities, challenges, and strategy, instead of mere management reporting.

You may also include any key hires or fires in the newsletter. It's important to let investors know when people leave and not just celebrate new hires. You wouldn't want an investor to find out from LinkedIn, for example, that an executive had departed the company. You may also include any significant emerging industry stats or trends or new regulations, as well as key lessons learned recently. You not only want to keep your investors abreast of what's happening in the business, as an expert in your space you also want to constantly play the role of educator. You want to make it easy for your investors to learn about your business and your space, especially in dynamic, fast-paced sectors where there are many moving parts, ongoing innovations, and new market entrants.

The format of the newsletter can be text only, it doesn't need to be designed or include nice graphs or illustrations. This newsletter format can then be tailored to engage potential investors, as well as update other outside partners and advisors. This will serve to plant a seed well in advance for when you approach them for future fundraising or collaboration. Of course, the newsletter can also be used internally to inform your team, particularly your management team, to make sure everyone is on the same page and up to speed on the current state of the business and what's on the near horizon.

The last thing you want to have in board meetings is surprises, whether it's a new launch, a major HR decision, or whatever. As much as you can, you want to warm up the board well in advance of what's to come. Communication between board meetings, such as newsletters, can serve as a prelude to such announcements or discussion. You don't want to catch them off guard in the board meeting if the issue at hand is big, especially if it's bad news like a major account or key executive loss. This communication can also take the form of a private, one-on-one conversation or a WhatsApp communication. Regardless of what form you use for communication with the various board members individually or as a group, the main goal is to give a heads-up to your board in order to manage expectations.

Leverage Integrity and Transparency to Seed and Grow Your Board Relationships

By Bill Liao, General Partner at SOSV

At the risk of stating the obvious, have integrity, be truthful, and actually do what you said you were going to do. In the context of entrepreneurship and fundraising, there is this notion out there of "fake it till you make it." The fact that there is a nice rhyme in there does not make those words wise or useful for your journey. You can tell your best truth, just make sure it is the truth. You need to really respect the people that you are going to be getting investment from and working with for a long time. Part of that respect is being a truth-teller and saying it early. It's about setting off goals, executing, and being super upfront with your board about the state of the business and where you fail.

As an investor or board member, if you come to me and tell me, "My projections were overambitious and I've run into problems," there is a lot that we can do, as stakeholders, to assist you. If you don't tell us that until the business falls over, by that time there is nothing we can do to save you because we are certainly not going to throw good money after bad money if you haven't communicated to us.

Integrity doesn't just mean telling the truth; it means making up for the deficiencies in those truths when you have them. In other words, if you make a mistake, own up to it early. If you do, you are going to get a much better outcome than if you don't—that's true integrity. True integrity isn't about being quiet and hiding to look like you're not failing on your promises. True integrity is making big promises, following through, and if you mess up, owning up and making up for it. Integrity and trust are the bedrock of every meaningful business relationship, especially when it comes to your investor and board relationships.

Think of Liquidity as Another Chapter in Your Startup's Growth

By Noor Sweid, Founder of Global Ventures

An age-old adage in the entrepreneur community is that a startup's success culminates in an exit. However, if you think of an exit as the ultimate end goal, you are implying that growth ends post-exit. It is more useful to think of it as yet another phase in your company's growth journey as it changes hands privately in a transaction or publicly in the capital markets. Instead of an ending, consider liquidity events as a core part of your long-term business plan.

On a practical level, your investors will look to cash in on their investment at some point as you build your business. For VCs, this is how they return money to their limited investors. When you accept money from a VC, you are explicitly agreeing to a redemption clause or implicitly agreeing to make their shares valuable and liquid at some point, so they can share returns with their investors. Even your employees and co-founders will eventually want to taste the fruits of their labor. A liquidity event may be an exit for some investors who sell their ownership stakes and move on, but more importantly it offers a financing opportunity for your company, leading to a new stage of growth.

When considering a liquidity event, you can take one or more of three routes, each of which comes with its own set of benefits and drawbacks. Before that, however, it is important to determine who the liquidity is meant for and how it serves the purpose of your company within its lifecycle.

First, you have the classic sale, merger, or acquisition, often referred to as M&A. It is the road most traveled by entrepreneurs, whether in emerging or more mature markets. Of all the exit options, M&A typically carries the lowest risks and greatest strategic rewards. The consolidation of two businesses creates unique operational synergies through which the unified whole becomes greater than the sum of its parts. M&A allows companies to expedite growth that would otherwise be inaccessible, time-consuming, or expensive. It offers avenues for startups to increase their user base, expand their geographic footprint, or broaden or refine their product offering.

In a merger, two entities come together as one. In an acquisition, parts of the selling company's assets are transferred to the buyer, with the retention of key personnel, including the founder, typically built into the deal structure. In certain cases, startups are acquired purely for their talent. Known as an "acquihire," this type of acquisition serves to bridge the gap between the demand and supply of talent.

Although there are a host of benefits that come with M&A as a growth strategy, there are key considerations to factor into your decision, including timing, market context, and strategic fit. Mergers and acquisitions are not simply meetings of two businesses, but also meetings of different minds; alignment on vision and mission is a critical prerequisite in the decision to merge or be acquired.

Second, you can take your company public by selling its shares on the stock market in what is commonly known as an initial public offering or IPO. This is often a goal and aspiration for founders globally, but it's very time-consuming and tedious as well. On average, it takes anywhere between three and nine months to go public, costs an exorbitant amount in time and legal, accounting, and investment banking fees, and is subject to stringent regulatory and reporting compliance.

A newer alternative is a special purpose acquisition company, or SPAC, where a company is formed for the sole purpose of raising capital through an IPO to then acquire a private company within a predetermined cut-off period. Typically, this approach carries lower risks and higher certainty than the traditional IPO route.

Liquidity is an important strategic event for you and your shareholders. While M&As and IPOs create liquidity for your entire cap table, some shareholders may need liquidity for reasons that are entirely separate from your funding strategy. The third option, secondaries, will allow you, your employees, or your investors to sell a partial stake in the business. There are a few tools that you can leverage that enable your stakeholders to benefit from more liquidity events while you continue to grow your venture. Inside investors can buy back the stock of other shareholders in either a primary sale, where the company sells shares and receives the proceeds, or a secondary sale, where a shareholder sells their shares and receives the proceeds. Another liquidity event occurs when shareholders can sell stock individually as part of a company-wide fundraise. Alternatively, and this requires careful management, your venture can also use its own cash to buy back stock from shareholders.

In conclusion, to properly prepare for an exit, you should be methodical in your approach and check all the boxes in your planning. You need to make sure your timing is right, based on both internal factors and external, market-related factors. Depending on your exit strategy, your exit could take between 6 and 24 months. You need to hire the right advisors to help you navigate this intelligently and efficiently. Be prepared for financial and legal due diligence. You will also want to optimize results without jeopardizing long-term value. You need to retain and incentivize key management and demonstrate a post-exit vision that lays out the integration for M&A, advantages and disadvantages of public scrutiny with an IPO, and strategic advantages for new investors during secondaries. Finally, make sure to communicate extensively with your stakeholders at every step in the process.

———

Be Open with Your Investors and Board About Your Liquidity Needs

By Tim Levene, CEO at Augmentum Fintech

For many first-time entrepreneurs, their entire net worth is tied up in their business. There are countless examples of a founder being worth a significant amount on paper, yet struggling from a cash flow perspective to make ends meet and provide for their family, especially in the face of unexpected conditions or emergencies. They may be "paper millionaires," but the reality is that they may have little liquidity and be struggling with their personal finances.

It is healthy to have a conversation about this with your investors rather than brushing the issue aside and letting it create further stress, ultimately distracting you from doing your job. When conveying this problem to investors, I suggest framing the conversation with a reassurance that you are totally committed to the business and believe in its long-term growth, but the opportunity to take a small amount of liquidity off the table once the business has become established is something that you'd like them to consider. It is unusual to see partial founder liquidity before Series B. But assuming that the business is performing well, your founder equity is still vesting, and your investors are still buying into the long-term vision, it is perfectly reasonable for a founder or for a group of founders to seek some early liquidity so that they can continue to focus on taking the business forward.

Investors recognize that startups are all-consuming endeavors that take a toll on their founders and management teams. They understand that it takes an exceptional level of dedication, commitment, and execution to build a successful venture-backed business and that it is an extraordinarily hard journey. They should want the entrepreneurs and the management team to be totally focused on delivering success. Any good VC investor will recognize this and work with the founder to find an appropriate solution. They may ask what it might look like when they next raise capital. This could involve raising a minimum amount of primary equity, and once that minimum has been hit, the door opens for some secondary founder stock to be sold with a cap on the amount. In addition, when you are off-cycle and there is no immediate need to raise additional capital, there might be an opportunistic enquiry from a prospective investor who is looking to find a way to buy equity in the company. Secondary stakes are far more common in venture in 2022 than they were 5 years earlier.

Selling a small amount of equity as a founder shouldn't send negative signals as long as you clearly articulate your position and you can have an open, frank discussion within the context of a high-trust relationship. It's not just about waiting for the ultimate exit—you need to navigate the situation as you progress. Reasonable investors should absolutely be supportive of that, and if handled correctly it will benefit all shareholders over the long term.

Know When to Stand Your Ground in the Boardroom

By Tim Draper, Founder of Draper Associates and DFJ

The best entrepreneurs form great personal relationships with their board members and have open, direct lines of communication with them. They often call their board members, and they talk to them one-on-one to discuss the business and to brainstorm. They know what each of their board members is looking for and thinking about. Then they incorporate that thinking into their business without losing their way. A board member can indeed be a very strong voice. Sometimes, that strong voice can throw you off track—then you get lost. That's because that board member is not running the business, you are. So when you're talking to your board, make sure to listen very carefully, but then do what you know you need to do to make your business successful. There are endless examples of very bad advice given by board members to entrepreneurs, who were enamored of the seniority of the board member or the strength of their voice. Yet, the advice turned out not to be in the best interest of the company. I, myself, have given out advice that played out poorly in retrospect. Blindly following the advice of a board member can really destroy an entrepreneur who has an original vision, but doesn't have the confidence to stick with it over board objections.

You've got to have that confidence to stick with your position when you have strong convictions and you've already carefully considered opposing views, no matter what your board says and what the issue at hand is. When you are talking to people about selling your business, for example, you should listen to your board's input. Then you have to make up your mind and do the right thing for the business. Most board members tend to align with entrepreneurs and give them extra leeway, knowing that founders are closer to the action, and try not impose their outside point of view. Every situation is different, and your job as an entrepreneur is to distinguish between when you should listen and follow your board's advice and when you should stand your ground and not give in to the board's pressure.

Also, understand that board members themselves can be under pressure. Some board members may have immediate pressure. They may need the cash, so they have to pressure you to sell, for instance. Usually, you're going to want to find somebody to buy out those board members. There are also board members who are not fully engaged with the business and therefore are not in a great position to give relevant advice. There are board members who are risk-averse and watch over every dollar spent very carefully and ask, "Why did you spend $3.50 on this coffee mug?" On the other hand, there are board members who give amazing advice, who have marketing vision, or who dig deep into the technology and really help you. Make sure you surround yourself with a board that you enjoy working with and you think might occasionally come up with something that can help your business, but don't think of your board as the people who are running your business, because that's your role. Remember, the buck stops with you, not with your board.

---

25. BUILDING FOR THE FUTURE

Remember Closing a Round is Not the End Game

By Kelly Perdew, Managing Partner at Moonshots Capital

A lot of entrepreneurs, especially first-time entrepreneurs, get overly excited about closing a round of financing and react as if they have achieved a major business milestone. It's exacerbated even more when the funding is in the seven-figure range and valuation is remarkably high for such a young company, and they get coverage from TechCrunch, Bloomberg, or other major media outlets. Granted, raising $10 million, $20 million, or $50 million from the outset is quite an accomplishment for an entrepreneur at the beginning of their startup journey, and it can certainly feel like a major milestone. However, the reality is that it's only an indicator that you have been able to convince someone that your long-term vision is possible and that you are going to be capable of executing against it.

While that should be comforting, it can't be the end game. It is not the finish line. If anything, it's an indication that you now have your work cut out for you, and it's more critical than ever to deliver on your promise—to buckle up and execute. All too often, entrepreneurs believe their own hype and the ongoing validation of the market, the press, and their colleagues, and start thinking they're invincible. They fail to see their business flaws or shortcomings. They begin overspending or rest on their laurels and lose a bit of the hunger and the edge they had when they were bootstrapping. These warnings are especially poignant when the cash raised is significant—you need to maintain the hunger and the edge. As we've seen so frequently, raising capital does not equal success.

Moreover, fundraising never stops. After raising a round, you must execute against your new, more difficult KPIs to scale to the next level. It is very important that you infuse your team with a greater sense of responsibility and be efficient and frugal with the money that investors entrusted you with. You've likely also added new investors to your board, so you'll have an extra set of eyes interested in holding your feet to the fire. So remember, raising money isn't the end of the road, nor does it guarantee smooth sailing. If anything, it's actually the beginning of a more challenging journey.

Keep in Mind the Cyclical Nature of Venture Capital and Invest in Relationships

By Uzma Choudry, Investor at Octopus Ventures

Almost all founders will raise capital a number of times before they exit or go public. There are also lots of serial entrepreneurs who will get their business to a certain stage and then start a new business, and start fundraising all over again. This means that, as an entrepreneur, you might need to knock on the doors of the same VCs for a second, third, or umpteenth time in your lifetime.

The best entrepreneurs increasingly have a choice as to where they get their capital from, and investors have to earn the right to be on their cap table; the balance of power has shifted somewhat in founders' favor. Despite this, it's still worthwhile to maintain friendly relationships with the VCs you don't end up working with.

Clearly, this goes both ways, and VCs should treat founders with the respect they deserve after saying no to a potential investment. Naturally, it can be frustrating for founders who were counting on a VC to lead the round when they change their mind late in the process, because the collateral damage can be significant. At the very least, it means a lot of time is lost, but it can also lead to other investors pulling out. The good and reputable VCs do their best to avoid these situations and typically operate on the basis of transparency, because they don't like to lead founders on.

There is no justification for genuinely bad behavior, which unfortunately does exist in the industry. However, there are also many instances where things just don't work out for all sorts of reasons, and it's not always in investors' control. Even in these situations, frustrating as it might be, it pays to act with integrity and maintain the relationship. Whether you have just received a rejection from a VC, or you have to tell a VC that you can't work with them on this occasion, you should not take it personally and should aim to keep in contact.

It's worth remembering that VCs are in the business of saying no, since they typically only invest in 1 or 2 percent of the businesses they see. So you shouldn't be afraid of saying something like, "Sorry we couldn't make it work this time for XYZ reasons, but let's stay in touch." That's much better than just ignoring their messages for fear of an awkward conversation. Even when it's the VC that has said no, they can be very helpful in other ways because good VCs have strong networks. For example, they might still offer to put you in touch with other investors, customers, potential hires, or people who can help in other ways, so it can be worth keeping them onside. Often enough, it's simply a case of timing, and these VCs may go on to invest in your next fundraise.

Ultimately, the VC and startup world is still quite small and much of it is built on networks. You stand to lose more than you gain by burning bridges, so always optimize for the long term while keeping in mind the cyclical nature of venture capital

———————

EPILOGUE

No Fundraising Advice is Set in Stone

By David Hornik, Founding Partner at Lobby Capital

Great entrepreneurs are creative and flexible. They're great listeners and they react to the circumstances. You can be handed countless rules on fundraising, as is the case in this book, and you can feel you're well prepared for every circumstance, but then you will find yourself faced with something that no one had anticipated. As such, there's no single set of rules that applies to all entrepreneurs all the time. Similarly, there is no single set of rules that applies to all venture capitalists all the time. The ability to listen and to understand the impact of what you're presenting on the investor audience will really matter. For example, there are many entrepreneurs, and even investors, who will tell you that you should always present a pitch deck, because it creates structure, and it creates a simple framework to help investors follow what you're presenting. However, there are entrepreneurs who are astonishing storytellers who have never used a single slide. They simply tell a compelling story of how they came up with the idea, why they're the perfect people to build this business, what they know about the business, and how big this business can be—and before you know it, investors are entranced and hand them a big check.

Granted, those are outlier scenarios that you should not necessarily follow unless, of course, you're a great storyteller who you can skip the advice on presenting a pitch deck and talk your way to fundraising.

The point is that no advice on fundraising—or company-building for that matter—is set in stone. It's only meant to provide practical guidelines for a general audience, and by no means should you follow it blindly or let a generic tip on some aspect of your fundraising or your business interfere with your own judgment in a given situation.

Always be creative and thoughtful about how you approach your fundraising and your business and continue to learn and tweak things. You always need to be gathering information and doing your homework to read and understand the investors you're pitching to and dealing with. Then you need to be constantly reacting to additional information or findings you encounter along your fundraising journey, and ultimately develop your own approach and style and go on to secure capital and build an impactful and successful business.

CONTRIBUTOR PROFILES

AHMED EL ALFI
Co-Founder and Chairman at Sawari Ventures
www.sawariventures.com

Ahmed El Alfi is the Co-Founder and Chairman at Egypt-based Sawari Ventures, a leading venture capital firm in North Africa. He is also the Founder and Chairman at The GrEEK Campus, a startup innovation hub, as well as the Co-Founder of Flat6Labs, the largest accelerator in the Middle East and North Africa (MENA). He was named one of the most creative people in the world by *Fast Company* magazine. Ahmed has been an investor for the past 25 years and has extensive experience in funding and supporting the growth of early-stage companies. He grew up in California and relocated to Egypt in 2006 as the CEO at EFG-Hermes Private Equity. Prior to that, he co-founded Hybrid Capital Partners, a private investment partnership. In 2011, Sawari created and funded Flat6Labs, which has since grown to become the region's premier startup accelerator, with operations in five countries.

AHMAD ALNAIMI
General Partner at STV
www.stv.vc

Ahmad Alnaimi is a General Partner at Saudi Arabia-based STV, a leading venture capital firm in the MENA region that's focused on the technology sector. His investments and board memberships include numerous category leaders, including Trukker (tech-enabled land freight), Foodics (point of sale), Floward (social gifting), and several others. Prior to STV, Ahmad was part of an early-stage company based in Seattle that develops infrastructure software for machine learning. Prior to that, Ahmad led the business incubation function of Aramco Entrepreneurship Center. He holds an MBA from MIT and a Computer Science degree from KFUPM.

FEDERICO ANTONI
Founder and Managing Partner at ALLVP
www.allvp.com

Federico Antoni is the Founder and Managing Partner at Mexico-based ALLVP, one of the most active Series A funds in the venture capital industry in Latin America. ALLVP's investment thesis revolves around the Fintech, future of commerce, human capital, and smart cities sectors. Federico is one of the most notable figures and early capital investors in Mexico's ecosystem. He has held senior management positions in large and complex organizations. Federico holds an undergraduate degree in Economics from Paris Dauphine and an MBA from Stanford Graduate School of Business. He is also a lecturer at the Stanford MBA program and a professor at ITAM. Federico is board member of AMEXCAP and President of AFICO, the Mexican Association of Crowdfunding Platforms. He was named Co-President of the Entrepreneurship division of COMFEI, the Franco-Mexican Council for Entrepreneurship and Innovation.

CAIO BOLOGNESI
Partner at Monashees
www.monashees.com.br

Caio Bolognesi is a Partner at Brazil-based Monashees, a globally active venture capital firm that invests in entrepreneurs committed to creating innovative solutions for a new world. Caio has been with Monashees since 2014. He co-leads investments in the health, SaaS, and B2B segments. Previously, he served as a consultant for three years at Kearney in the consumer goods sector and in the financial industry. Caio graduated from USP with a degree in Administration and, while still at college, created and consolidated the first relationship club between schools and markets, in the Marketing and Finance department.

SIMON CANT
Co-Founder and Managing Partner at Reinventure Group
www.reinventure.com.au

Simon Cant is the Co-Founder and Managing Partner at Australia-based Reinventure Group. Founded in 2013, Reinventure is a founder-first corporate venture fund with $150 million under management, with Westpac as the primary investor. To date, Reinventure has invested in over 30 companies, primarily focused on Fintech and adjacent areas. Simon led a number of those investments, including the 2015 investment in Coinbase. Simon also founded and was the inaugural President of Fintech Australia, the industry's peak representative body. Simon has built his career around venture and innovation. He was a founding team member at Social Ventures Australia, Tinshed Angel Group, ninemsn, and AustLII. Simon began his career as a solicitor with Allens.

JASON CHAPMAN
Managing Partner at Konvoy Ventures
www.konvoy.vc

Jason Chapman is Managing Partner at Colorado-based Konvoy Ventures, a venture fund investing in early-stage companies in the video gaming industry. Konvoy Ventures invests in the infrastructure technology, tools, and platforms of tomorrow's video gaming industry. Some of its investments include Game of Whales (March 2019), Askott Entertainment (April 2019), Opera Event (April 2019), and Upcomer (May 2019).

SHUO CHEN
General Partner at IOVC
www.iovc.io

Shuo Chen is a General Partner at San Francisco-based IOVC, where she focuses on early-stage venture investments in Silicon Valley with a focus on future of work and enterprise/SaaS. She is also a faculty member at UC Berkeley and Singularity University. Shuo was appointed by Governor Gavin Newson to serve as 1 of 13 voting members on California's Mental Health Commission, which oversees approximately $2.6 billion annually. In her venture role, Shuo has invested in companies acquired by Goldman Sachs, Ford, Caterpillar, Binance, and Dialpad, as well as now-unicorns including Boom, Checkr, Grubmarket, Instacart, and Rescale. Prior to that, Shuo worked at Goldman Sachs and PwC, where she worked on Google's $12.5 billion acquisition of Motorola and LinkedIn's $119 million acquisition of SlideShare. Shuo has also co-authored a leading book on financial regulations, and sits on the advisory board of Forbes China.

SHANE CHESSON
Founding Partner at Openspace Ventures
www.openspace.ai

Shane Chesson is a Founding Partner at Singapore-based Openspace Ventures, a venture capital fund manager focused on backing and building early-stage and mid-stage technology companies in Southeast Asia. Openspace Ventures manages over US$550 million across four funds and has invested in 35 companies since 2014. Shane was previously Managing Director and Co-Head of Technology Group at Citigroup Investment Banking, Asia-Pacific. Shane previously worked with Merrill Lynch Singapore and began his career as a strategy consultant with Bain and Company and GEM Consulting in Australia. Shane graduated with an MBA with Distinction from INSEAD and has an LLB/BCom from the University of Western Australia. He is also Chairman of the Investment Committee for Aidha Accelerator, working with migrant workers on entrepreneurship opportunities.

UZMA CHOUDRY
Investor at Octopus Ventures
www.octopusventures.com

Uzma Choudry, PhD, is an Investor at London-based Octopus Ventures. Uzma is an academic turned VC. She started her academic career in a synthetic biology and biophysics lab as a PhD scientist. While working for the tech transfer and innovation arm of the University, she quickly became interested in the exciting challenge of commercializing breakthrough research to help address global issues facing the planet. She now leads the bio investment strategy, managing origination, network, and portfolio, at the European venture capital firm Octopus Ventures.

DAVID COHEN
Founder and Chairman at Techstars
www.techstars.com

David Cohen is the Founder and Chairman at Colorado-based Techstars, a worldwide network that helps entrepreneurs succeed. David has been an entrepreneur and investor for his entire life. He has only had one job interview in his career, successfully got that job, but then quit shortly thereafter to start his first company. Since then, he has founded several companies and has invested in hundreds of startups, such as Uber, Twilio, SendGrid, DigitalOcean, Pillpack, Classpass, Zipline, Scopely, Outreach, Remitly, SalesLoft, and DataRobot. In total, these investments have gone on to create more than $210 billion in value. Prior to that, David was Co-Founder of Pinpoint Technologies, which was acquired by ZOLL Medical Corporation in 1999. David was the founder and CEO at earFeeder, a music service that was sold to SonicSwap. David is the co-author, with Brad Feld, of *Do More Faster: Techstars Lessons to Accelerate Your Startup.*

JAMES CURRIER

General Partner at NFX
www.nfx.com

James Currier is a General Partner at San Francisco-based NFX, an early-stage venture capital firm, investing $1 million to $3 million for 15 percent of startups, with a focus on companies that have network effects. He is one of Silicon Valley's foremost experts in growth and network effects. He is also a pioneer of user-generated models, viral marketing, a/b testing, and crowdsourcing. James co-founded and served as CEO at Tickle, which he grew to become the 18th-largest website in the world, with over 150 million registered users. It was acquired in 2004 by Monster for $110 million. James also co-founded three other companies: Wonderhill (online video games, merged with Kabam in 2010, which then sold for $800 million), IronPearl (growth analytics SaaS, acquired by PayPal in 2013), and Jiff (enterprise healthcare software, raised $68 million from Venrock, GE, J&J, and merged with Castlight in 2017. NASDAQ: CSLT).

FILIP DAMES

Founding Partner at Cherry Ventures
www.cherry.vc

Filip Dames is a Founding Partner at Berlin-based Cherry Ventures, an early-stage venture capital firm led by a team of entrepreneurs with experience building fast-scaling companies such as Zalando and Spotify. Prior to that, he founded an online auction house for antiques and collectibles. He then joined the founding team of Zalando as CEO of the group's shopping club. Until 2014, Filip led Zalando's business development, including the international expansion and the overall product/mobile strategy for online shops, until the IPO. Filip is also an active supporter of the Ashoka network, helping founders start social businesses around the world. He holds an MSc (Diplom) from WHU-Beisheim School of Management. Filip loves to spend his time around product-focused companies and has particular interests in digital health, AI, Fintech, and next-gen retail technology.

BYRON DEETER
Partner at Bessemer Venture Partners
www.bvp.com

Byron Deeter is a Partner at San Francisco-based Bessemer Venture Partners, a venture capital firm that funds consumer, enterprise, and healthcare startups. The firm has over $10 billion under management and invests globally. At Bessemer, Byron is a leading investor in cloud and the internet. He co-authors Bessemer's iconic *10 Laws of Cloud Computing* and the annual *State of the Cloud Report*. He created the Bessemer *Forbes Cloud 100* and *BVP Nasdaq Emerging Cloud Index*. He is the host of Bessemer's newest podcast, "Cloud Giants." To date, 19 of Byron's investments are valued above $1 billion, including 10 IPOs and counting. Byron first raised a Series A with Bessemer Venture Partners back in 2000, as CEO and founder at Trigo Technologies. His company grew to be one of the first global SaaS companies, reached profitability, and was successfully sold to IBM.

FRED DESTIN
Co-Founder and General Partner at Stride.VC
www.stride.vc

Fred Destin is a Co-Founder and General Partner at London-based Stride.VC, a seed-stage tech fund that backs small teams of passionate entrepreneurs. He serves as a board member at Impala, Unibuddy, Cazoo, Huboo, and WeGIFT. Previously, he served as General Partner at Accel (Palo Alto) and at GoCardless, EnglishCentral, and Deliveroo. He serves as a board member at Hofy. He also invested or served on the boards of Rainfinity (acquired by EMC), CapitalIQ (acquired by S&P), and Xerox-PARC spinoff Inxight Software (acquired by BOBJ). He was previously an Executive Director at Goldman Sachs and also worked at JP Morgan in hybrid derivatives. He was selected among *Forbes Europe*'s Midas List 2020. He holds a master of finance, magna cum laude, from Solvay Business School (University of Brussels).

CAMILLA DOLAN
Partner at Eka Ventures
www.ekavc.com

Camilla Dolan is a Partner at London-based Eka Ventures, which invests in founders creating positive systemic change through focusing on an environmental or social objective. The firm focuses on Series A and earlier. Previously, she was an Investment Manager at MMC Ventures, responsible for sourcing new deals and deal execution. Before joining MMC, she was a Consultant and Case Team Leader at Bain & Co where she specialized in Fintech. Camilla has a master's degree in Law from Merton College, Oxford University. Prior to university she set up and ran a small equine business.

TIM DRAPER
Founder of Draper Associates and DFJ
www.draper.vc; www.dfj.com

Tim Draper is the Founder of Silicon Valley-based Draper Associates and DFJ, venture capital firms that are focused on investments in enterprise, consumer, and disruptive technologies. He is the Founder of Draper University, creator of the popular show, "Meet The Drapers," and Author of *The Startup Hero*. The firms' investments include Coinbase, Skype, Tesla, Baidu, Hotmail, Robinhood, SpaceX, and others. Time is a leading spokesperson for Bitcoin, blockchain, ICOs, and cryptocurrencies. He created viral marketing. He is regularly featured on major networks and has received many awards, including the World Entrepreneurship Forum's Entrepreneur of the World. He is listed among the top 100 most powerful people in finance by *Worth Magazine* and the top 20 most influential people in crypto by CryptoWeekly, and he is number seven on the *Forbes* Midas List. Tim served on the California State Board of Education. He received a BS from Stanford University and an MBA from Harvard Business School.

BRAD FELD

Co-Founder of Foundry Group and Techstars, and
Author of *Venture Deals*
www.foundrygroup.com; www.techstars.com

Brad Feld is the Co-Founder of Colorado-based Foundry Group and Techstars. He has been an early-stage investor and entrepreneur since 1987. Prior to co-founding Foundry Group, he co-founded Mobius Venture Capital and, prior to that, founded Intensity Ventures. Brad is also a Co-Founder of Techstars. Brad is a writer and speaker on venture capital investment and entrepreneurship. He has written a number of books as part of the Startup Revolution: *Venture Deals: Be Smarter Than Your Lawyer and Venture Capitalist*, *Startup Communities*, *Startup Boards*, *Do More Faster*, *Startup Opportunities*, *Startup Life*, and others. He also writes the blogs "Feld Thoughts" and "Venture Deals." Brad holds BSc and MSc degrees in Management Science from the Massachusetts Institute of Technology.

JENNY FIELDING

General Partner at The Fund
www.thefund.vc

Jenny Fielding is a General Partner at New York-based The Fund, a pre-seed fund and international founder community with a special focus on Fintech, healthcare, automation, and future of work. Her portfolio includes over 160 tech-enabled companies. Previously, Jenny was Managing Director at Techstars New York, where she led the program. Before that, Jenny headed up Corporate Venture and Digital Innovation at BBC Worldwide, where she made strategic investments and led business development deals. She has started several tech companies, most notably Switch-Mobile, a mobile VoIP company that was acquired in 2009. Jenny began her career as a lawyer, spent time at JP Morgan and is a graduate of Columbia University where she is an Adjunct Professor. She is also a Kauffman Fellow.

ZACH FINKELSTEIN
Co-Founder and Managing Partner at Class 5 Global
www.class5global.com

Zach Finkelstein is Co-Founder and Managing Partner at San Francisco-based Class 5 Global, an emerging market-focused venture capital fund. At Class 5, Zach focuses on early-stage tech investments in Latin America, the Middle East, and Southeast Asia. Previously, Zach was the Vice President of Corporate Development at Careem (acquired by Uber for $3.2 billion). In addition to his M&A and investor relations responsibilities, Zach helped to launch Careem's food delivery businesses and expand to several new geographies. He was also a partner at Lumia Capital, where he focused on emerging market portfolio-leading investments in Careem, CargoX, and Fresha, among others, and was recognized by *Forbes* as a top 30 under 30 venture capital investor. Earlier, Zach worked at Citigroup and at the Federal Reserve Bank of New York. Zach earned a BA magna cum laude from the University of Pennsylvania.

ISABEL FOX
General Partner at Outsized Ventures
www.outsized.vc

Isabel Fox is a General Partner at London-based Outsized Ventures, an early-stage VC fund that partners with founders pushing the boundaries of science and technology to solve the world's greatest challenges for the future of the planet, health, and society. She previously founded Luminous Ventures, where she had the opportunity to invest in visionary founders with breakthrough technologies and back deep tech and science that matters. She was also Head of Venture Capital at White Cloud Capital, where she focused on early-stage investments in life sciences and healthcare. With a background in investment banking and private equity turnarounds, Isabel founded and exited two corporate communications firms focused on the route to exit, co-founded two software startups (one exit) and was an active angel investor in the UK and the US. She has worked in New York, San Francisco, and London.

FABRICE GRINDA
Founding Partner at FJ Labs
www.fjlabs.com

Fabrice Grinda is a Founding Partner at New York-based FJ Labs, a stage-agnostic investment firm that focuses on marketplaces and consumer-facing startups. He has over 250 exits on 700 angel investments. Fabrice was an early investor in Alibaba, Coupang, Airbnb, Instacart, Flexport, Delivery Hero, and many more. Fabrice was named the #1 Angel Investor in the world by *Forbes*. He was Co-Founder and Co-CEO at OLX, one of the largest websites in the world with over 300 million unique visitors per month. The company operates in 30 countries and has over 10,000 employees. Prior to OLX, he was the CEO and founder of Zingy, a mobile content company, which he grew to over $200 million in annual revenues. Before that, he was the CEO at Aucland, one of the largest auction sites in Europe. Fabrice holds a BA in Economics from Princeton University where he graduated summa cum laude.

MARY GROVE
Managing Partner at Bread and Butter Ventures
www.breadandbutterventures.com

Mary Grove is the Managing Partner at Minneapolis-based Bread and Butter Ventures, an early-stage firm that invests in Healthtech, Foodtech, and enterprise SaaS. She began her career working on the Google IPO and went on to lead new business development partnerships, negotiating early-stage product and technology deals worldwide. Mary then served as the founding director of Google for Startups, leading the company's global efforts to support entrepreneurs in over 100 countries. Earlier, she was an investment partner at Revolution's Rise of the Rest Seed Fund. She is also the Co-Founder and Executive Director at Silicon North Stars. Mary serves on the boards of Vital Voices, the Minneapolis Foundation, the Bush Foundation, and the Techstars Foundation. She earned her BA and MA from Stanford University.

OLIVER HOLLE
Co-Founder and Managing Partner at Speedinvest
www.speedinvest.com

Oliver Holle is a Co-Founder and Managing Partner at Austria-based Speedinvest. Speedinvest is one of Europe's most active early-stage investors with more than €600 million in assets under management; 40 investors based in Berlin, London, Munich, Paris, Vienna, and San Francisco; and more than 200 portfolio companies. With over 15 years of entrepreneurial experience in the mobile and internet industries and 10 years as Co-Founder of Speedinvest, Oliver Holle is a leading expert in Europe's technology startup scene. In 1997, he founded one of the first European internet startups. After two successful mergers, 3united was sold for €55 million to US giant VeriSign in 2006, and Oliver worked for the company in Silicon Valley for several years, overseeing their mobile business and more than 600 employees.

DAVID HORNIK
Founding Partner at Lobby Capital
www.lobby.vc

David Hornik is a Founding Partner at San Francisco-based Lobby Capital and the creator and Executive Producer of The Lobby Conference. He invests broadly in information technology companies, with a focus on consumer-facing software and services, enterprise applications, and infrastructure software. He is the author of the first venture capital blog, "VentureBlog" and creator of the first venture capital podcast, "VentureCast." Prior to Lobby Capital, David was a General Partner at August Capital for 20 years. David teaches business and law at Harvard Law School and Stanford's Graduate School of Business

ALI KARABEY
Co-Founder and Partner at 212
www.212.vc

Ali Karabey is a Co-Founder and Partner at Istanbul-based 212, Turkey's first venture capital firm, with offices in Istanbul, Doha, and San Francisco. 212 invests in unique teams with global ambitions to scale B2B technology. He has spent his career focused on technology and communications investments. After graduating from the University of Michigan in 1999, Ali joined Arthur Andersen in New York. In 2002, he joined Morgan Stanley Capital International, where he managed the North American and European finance teams. In 2007, he joined Deutsche Bank and served on its principal investments team. He then worked with the Turkish government. At 212, Ali serves on the boards of Avatao, App Samurai, Fazla Gida, Insider, Metrobi, Solvoyo, and Smartmessage. Ali also sits on the Advisory Board of Endeavor and is a member of the Istanbul chapter of the Entrepreneurs Organization.

ROB KNIAZ
Co-Founder and Partner at Hoxton Ventures
www.hoxtonventures.com

Rob Kniaz is a Co-Founder and Partner at London-based Hoxton Ventures, an early-stage technology venture capital firm that partners with founders seeking to invent new market categories or transform large existing industries. He represents the firm on the boards of Assetario, FabricNano, Kheiron Medical, LiliumX, NoMagic, Pear Bio, Preply, Spacelift, and Vatic, and previously was on the board of Immunio (acquired by Trend Micro) and Campanja (acquired by 24/7 Media). He also works on Hoxton's interests in Deliveroo, Babylon Health, Ochre Bio, Optimoroute, Raptor Supplies, and Wanted. In 2008, he joined join the investments team at Fidelity Ventures. Before that, he was on the new business development team at Google, where he launched the AdWords pay-per-action product and helped with the acquisition of Feedburner. He holds a BSc in Computer Science from the University of Maryland and a master's certificate in Management Science and Engineering from Stanford University.

VINNIE LAURIA
Founding Partner at Golden Gate Ventures
www.goldengate.vc

Vinnie Lauria is a Founding Partner at Singapore-based Golden Gate Ventures, an early-stage VC firm in Southeast Asia with US$250 million in assets under management and more than 60 investments to date. He is a Kauffman Fellow and a guest lecturer at the National University of Singapore. He was rated by the Founder Institute as the best startup mentor in Asia from a pool of 2,500 mentors. Prior to setting up Golden Gate Ventures, Vinnie built two startups in Silicon Valley: Meetro, a location-based chat service, which was dissolved with many lessons learned in 2007; and Lefora, a forum-hosting platform, which grew to over 100,000 communities and was acquired by CrowdGather in 2010. He founded the Silicon Valley NewTech meetup, featuring hundreds of startups to a monthly audience with more than 10,000 members. Vinnie is a graduate of Boston University's College of Engineering.

JENNY LEFCOURT
General Partner at Freestyle Capital
www.freestyle.vc

Jenny Lefcourt is a General Partner at San Francisco-based Freestyle Capital, an early-stage VC firm whose investments include Airtable, Intercom, Patreon, BetterUp, Snapdocs, Digit, and many others. Jenny is also a founding member and board member of All Raise, a non-profit dedicated to increasing diversity in tech. Prior to Freestyle Capital, Jenny co-founded WeddingChannel.com (acquired by The Knot) and Bella Pictures (acquired by CPI). She also has angel invested and/or advised companies such as Discord, MainStreetHub, and Minted. Jenny received a BSE from The Wharton School and attended Stanford Graduate School of Business before dropping out after her first year to co-found WeddingChannel.com

TIM LEVENE
CEO at Augmentum Fintech
www.augmentum.vc

Tim Levene is the CEO at London-based Augmentum Fintech, one of Europe's leading venture capital investors focusing exclusively on the Fintech sector. Tim co-founded juice bar business Crussh and was the founding employee at Flutter.com, which became one of the highest-profile digital businesses in the UK after it merged with Betfair.com in 2001. In 2010, Tim co-founded Augmentum Capital with the backing of RIT Capital and Lord Rothschild. In 2018, Tim and co-founder Richard Matthews successfully launched Augmentum Fintech PLC on the main market of the London Stock Exchange. Tim sits on multiple Fintech boards including Interactive Investor, Tide, Zopa, Farewill, iwoca, and Monese. He is active in cross-industry initiatives including the UK Fintech Strategy Group. Tim was elected as a Common Council member to represent Bridge, one of the 25 wards in the City of London's Local Authority.

SETH LEVINE
Co-Founder and Managing Director at Foundry Group
www.foundrygroup.com

Seth Levine is a Co-Founder and Managing Director at Colorado-based Foundry Group, a venture capital firm he co-founded in 2006, with almost $3 billion in assets under management. He is a passionate advocate for entrepreneurship. He spends time as an advisor to venture funds and companies around the world. He co-founded Pledge 1%, a global network of companies that have pledged equity, time, and product back to their local communities. He is on the board of StartupColorado. He is a trustee of Macalester College in St. Paul, Minnesota, where he helped found their entrepreneurship program. He also works with a number of funds and companies, especially in the Middle East and Africa, to help promote entrepreneurship and economic development globally. He is the author of *The New Builders: Face to Face with the True Future of Business.*

BILL LIAO
General Partner at SOSV
www.sosv.com

Bill Liao is a General Partner at Ireland-based SOSV, an investment management and venture capital firm that provides funding in the technology sector. He is responsible for over $1 billion under management as one of eight partners managing various global accelerator programs. He is also the Founder of the SOSV Momentum pre-accelerator program. Bill is a Chinese-Australian-Irish entrepreneur, investor, former diplomat, business mentor, author, passionate leader, and speaker, with a distinguished record in business development and community activism. Co-founder of the CoderDojo movement and of Weforest, his career in tech and business encompasses two unicorn companies and launching the world's first biotech accelerator. Bill's current focus is quantum software.

NATHAN LUSTIG
Managing Partner at Magma Partners
www.magmapartners.com

Nathan Lustig is the Managing Partner at Chile-based Magma Partners, a seed-stage venture capital fund based in Latin America, the US, and China. He founded ExchangeHut during his sophomore year at the University of Wisconsin and ran it until his senior year, when ExchangeHut was acquired. In 2008, he co-founded Entrustet. In 2010, Nathan was part of the pilot program of Startup Chile and grew Entrustet to the market leader in the industry. In 2012, Entrustet was acquired by a European competitor. Nathan is also the founder of Capital Entrepreneurs, an organization of high-tech entrepreneurs in Madison, Wisconsin dedicated to making Madison a new startup hub. He also worked as the Head of Marketing for Welcu and taught entrepreneurship at several Chilean universities. He is the author of *Startup Chile 101*.

MANUEL SILVA MARTINEZ

General Partner at Mouro Capital
www.mourocapital.com

Manuel Silva Martinez is a General Partner at London-based Mouro Capital, a global venture capital fund investing in early-stage Fintechs across the Americas, Europe, the Middle East, and Africa. Manuel has been investing in Fintech since the early 2010s, first with BBVA Ventures in San Francisco, then with Santander InnoVentures based out of London. Before that, he occupied several positions in Corporate Development and Innovation at BBVA. Manuel holds a BA in Business Administration from CUNEF (Madrid) and a Diplome from Sciences Po (Paris). He has conducted doctoral research in Paris, Hong Kong, and Beijing.

ELISA MILLER-OUT

Co-Founder and Managing Partner at Chloe Capital
www.chloecapital.com

Elisa Miller-Out is a Co-Founder and Managing Partner at New York-based Chloe Capital, which she established in 2017. Chloe Capital is an early-stage venture capital fund on a mission to bring more women into technology investing and leadership. To date, Chloe Capital has funded 10 companies with a combined portfolio value of $70 million and drawn more than 15,000 members to its #InvestInWomen movement. She is Chair of the board for Singlebrook. Beyond leading her own companies, Elisa has mentored several hundred business leaders recently through her various roles, such as managing partner for Chloe Capital, Entrepreneur in Residence at Cornell University and Launch NY, Instructor for the National Science Foundation, and Innovation Advisor to the New York State Energy Research & Development Authority (NYSERDA). Elisa has served on the boards of numerous commercial enterprises, as well as the New York State Climate Action Council.

GREG MOON
Managing Partner at SoftBank Investment Advisers
www.visionfund.com

Greg Moon is the Managing Partner of Japan-based SoftBank Investment Advisers (the Vision Fund management company), covering Asia-Pacific regions including Singapore, Indonesia, Vietnam, Korea, and Oceania. Greg serves on the board of many portfolio companies, including Grab, and is working to expand investment in Southeast Asia. Prior to the Vision Fund, he served as the CEO and Managing Director at SoftBank Ventures Asia (SBVA), which is a corporate venture capital firm, and as CEO and President at SoftBank Korea (SBK), which is an investment holding company owned by Japan's SoftBank Group. Greg draws on 32 years of experience in the dynamic field of information technology. He attended Korea University and has a degree in Literature and an MBA from Drexel University in Philadelphia, Pennsylvania.

PATRICIA NAKACHE
General Partner at Trinity Ventures
www.trinityventures.com

Patricia Nakache is a General Partner at San Francisco-based Trinity Ventures, where she invests in early-stage consumer and business tech startups. Her current investments include Turo, Side, Bevi, Beautiful.ai, Life House, ManiMe, and Relish. She has previous investments in thredUP (TDUP), where she is Chairperson of the board, Care.com (CRCM), LoopNet (LOOP), PayScale (acquired by Warburg Pincus), and Sabrix (acquired by Thomson Reuters), among others. Patricia is a board member at the National Venture Capital Association and a Lecturer in Management at the Stanford Graduate School of Business, where she teaches Formation of New Ventures and Startup Garage. She earned an MBA from Stanford University and an AB from Harvard University.

JIMMY FUSSING NIELSEN
Co-Founder of Heartcore Capital
www.heartcore.com

Jimmy Fussing Nielsen is a Co-Founder of Denmark-based Heartcore Capital. The firm was founded in 2007. Today, Heartcore is Europe's leading consumer tech VC, investing from offices in Berlin, Copenhagen, and Paris. Heartcore has backed several category winners, including GetYourGuide, Tink, Neo4j, Boozt, Travelperk, Kaia Health, Podimo, and many more. Jimmy's passion for technology investing and entrepreneurship started in asset management, where he earned his investment cred. Jimmy holds an MSc in Finance from CBS.

SAJITH PAI
Director at Blume Ventures
www.blume.vc

Sajith Pai is a Director at India-based Blume Ventures, an early-stage venture fund that backs tech-led startups with both funding and active mentoring. Sajith is a long-time media executive turned VC. At Blume, Sajith supports investments in EdTech, HRTech, SMB SaaS, and B2B marketplaces, while simultaneously helping Blume build a research and knowledge platform. Sajith is a prolific writer on topics ranging from startups and e-commerce to culture and education. His work has been published in Scroll, Quartz, Buzzfeed, and The Times of India. Sajith was among LinkedIn's Top Voices 2020 for sharing "insights from the intersection of technology, business, and culture."

KELLY PERDEW
Co-Founder & Managing General Partner at Moonshots Capital
www.moonshotscapital.com

Kelly Perdew is a Co-Founder and Managing General Partner at Los Angeles-based Moonshots Capital, a seed-stage venture capital firm that invests in extraordinary leadership. Kelly has served in every capacity: Founder, board member, CEO, COO, CFO, business development, and sales. He has raised institutional financing, grown businesses, downsized businesses, and sold businesses for eight-figure exits. Kelly was the winner of the second season of *The Apprentice*. This granted him access to work with the Trump brand across its different businesses. He holds an MBA and JD from the UCLA School of Law and graduated from West Point.

BILL REICHERT
Venture Partner at Pegasus Tech Ventures
www.pegasustechventures.com

Bill Reichert is a Venture Partner at San Francisco-based Pegasus Tech Ventures, a global venture capital firm that manages a $1.7 billion fund. It invests in emerging technology companies, working with them to expand sales in North America, Asia, and Europe. Prior to Pegasus, Bill was Co-Founder of Garage Technology Ventures. Prior to that, Bill was a co-founder or senior executive in several venture-backed technology startups, including Trademark Software, The Learning Company, and Academic Systems. Bill earned a BA from Harvard College and an MBA from Stanford University. He was a founding board member and Chairman of the Churchill Club, and a charter member of the Silicon Valley Association of Startup Entrepreneurs.

GARY RIESCHEL
Founding Managing Partner at Qiming Venture Partners
www.qimingvc.com

Gary Rieschel is the Founding Managing Partner at Shanghai-based Qiming Venture Partners, which invests in technology and healthcare. The firm has over $9 billion in assets under management, including Xiaomi, Meituan Dianping, UBTech, Bilibili, Roborock, and others. Previously, Gary was a senior executive at Intel, Sequent Computer, and Cisco Systems. He created and grew SoftBank's US venture group to over $1 billion in market capitalization and served on SoftBank's board of directors. He helped found the China Greentech Initiative and sponsored the Rocky Mountain Institute's entry into China. Gary actively supports the Asia Society, the Council on Foreign Relations, The Nature Conservancy, PERC, the Climate Leadership Council, the US Olympic Foundation, and the Fudan University International Advisory Board. Gary attended Reed College (BA) and Harvard Business School (MBA).

ANDREW ROMANS
Co-Founder, CEO, and General Partner at 7BC Capital
www.7bc.vc

Andrew Romans is the Co-Founder, CEO, and General Partner at San Francisco-based 7BC Capital. He is a successful, consistently top-quartile-performing VC, VC-backed entrepreneur, former tech VC and M&A investment banker, and co-founder of an angel group. He was the Founder and General Partner at Rubicon Venture Capital. He is a published author of three books on VC and crypto. Andrew also advises large corporations and governments on policies about venture capital and corporate venture capital. He raised over $48 million for tech startups he founded by the age of 28. Andrews has founded numerous startups, raised hundreds of millions of dollars in VC funding, and led startups to exits. He is a frequent guest speaker on MSNBC, CNBC, and ABC. Andrew holds an MBA in finance from Georgetown University.

JENNY ROOKE
Managing Director at Genoa Ventures
www.genoavc.com

Jenny Rooke is the Managing Director at San Francisco-based Genoa Ventures, which invests in early-stage companies innovating at the intersection of biology and technology, with a focus on opportunities in research tools, molecular diagnostics, synthetic biology, ag biotech, and industrial biology. She has over a decade of investing experience at Fidelity Biosciences, and in 2006 was named a Kauffman Fellow. After Fidelity, Jenny helped establish the investing function at the Gates Foundation, funding companies involved in genetic engineering, diagnostics, and synthetic biology. Jenny began 5 Prime Ventures in 2014 using the largest life sciences syndicate on AngelList and achieving one of the highest-performing AngelList syndicates in any sector. Her prior investments include Zymergen, Caribou, Accuri, and Topaz. Jenny studied physics at Georgia Institute of Technology and has a PhD in genetics from Yale.

DANIEL ROSEN
Founder and General Partner at Commerce Ventures
www.commerce.vc

Daniel Rosen is the Founder and General Partner at San Francisco-based Commerce Ventures, an early-stage venture capital firm focused on investing in and empowering the next generation of technology innovators in the retail and financial services industries. He is an experienced venture capitalist with a strong, 20-year investing track record across every stage of private equity. He made investments in pioneering startup companies such as Bill.com, BillGO, ClickSWITCH, InAuth, Kin, Forter, Marqeta, MX, Narvar, Quattro Wireless, Snapsheet, Socure, Vestwell, and WePay. Daniel has deep expertise in commerce, entrepreneurship, financial services, Fintech, venture capital, go-to-market strategy, and strategic partnerships.

CHRISTOPHER M. SCHROEDER
Co-Founder of Next Billion Ventures
www.nextbillionvc.com

Christopher M. Schroeder is a Co-Founder of Next Billion Ventures. He is also an Advisor and Network Partner of Village Global and other leading Silicon Valley enterprises. He is a leading global venture investor and advisor with particular expertise in rising markets. Previously, Christopher was CEO at washingtonpost.com and a Co-Founder of the Sequoia-backed healthcentral.com, sold in 2012. He serves on the investment committees of Saudi Telecom Ventures and Wamda Capital. Christopher authored the bestselling *Startup Rising: The Entrepreneurial Revolution Remaking the Middle East*, the first book on startups in the Arab world. He has written and speaks extensively on startups and innovation globally and in the Middle East. Christopher has also been featured regularly on leading news shows. He was named in LinkedIn's Top 50 Influencers and his blog can be read on LinkedIn and Substack.

IZHAR SHAY
Venture Partner at DisruptAI
www.disruptiveai.fund

Izhar Shay is a Venture Partner at Israel-based DisruptAI, an early-stage, deep tech VC focused on AI investments. He is Israel's former Minister of Science and Technology, and he was a member of the country's special Coronavirus Cabinet. Izhar is the Chairman of Kendago, as well as an advisor, board member, and mentor for CEOs and entrepreneurs. He was elected as a member of the Israeli Parliament (Knesset). Izhar founded Israel's largest digital community for entrepreneurs (Startup Stadium) with 45,000 members. He also anchored a popular radio program ("High-Tech Ba'Pkakim"). Izhar was a professor in the Kellogg-Recanati International Executive MBA Program. He was named one of Israel's top 20 investors for early-stage ventures by the VCFORU community. He was a Founding Managing General Partner at Canaan Partners Israel. He holds a BSc in Electronic Engineering from the Technion.

WAYNE SHIONG
Partner at China Growth Capital
www.chinagrowthcapital.com

Wayne Shiong is a Partner at Beijing-based China Growth Capital, an early-stage and seed-stage venture investor with over $1 billion under management. Wayne leads frontier technologies and life science investments at the firm. His notable portfolio includes PlusDrive, WeRide, Innovusion, DeePhi (NASDAQ: XLNX), Biren Technologies, Mech Mind, Tezign, Nreal, Landscape Aerospace, Raysight, Immorna, KOKA, and Singleron. Wayne was a partner at Bertelsmann Asia Investments (BAI Capital). Prior to BAI Capital, Wayne was a partner at WI Harper Group, a cross-border early-stage investor in technology and healthcare, where he worked on Maxthon, Go Mobile (NASDAQ: GOMO), Mapbar (sold to NavInfo; SZSE: 002405), ChIVD (STAR: 688468), and Edan Instrument (SZSE: 300206). Wayne majored in Economics at Peking University.

JON SOBERG
Managing Partner at MS&AD Ventures
www.msad.vc

Jon Soberg is a Managing Partner at San Francisco-based MS&AD Ventures, an early-stage venture capital firm focused on the future of finance, risk assessment, and building a sustainable society. Jon has made over 120 investments across five continents and has held more than 40 board positions. Prior to becoming an investor, Jon was a serial entrepreneur and operator, with an IPO exit at Adforce. Jon has a master's degree in Engineering, a CFA, and is an MBA and Palmer Scholar at Wharton. Jon is ranked #13 on Business Insider's Seed 100 list of top seed investors.

THOMAS SPERRY

Managing Director at Rogue Venture Partners
www.roguevp.com

Thomas Sperry is a Co-Founder and Managing Director at Oregon-based Rogue Venture Partners, a private equity fund. Prior to Rogue, he was CEO at Exit Games Inc. Exit Games is a venture capital-backed technology company with a focus on the video game industry. Prior to Exit Games, he was CEO at the venture-backed company Blade3D, headquartered in Shanghai, China. Prior to that, Tom held senior management positions with HNC Software (Executive Director) and Looking Glass Studios (Director). Tom began his career at Microsoft Corporation, where he was a founding member of the Games Division.

NOOR SWEID

Founder of Global Ventures
www.global.vc

Noor Sweid is the Founder of Dubai-based Global Ventures, a growth-stage venture capital firm focusing on investing in emerging markets. Previously, Noor was the Chief Investment Officer at Dubai Future Foundation and a Managing Partner at Leap Ventures. Noor led the IPO for Depa on the London Stock Exchange and NASDAQ Dubai, scaling the business to $600 million in revenues. Noor also founded and exited ZenYoga to a private equity firm. Noor is Chairperson of the Middle East Venture Capital Association. She on the founding board of Endeavor UAE and serves as a director for MIT Sloan and TechWadi. Recently, Noor was listed as one of the World's Top 50 Women in Tech by *Forbes*, received the Arab Woman Award for Finance, and was named in the *Arabian Business* 100 Most Powerful Arab Women list. Noor holds bachelor's degrees in Finance and Economics from Boston College and an MBA from MIT Sloan.

YINGLAN TAN

CEO and Founding Managing Partner at Insignia
Ventures Partners
www.insignia.vc

Yinglan Tan is the CEO and Founding Managing
Partner at Singapore-based Insignia Ventures Partners. He also serves on
the Singapore government's Pro Enterprise Panel and is a member of the
international board for Stars and the board for Hwa Chong Institution. He
was honored as a Young Global Leader by the WEF and serves on its
Technology Pioneer Selection Committee Panel. He was also named to the
Young Leader Circle by the Milken Institute and Top 40 leaders under 40 by
Prestige Magazine. Yinglan is one of 100 Leaders of Tomorrow listed by the St
Gallen Symposium, and 100 Global Thinkers listed by think-tank Lo Spazio
della Politica. He is also a World Cities Summit Young Leader, a WEF Global
Agenda Council member on Fostering Entrepreneurship, and a Kauffman
Fellow. He is the author of *The Way of the VC*, *How Chinese Innovators are
Changing the World*, and *New Venture Creation*. Yinglan was educated at
Harvard, Stanford, and Carnegie Mellon.

ANIS UZZAMAN

Founder and CEO at Pegasus Tech Ventures
www.pegasustechventures.com

Anis Uzzaman is the Founder and CEO at San Francisco-based Pegasus Tech
Ventures, a global venture capital firm that manages a $1.7 billion fund.
The firm invests in emerging technology companies, working with them
to expand sales in North America, Asia, and Europe. Anis also serves as
the Chairman of Startup World Cup, a global entrepreneurship platform.
Anis has invested in over 200 startups, including SpaceX, Airbnb, Doordash,
and 23andMe. He serves on the boards of Lark, Asteria, Zuu, Tech in Asia,
Affectiva, and others. Anis holds a BSc in Engineering from Tokyo Institute
of Technology, an MSc in Engineering from OSU, and a PhD in Computer
Engineering from Tokyo Metropolitan University. Anis is a Forbes Finance
Council member and contributor at *Forbes*. Anis is also a contributing editor
at *Inc.* and an Entrepreneur Leadership Network Contributor at *Entrepreneur*.
Anis is an honored guest speaker at international conferences, has published
more than 30 technical papers, and is the author of several books.

BILAL ZUBERI
Partner at Lux Capital
www.luxcapital.com

Bilal Zuberi is a Partner at New York-based Lux Capital, a venture capital firm that helps entrepreneurs turn breakthroughs into world-changing businesses within energy, healthcare, and technology. Bilal leads Lux's investments in DesktopMetal, Evolv Technology, Saildrone, Applied Intuition, Ironclad, Nozomi Networks, Meter, Fiddler Labs, Happiest Baby, Commure, OpenSpace, Zededa, Orbital Insight, Veo Robotics, High Arc, AirMap, and others. Prior to joining Lux, Bilal was an investor at General Catalyst Partners. Before becoming an investor, he was an entrepreneur and co-founded GEO2 Technologies. Earlier in his career, Bilal was a strategy consultant at BCG and a visiting scientist at PNNL/DOE Labs. He also served as member of the founding team of the School of Science and Engineering at LUMS University. Bilal earned a PhD from the Massachusetts Institute of Technology.

KEET VAN ZYL
Co-Founder and Partner at Knife Capital
www.knifecap.com

Keet Van Zyl is a Co-Founder and Partner at South Africa-based Knife Capital, an independent growth equity investment firm focusing on innovation-driven ventures with proven traction. He has extensive high-growth investment experience. Keet structured various private equity funds in Southern Africa for a US fund-of-funds investor and worked at industry-leading companies such as Procter & Gamble, Investec Bank, and Here Be Dragons Venture Capital (HBD). In 2010 he co-founded Knife Capital to continue the active management of HBD's South African portfolio of investments and raise third-party funds for growth equity investments. Keet co-founded other companies, including AngelHub, Grindstone Accelerator, and KNF Ventures. Keet is passionate about building the early-stage funding ecosystem in Sub-Saharan Africa.

ACKNOWLEDGMENTS

This book was a collective effort in every sense of the word. As such, I'm very grateful to the dozens of people who were involved in various capacities and who, in effect, helped bring this book to life. Without them, this project would have never gotten off the ground.

First and foremost, thank you Brad Feld for your invaluable inspiration and support for this book and over the years. You truly practice what you preach, and you're a true mentor and inspiration to me and countless others.

Thank you, Christopher Schroeder, for your generosity and support throughout this project. It means a lot to me.

I am grateful and thankful to all the interviewees and contributors featured here for their time, patience, and valuable input. I would also like to acknowledge those who committed to be part of this work and were not featured in the book due to space limitations. Please forgive me. I'm appreciative of your time and well intentions.

To my great editor Michelle Waitzman: thank you very much for all your diligence and great attention to detail. I trust you'd be proud of the final product.

To Andy Meaden, Kristin Muller, Milan Trninic, Caroline Lips, and Yei Philip: thank you for all your valuable help and patience.

Special thanks to the following people: Muhammed Mekki, as always, for your astute eye and priceless feedback and generosity; my partners in crime—Tarek Sadi, Karim Kobrossi, and Omar Christidis—for being a class act first and foremost and for your mentorship, as well as your overall encouragement and support; Aaron

Valverde for providing the right environment to focus on this project and for all your great accommodation and service; Erika Vericima, Aysha Espada, and Juve Oreo for your wonderful support and great encouragement every step of this journey with all of its ups and downs; Elisa Jouttunpaa for your thoughtfulness and timely help; Samantha Cook, Bernadette Valdivia, and Claudia Bueno—for all your great encouragement in this project and over the years; and Nash Salah for your priceless friendship and all your help when it matters most.

Finally, thank you to my beloved family: Rawia Helmy, Omar Soudodi, Ahmed Soudodi, Reem Soudodi, Mostafa Hegazi, Rimy Allam, Amal Elsayed, and Maryam Allam. To my mother and father, may they rest in peace—beyond any gratitude or words can express, I owe my best to you.

Special thanks and appreciation to everyone else who helped me in this journey, even if you're not mentioned here by name.

INDEX

INDEX

ABOUT THE AUTHOR

AMIR HEGAZI is the Co-Founder and Managing Partner at CapitalDemocracy, a global professional advisory firm that helps outstanding founders and startups raise venture capital. He also serves as an advisory board member for multiple startups across diverse sectors and geographies. Amir was previously the Co-Founder and Managing Partner at intoMENA Group and the Director of Marketplace at Souq.com, MENA's largest e-commerce platform (acquired by Amazon.com). He is also one of the early pioneers of digital media in the Arab world, having launched the region's largest online TV networks at JumpTV and Talfazat. (JumpTV raised $150 million and completed an IPO dual listing on the Toronto Stock Exchang and the AIM Market of the London Stock Exchange before being acquired by Neulion in 2008.) He is also an advisor on tech startups, entrepreneurial ecosystems, go-to-market, and e-commerce strategies for ministers, policy-makers, and founders. Amir is the author of Amazon.com bestsellers *Startup Arabia* and *Ecosystem Arabia*, both of which were recognized as "Startup Books to Read" in 2019 and 2020, respectively, by Book Authority.

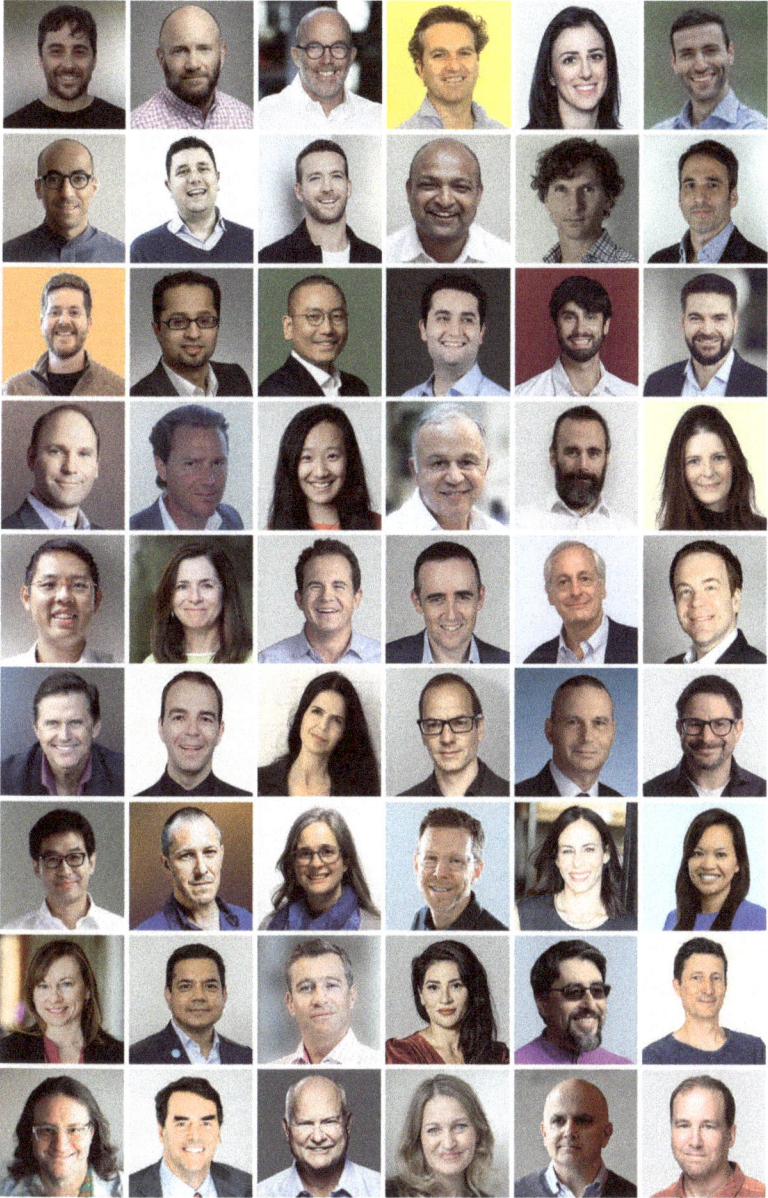